全国高等教育商务英语规划系列教材

商务英语函电与沟通
English for Business Communication

主 编 孙志祥 谢竞贤
副主编 孙亚玲 王红华 方小勇
　　　 潘 珺 谢 晴

苏州大学出版社

图书在版编目(CIP)数据

　　商务英语函电与沟通 = English for Business Communication / 孙志祥,谢竞贤主编. —苏州：苏州大学出版社,2022.3
　　全国高等教育商务英语规划系列教材
　　ISBN 978-7-5672-3760-5

　　Ⅰ.①商… Ⅱ.①孙… ②谢… Ⅲ.①国际商务-英语-电报信函-写作-高等学校-教材 Ⅳ.①F740

　　中国版本图书馆 CIP 数据核字(2022)第 005110 号

书　　　名：	商务英语函电与沟通 English for Business Communication
主　　　编：	孙志祥　谢竞贤
策划编辑：	汤定军
责任编辑：	汤定军
装帧设计：	吴　钰
出版发行：	苏州大学出版社(Soochow University Press)
社　　　址：	苏州市十梓街 1 号　邮编：215006
印　　　刷：	广东虎彩云印刷有限公司印装
邮购热线：	0512-67480030
销售热线：	0512-67481020
开　　　本：	787 mm×1 092 mm　1/16　印张：15.5　字数：360 千
版　　　次：	2022 年 3 月第 1 版
印　　　次：	2022 年 3 月第 1 次印刷
书　　　号：	ISBN 978-7-5672-3760-5
定　　　价：	49.00 元

凡购本社图书发现印装错误,请与本社联系调换。服务热线：0512-67481020
苏州大学出版社网址　http://www.sudapress.com
苏州大学出版社邮箱　sdcbs@suda.edu.cn

全国高等教育商务英语规划系列教材

顾　问	徐青根　鲁加升

编　委（以姓氏笔画为序）

于延梅	王　娅	王　翔	王红华
王金华	王德丽	毛卫强	文　格
方小勇	朱冬梅	刘　萱	孙亚玲
孙志祥	李卫东	李太志	李甜甜
杨　晓	步阳辉	张　莹	张　涛
张夏菲	陈　羔	陈　培	陈东东
林又佳	季　宇	金焕荣	郑　骏
施　翔	姚春宁	姚菊霞	袁海燕
顾　红	顾　薇	顾秀梅	徐　健
徐　源	董　坤	程进军	曾　艳
潘　珺	穆连涛		

策　划　汤定军

编者的话

在21世纪的今天，经济和文化的全球化态势给人类带来了巨大的发展机遇和挑战。随着国际交往的频度、广度和深度的不断加强，既精通英语又熟悉商务的外语类实用型人才备受用人单位青睐。在我国，自2007年开设商务英语本科专业以来，开设商务英语课程的院校与日俱增，对优秀教材的需求越来越迫切。《商务英语函电与沟通》一书正是在这样的背景之下编写的。

在本书的编写过程中，我们本着理论联系实际的原则，重在提高读者在国际商务语境中熟练运用英语处理国际商务的能力。在章节安排上沿用了以交易环节为线索的思路，但不满足于信函与练习简单相加的编写体系。本书的特点可以概括为以下几点：（1）除了范文阅读之外，每章都有较详细的相关环节知识要点和写作要领，体现了"以英语学专业，通过专业知识巩固英语基础"的思路；（2）突出了信函、合同、单证等形式在书中的合理安排，让读者能以规范的英语和格式撰写信函、缮制合同和制作单证；（3）在练习的安排上，除了配有翻译、完形填空等语言知识型练习外，还安排了案例分析，旨在提高读者分析和解决问题的能力和创新能力；（4）每章附有常见的术语和表达方式，还适当加入了各类公司名称、纺织服装类商品名、轻工类商品名、机械设备类商品名、土畜食品类商品名、五金矿产类商品名、文体类商品名和医药保健类商品名；（5）考虑到对外经贸活动中涉及很多国际惯例和法律法规，本书在附录中安排了《中华人民共和国对外贸易法》《跟单信用证统一惯例（国际商会第600号出版物）》《联合国国际货物销售合同公约》等最新英文版本，读者可以有针对性地进行深入阅读，加深对相关环节的认识和了解。

本书主要编写人员为孙志祥、孙亚玲、方小勇、王红华、潘珺等。本书编者衷心感谢苏州大学出版社汤定军先生的大力支持，感谢丁锡芬、赵洪娟等的热心帮助。

由于作者水平有限，书中错误或不妥之处在所难免，敬请读者不吝赐教。

孙志祥
2021 年 10 月于江南大学

使用说明

　　本书可以作为本专科商务英语专业、英语专业、国际经济与贸易专业、涉外文秘专业、对外汉语专业及其他涉外专业的函电或应用写作教材。本书同时可以作为企业在职人员培训时使用，以及有志于从事国际商务活动的人士自学之用。

　　本书共由 12 个单元和附录组成。每单元均由相关知识与写作指南、示范阅读、常用术语和表达、交际园地等部分组成。相关知识和写作指南部分适当介绍了与主题相关的专业知识，详细阐述了写作原则和要领。示范阅读部分主要选取了具有代表性的范例供读者阅读与赏析，在阅读中体味与把握写作原则和要领。常用术语和表达部分主要是常见的专业术语和表达方式，供读者查询与记忆。交际园地部分包括翻译、完形填空和案例分析。其中，英汉翻译练习旨在在翻译的同时熟记一些常用句型，汉英翻译练习旨在盘活一些常用词汇和句型；完形填空部分旨在巩固常用词汇结构，增强商务英语语感；案例分析部分重在通过具体商务情形分析磨炼在商务语境下应用英语解决实际问题的能力。此外，附录部分主要供教学拓展之用。

　　全书共 12 个单元，用作全日制学生的教材时，建议一周开设 4 个课时，每 4—6 个课时讲解一个单元。此外，教师可根据自己学校的专业特点，自行安排讲解课时和顺序。

Contents

Unit 1   Introduction to Business Communication   1

1.1	Principles for Business Writing	1
1.2	Business Letter Style and Format	6
1.3	Sample Letters	12
1.4	Useful Terms and Expressions	14
1.5	Communication Laboratory	15

Unit 2   Establishing Business Relations   18

2.1	Introduction	18
2.2	Credit Enquiries	19
2.3	Information to Be Contained	20
2.4	Sample Letters	20
2.5	Useful Terms and Expressions	22
2.6	Communication Laboratory	23

Unit 3   Enquiries and Replies   34

3.1	General Introduction to Enquiries and Replies	34
3.2	Basic Principles for Sending Enquiries and Replies	35
3.3	Structures of Enquiries and Replies	36
3.4	Sample Letters	39
3.5	Useful Terms and Expressions	41
3.6	Communication Laboratory	42

Unit 4 Quotations, Offers and Counteroffers — 46

- 4.1 General Introduction to Quotations, Offers and Counteroffers — 46
- 4.2 Difference between Quotations and Offers — 48
- 4.3 Guidelines for Offers — 48
- 4.4 Guidelines for Counteroffers — 49
- 4.5 Sample Letters — 50
- 4.6 Useful Terms and Expressions — 52
- 4.7 Communication Laboratory — 54

Unit 5 Orders and Their Execution — 56

- 5.1 General Introduction to Orders — 56
- 5.2 Basic Contents of Orders — 57
- 5.3 Replies to Orders — 58
- 5.4 Sample Letters — 58
- 5.5 Useful Terms and Expressions — 60
- 5.6 Communication Laboratory — 62

Unit 6 Payment — 65

- 6.1 Payment Methods for International Trade — 65
- 6.2 Examples of Terms of Payment in Contracts — 66
- 6.3 Letter of Credit — 67
- 6.4 Sample Letters — 70
- 6.5 Useful Terms and Expressions — 71
- 6.6 Communication Laboratory — 73

Unit 7 Packing — 76

- 7.1 General Introduction to Packing — 76
- 7.2 Packing Containers Used in International Trade — 77
- 7.3 Marks — 78
- 7.4 Examples of Terms of Packing in Contracts — 82
- 7.5 Packing List — 82
- 7.6 Letters on Packing — 83
- 7.7 Sample Letters — 84
- 7.8 Useful Terms and Expressions — 85

7.9	Communication Laboratory	88

Unit 8　Shipment　　　　　　　　　　　　　　　　　　　90

8.1	Tramp and Liner	90
8.2	Transport Documents	90
8.3	Shipping Advice	94
8.4	Terms of Shipment in Contracts	95
8.5	Sample Letters	96
8.6	Useful Terms and Expressions	98
8.7	Communication Laboratory	102

Unit 9　Insurance　　　　　　　　　　　　　　　　　　　105

9.1	Introduction	105
9.2	Writing Guide	111
9.3	Sample Letters	112
9.4	Useful Terms and Expressions	114
9.5	Communication Laboratory	115

Unit 10　Complaints, Claims and Adjustments　　　　　119

10.1	General Introduction to Complaints, Claims and Adjustments	119
10.2	Principles for Making Complaints, Claims and Adjustments	120
10.3	Structures of Complaints, Claims and Adjustments	121
10.4	Sample Letters	123
10.5	Useful Terms and Expressions	125
10.6	Communication Laboratory	127

Unit 11　Contracts　　　　　　　　　　　　　　　　　　130

11.1	Drafting Contracts	130
11.2	Sample Contracts	132
11.3	Useful Terms and Expressions	145
11.4	Communication Laboratory	148

Unit 12 Documentation in International Trade — 152

12.1	Introduction	152
12.2	Commercial Documents	153
12.3	Transportation Documents	157
12.4	Finance Documents	163
12.5	Other Documents	166
12.6	Useful Terms and Expressions	170
12.7	Communication Laboratory	170

Appendix 1 Foreign Trade Law of the People's Republic of China — 173

Appendix 2 Uniform Customs and Practice for Documentary Credits, UCP 600 — 184

Appendix 3 UN Convention of Contracts for the International Sale of Goods — 206

Appendix 4 List of Common Imports and Exports — 229

References — 236

Unit 1　Introduction to Business Communication

1.1　PRINCIPLES FOR BUSINESS WRITING

1.1.1　Distinguishing Characteristics of Business Writing

Business writing is different from other kinds of writing in four fundamental ways.

People write in organizations to accomplish specific goals. Their purpose in writing is to achieve their goals. Broadly speaking, people write in organizations to ask for or impart some information or to persuade a business partner to act in a certain way. And at the same time, they build friendships or maintain old ones. In contrast, many other kinds of writing are not goal-oriented in this way. Poems are often written for the sheer enjoyment of the experience itself and not to accomplish some practical goals.

Once writing goals are identified and stated, success or failure depends largely on whether the message can accomplish its writer's goals. In this sense, good business writing is effective business writing where effectiveness is the single most important criterion for the evaluation of a business message. Writing is much more a matter of paying attention to the reader than of paying attention to your good English, even though good English mechanics are still very important.

Another important difference between business writing and other kinds of writing is that business writing takes place in real-life situations. In business, it would be time-consuming and expensive to make a trip every time to exchange news and information. Letters are then substitutes for personal visits. A typical reader is a busy executive with a heavy daily reading load. Therefore, a message must communicate quickly and efficiently.

As stated above, people in business write to achieve certain goals. The writer of a business letter has an inherent obligation, or liability, to make the message easy for the reader to grasp. Consider the far lesser degree of liability found in fiction writing. Here the author may want readers to pity a particular character, to dig out the meanings. In business settings, the audience shouldn't have to work hard to study the meanings of a letter or a report. It is the writer, not the audience, that is responsible for successful communication.

Business people depend on the written words to keep them in touch with their customers and business associates and to preserve on paper their conversations with them.

Thus business letters represent business people in dealing with their customers and business associates. It is important that the letters leave the reader with a good impression of the writer and his or her company. The message should encourage the audience to think favorably about the company. In other words, the image-building goals of every message shouldn't be overlooked. Business letters are in many cases an ambassador of goodwill.

1.2.1 Principles for Business Writing

As a manager who needs to communicate well with customers and business associates in order to be effective, you should have an attitude towards words that the musician has toward sound and the painter toward line and color. No one is "born" an accomplished writer, but every one can learn to be an effective communicator. The key to successful business writing is adhering to fundamental principles without making you a slave to rules.

The basic principles for business writing can be summed up in the six C's, i.e. (1) completeness, (2) clearness, (3) conciseness, (4) correctness, (5) courtesy and (6) consideration.

(1) Completeness

The message should be complete. Incomplete letters can be costly, for they lead to errors, often cause delays in filling orders, and call for other letters of clarification to be written. Answers to some fundamental questions help you see your audience and ensure that the message is complete. After writing, you can check the completeness of your message against the following questions:

- Who am I trying to influence? What special characteristics do they embody?
- Where are they located? How do I reach them? At what time?
- What do they want to know? What do they need to know? What do I want to tell them?
- What should I say? How do I get them to accept or appreciate my point of view? What arguments should I make? What facts should I incorporate? What enclosures?

(2) Clearness

If a message is not complete, it is not clear, either. Clarity is also influenced by the words you use and the way you use them. Take your cue from news stories, feature articles and editorials in newspapers or magazines. Journalists have pioneered most of the basics of good business writing. They normally write to be understood by the average teenager even when they are writing for the older, more sophisticated audience.

When you have a clear idea in your mind of what you want to say, say it in plain, simple words, and use short sentences rather than long, complicated ones.

Following is a list of difficult, out-of-date terms and modern alternatives.

Obscure Words	Easy Words
aforementioned	already discussed
initial	first

Obscure Words	Easy Words
in lieu of	in stead of
accede	agree
issuance	send
subsequent	later
ascertain	find out
pursuant to	after
forward	mail
endeavor	try
disclose	show
supersede	replace
pertain to	about

Most good writers find an average sentence length of fifteen to eighteen words works well. Contrast the following:

Poor: Good writing begins with an understanding of your audience and then proceeds to the use of words in a clear and logical fashion with the intention of giving your reader the easiest explanation of the subject you are covering, the end product being a communication that is taken seriously rather than casually and that makes the reader think or act differently as a result.

Better: Good writing begins with an understanding of the people you want to reach. By using the right words clearly and logically, you make it easy for them to grasp your message. The end product should be a communication that helps them to think and act differently.

Poor: It is obligatory that you confirm this outstanding indebtedness and, if no discrepancies exist, that you expedite remittance.

Better: Please let us know if your records and ours do not agree. If you find that they agree, won't you send us your check right away?

(3) **Conciseness**

To be efficient, business writing should be direct and get to the point quickly and cogently. Don't beat around the bush with verbiage or extraneous information. A concise letter is a letter that covers the subject in the fewest words possible. Brevity is the soul of wit, but brevity is only a part of conciseness. To be concise, a message must be both brief and complete. Conciseness means saying all that needs to be said and no more. Here are a few cautions to keep you on track:

- Use active, not passive, voice—"Thank you for" rather than "I would like to thank you for", or "I have learned that" rather than "It has recently come to my attention that";
- Omit needless words—put "since" or "because" in place of "owing to the fact

that", or "He is trustworthy" in place of "He is a person whom we can trust";
- Avoid clichéd or hackneyed expressions—"at this point in time", "it goes without saying";
- Avoid redundancies such as "rise up", "totally destroyed", "make perfectly clear", "drop down".

Hereunder is a list of wordy and concise phrases for reference:

Wordy	Concise
am in receipt of	received
enclosed herewith	enclosed
enclosed please find	enclosed is (are)
please don't hesitate to call upon us	please call upon us
please feel free to write	please write
prior to	before
under separate cover / by separate post	separately
during the year of 2008	during 2008
endorse on the back of this check	endorse this check
in (for) the amount of USD300	for USD300
for a price of USD30	for USD30
in the city of Chicago	in Chicago
according to our records	we find
at this time	now
due to the fact that	because
during the time that	while
for the purpose of	for, to
for the reason that	since (or because)
in accordance with your request	as you requested
in all cases	always
inasmuch as	since (or because)
in due course	soon
in spite of the fact that	even though
in such a manner that	so
in the matter of	about
in view of the fact that	because
it should be pointed out that	please notice that

(4) Correctness

Writers of business letters and documents continually strive to be correct in every detail. Some errors, such as those involving dates and amounts of money, can cause a great deal of harm.

Reasons for errors fall into two categories:
- Carelessness, such as the following: typographical errors (wrong letters, errors in spacing), poor margin balance (top and bottom and right and left margins out of balance), messy corrections (smudges);
- Failure to consult reference sources, with these results: misspelled words and names, errors in word selection, errors in dates and figures, errors in capitalization and punctuation, incomplete message.

(5) **Courtesy**

The most important reason for being courteous is to make communicating more pleasant. Good manners, however, are not reflected merely in a "please" or "thank you". Giving a prompt reply to his letter will please your customer or associate. The way you write or say "please" or "thank you"—the tone—also makes the difference. The following expressions help to give your letter a desirable tone:

> "You were very thoughtful to ... "
> "We appreciate your ... "
> "Thank you for ... "
> "You are entirely right in saying ... "
> "We were pleased to learn that ... "

Don't impose. Don't be brutally honest. Don't say:

> "You ought to ... "
> "Your letter is not clear at all ... "
> "Apparently you have already forgotten what I wrote you three weeks ago."
> "We demand immediate shipment from you."
> "We are disgusted with your manner of doing business."

Be friendly, enthusiastic, self-confident and sincere. Please say:

> "Perhaps you could ... "
> "If I understand your letter correctly ... "
> "As mentioned in my May 10 letter to you ... "
> "We request your immediate shipment."
> "We are not completely satisfied with your manner of doing business."

(6) **Consideration**

The word "business" contains both "u" and "i", but the "u" comes before the "i". To sell John Smith what John Smith buys, you must see John Smith with John Smith's eyes.

The key to successful communication is to make the reader feel that the most important person in our business relationship is You the reader, not "me/I", the writer.

This You Attitude is a style of writing which looks at things from the reader's point of view, shows reader benefit and focuses on the positive. The You Attitude, then, is more than using the "you" pronoun. It is truly an attitude that we believe, and, as a result, we make our readers believe that the most important person in our business relationship is you: our reader, our customer.

- Look at things from the reader's point of view.

> We Attitude: We shipped your order today.
> You Attitude: Your order will arrive on Thursday.

- Avoid starting letters with I or We.

> We Attitude: Dear Mr. Smith,
>   I am happy to inform you that we have approved your loan.
> You Attitude: Dear Mr. Smith,
>   Congratulations! Your loan is approved.

- Emphasize reader benefit.

> We Attitude: This laser printer prints 20 pages per minute.
> You attitude: This laser printer can turn out one of your 100-page proposals in five minutes.

- Focus on the positive and say "no" positively.

> We Attitude: No exceptions to this rule can be allowed.
> You Attitude: This rule must apply equally in all situations.

1.2 BUSINESS LETTER STYLE AND FORMAT

1.2.1 Business Letter Style

Although there is no standard by which the appropriateness and inappropriateness of a specific business letter style can be firmly established, business readers expect to receive letters that adhere to an existing format standard. There are several acceptable business letter styles available for use in the professional world. Three such business letter arrangement styles include:

- Full-Blocked Style: When using this business letter format, the entire letter is left justified and single-spaced except for a double space between paragraphs.
- Blocked Style: With this business letter format, the body of the letter is left justified and single-spaced. The date line, the complementary closing and the writer's identification usually start at the horizontal center of the page. However, the date may be aligned to end at the right margin, and the subject line may be centered or

indented five spaces.
- Semi-blocked Style: Similar to the blocked business letter style except that the first line of each paragraph is indented five spaces instead of left justified.

1.2.2 Business Letter Format

There are several main sections that are consistent with every business letter format. Each section contains several essential and a few optional parts. These sections are: (1) the heading, (2) the opening, (3) the body and (4) the closing.

(1) The heading

The heading refers to the company or organization letterhead and the date line.

The Letterhead. Almost every company uses high-quality stationary with its name, address, telephone number, fax number, and e-mail address printed on it. These identifying items not only provide identification of the writer's company but also help to project the company's image. Readers may form an opinion of the company based on its letterhead: old-fashioned or modern, middle-of-the-road or progressive and so on. Therefore, a company's letterhead is often designed by a professional artist to make the most favorable impression on the reader.

The Date Line. Every letter carries a date line consisting of the month, day and year. The month is often spelled in full. It is confusing and unacceptable to use a number to indicate the month as 8/12/2021. The day of the month is read an ordinal, but the ordinal suffixes, *st*, *nd*, *rd*, *or th*, are omitted in writing. There are two widely used date line styles, business and military. When writing to companies within the United States, use the business style or American date format.

Business (American)	Military (English)
December 8, 2021	8 December 2021

(2) The opening

The functions of an opening are to direct the letter to a specific individual, company, department or whatever (the inside name and address) and to greet the reader (the salutation).

The Inside Name and Address. The inside address is the recipient's address. It is always best to write to a specific individual at the firm to which you are writing. The name of the addressee, which should always be preceded by a courtesy title such as Ms., Mrs., Mr., or Dr. (except when followed by M. D. or another abbreviation), is usually the first line of the inside name and address. Follow a woman's preference in being addressed as Miss, Mrs., or Ms. If you are unsure of a woman's preference in being addressed, use Ms. If there is a possibility that the person to whom you are writing is a Dr. or has some other title, use that title. Usually, people will not mind being addressed by a higher title than they actually possess. It is common courtesy to include the person's job title when it is known, either on the same line as the name or on a separate line in the inside address.

The inside address includes the addressee's company, the street address, and the city, state(province), postcode number. For international addresses, type the name of the country in all-capital letters on the last line. The inside address begins one line below the sender's address or one inch below the date. It should be left justified, no matter which format you are using. The following are examples of accepted inside-address styles:

> Mr. John Grossman, President
> American Shipping Co., Inc.
> 140 Sylvan Avenue
> Englewood Cliffs, NJ 07632
> USA

> Ms. Helen L. McDonald, Head
> Home Sales Department
> American Drawback Service, LLC
> 15 Division Street
> Fairview, NJ 07022
> USA

> John Smith, M. D.
> American International Cargo Service Inc.
> 124 Sweeten Creek Road
> Asheville, NC 28803
> USA

The Attention Line. When a letter is addressed to a company or to a department within a company rather than to a specific individual, an attention line may be used to speed up handling of the letter. The attention line is typed in all-capital letters or in underlined uppercase and lowercase letters below the inside address and above the salutation. The following are accepted styles of attention lines.

> ATTENTION MR. J. R. SMITH
> ATTENTION SALES DEPARTMENT
> Attention Mr. J. R. Smith
> Attention Sales Manager

Remember to use one of the following salutations with an attention line: *Ladies:* or *Gentlemen:* or *Ladies and Gentlemen:* in the U. S. and *Dear Mesdames:* or *Dear Sirs:* or *Dear Mesdames* or *Sirs:* in the United Kingdom.

The Salutation. Just as it is extremely impolite to call a stranger by his first name or use familiar language with him, it is a bad mistake to use an inappropriate salutation in a letter. In all except the most formal letters in English, it is proper to begin with the word *Dear*, followed by the name of the person as you would say it in speaking to him directly. The following are examples of salutations and descriptions of their use:

Dear John	Used for informal business correspondence—implies a personal friendship.
Dear Mr. Gauss	Used in routine business correspondence addressed to a specific individual—formal but cordial.
Dear Sir or Madam	Used only for very formal correspondence.

(3) The body

The body of the letter consists essentially of the message and optionally a subject line.

The Message. The message is the most important part in a letter. By using the letter writing principles, the writer makes every effort to get his or her ideas across to the reader effectively. The message of every business letter usually consists of at least two paragraphs.

The Subject Line. The subject line gives the reader advance notice of what the letter is about. Like the attention line, the subject line is typed in all-capital letters or in underlined uppercase and lowercase letters immediately below the salutation. The word *Subject* or *Re* may be omitted, but when it is used it is followed by a colon:

SUBJECT: AMENDMENT TO L/C NO: 31819
Re: Homepage Design

(4) The closing

The closing consists of the complimentary closing, the company signature (an optional part), the writer's signature, the writer's identification, reference initials (an optional part), enclosure notation (an optional part), carbon copy notations (an optional part) and postscript (an optional part).

The Complimentary Closing. The complimentary closing is the writer's way to say "good-bye" to the reader. It is important to match the tone of the closing with that of the salutation. The complimentary closing begins at the same horizontal point as the date line and one line after the last body paragraph. Capitalize the first word only and leave four lines between the closing and the sender's name for a signature. If a colon follows the salutation, a comma should follow the closing; otherwise, there is no punctuation after the closing.

In the US, *Sincerely yours* is by far the most frequently occurring formula. It is used in personal letters, business letters—formal and informal. It is appropriate almost anywhere except in intimate letters, where it would sound overly formal. In the United Kingdom, *Yours faithfully* is preferred in most formal business letters. In most cases, American usage prefers to put the adverb before yours; British usage is the other way round, but both word orders are seen in both countries.

More commonly used forms are given below.

Formal	Informal
Respectfully yours	Sincerely
Very truly yours	Sincerely yours
Very sincerely yours	Cordially
Very cordially yours	Cordially yours
Yours very truly	Best regards

The Company Signature. The company signature is the typed name of the company. When company signature is used by some companies to emphasize that the company is legally sending the letter, the company signature is usually typed on the second line below the complimentary closing (Americans prefer to use all-capital letters).

The Writer's Signature. This is simply the handwritten signature of the writer. If the name does not indicate to the addressee whether the writer is a man or a woman, insert the proper title (for example, Mr. or Ms.) in parentheses before the typewritten name. Notice that to "sign" with a rubber stamp is a form of discourtesy.

The Writer's Identification. In most instances, the writer's name is typed for spaces below the complimentary closing. The writer's job title and/or department may also be typed beneath the typed name.

Sincerely yours

Henry Marshall

Henry Marshall

Manager, Sales Department

Reference Initials. The reference initials serve an administrative purpose only. If *HM* signed the letter, *hs* wrote it, and *mlm* typed it, the two acceptable reference-initials styles may be:

HM / hs / mlm

HM: hs: mlm

Enclosure Notation. When something is included with the letter in the same envelope or package, type the word *Enclosure* or an abbreviation of it (*Enc.*) with a figure indicating the number of enclosures to help writers, recipients and secretaries to confirm that all enclosures are included when the letter is sent or received. Some widely used styles are as follows.

Enclosures (4)

Enc.: B/L

Enclosures:

1. Sales Contract
2. Order No.: 3378
3. Invoice No.: ST 50819

Carbon Copy Notations. When the writer wishes to send a copy of the letter to other parties concerned and wishes the addressee to know, a carbon copy (*cc* or *CC*) notation is indicated on the original and all duplicate copies of the letter.

cc: Sales Department	cc Personnel Department
CC: Ms. Helen Keller	CC Mr. Harry Bush

Postscript. Some writers today deliberately add postscripts to the letter to draw the reader's attention to a particularly important point.

PS: To learn how to get the best security plus payment processing solution for your site from the most trusted name in Internet security, download the guide today.

1.2.3 Miscellaneous Matters

The Continuation Page. Business letters are usually one page long, but sometimes letters cannot be finished on one page and the message must be continued on plain (not printed letterhead) paper of the same size and quality as the head sheet. Second-page heading consists of the name of the addressee, the page number, and the date. Three blank lines should be left between the last line of the heading and the first line of the continued message. All continuation pages should have the same side margins as the first page. The top margin of a continuation page should be one inch.

Mr. Harry Bush	2	December 8, 2019
Mr. Harry Bush		
Page 2		
December 8, 2019		

Envelope addressing. Return address goes in the upper left hand corner of the front of the envelope. It should include a complete address so that the letter can be returned if necessary. If using an envelope with a double window, make sure the letter is folded and inserted so that the return address shows through the upper window.

The name and address of the recipient should be centered on the envelope. Make sure the address begins far enough down on the face of the envelope so that it will not be covered by the cancellation. If you are using envelopes with windows, make sure the address appears clearly through the window. When an attention line is used in a letter, it should be typed on the envelope. Addresses on envelopes are normally single-spaced.

Helen L. McDonald
American Drawback Service, LLC
15 Division Street, Fairview, NJ 07022
USA
Attention Manager, Accounting Department

                              Miss Helen Beecher
                              Department of Business Communication
                              Klondike Regional High School
                              Yellowknife, Yukon EFG 123
                              Canada

1.3 SAMPLE LETTERS

Sample Letter 1 (1): The Full-Blocked Business Letter Style

American International Cargo Service Inc.
124 Sweeten Creek Road
Asheville, NC 28803
USA

August 16, 2021

Ms. Helen L. Chan
Hong Kong Drawback Service, LLC
36/F, Room 3600, China Resources Building
26 Harbor Road
Wanchai
HONG KONG

Dear Ms. Chan,

Subject: Form of Full-Blocked Business Letter

This letter style is the most popular style in use today. Efficiency is the main reason for its popularity. The main characteristic of full-blocked business letters is that everything is flush with the left margin. Full-blocked letters are a little more formal than semi-blocked letters.

Unit 1　Introduction to Business Communication

If your letter is only one page, type the complimentary close and optional components as shown below. Otherwise, type them on the last page of your letter. Begin your full block continuation page three blank lines below the heading. Continuation pages should include at least three lines of text; otherwise, evaluate the contents of previous pages.

Sincerely yours,
American International Cargo Service Inc.
Henry Marshall
Henry Marshall
Manager, Sales Department

Sample Letter 1 (2): The Blocked Business Letter Style

American International Cargo Service Inc.
124 Sweeten Creek Road
Asheville, NC 28803
USA
　　　　　　　　　　　　　　　　　　　August 16, 2021

Ms. Helen L. Chan
Hong Kong Drawback Service, LLC
36/F, Room 3600, China Resources Building
26 Harbor Road
Wanchai
HONG KONG

Dear Ms. Chan,

Subject: Blocked Business Letter

This letter style is very popular for two reasons:
1. Many people feel comfortable with the traditional appearance;
2. The blocked paragraphs make it slightly more efficient to type.

If your letter is only one page, type the complimentary close and optional components as shown below. Otherwise, type them on the last page of your letter. Begin your continuation page 3 blank lines below the heading. Continuation pages should include at least three lines of text; otherwise, evaluate the contents of previous pages.

　　　　　　　　　　　　　　　　　Sincerely yours
　　　　　　　　　　　　　　　　　American International Cargo Service Inc.
　　　　　　　　　　　　　　　　　Henry Marshall
　　　　　　　　　　　　　　　　　Henry Marshall
　　　　　　　　　　　　　　　　　Manager, Sales Department

Sample Letter 1 (3): The Semi-Blocked Business Letter Style

American International Cargo Service Inc.
124 Sweeten Creek Road
Asheville, NC 28803
USA

               August 16, 2021

Ms. Helen L. Chan
Hong Kong Drawback Service, LLC
36/F, Room 3600, China Resources Building
26 Harbor Road
Wanchai
HONG KONG

Dear Ms. Chan,

<u>Form of Semi-Blocked Business Letter</u>

 The semi-blocked letter is still popular of its traditional appearance. In the semi-blocked letter, the first line of each paragraph is indented.

 If your letter is only one page, type the complimentary close and optional components as shown below. Otherwise, type them on the last page of your letter. Begin your full block continuation page 3 blank lines below the heading. Continuation pages should include at least three lines of text; otherwise, evaluate the contents of previous pages.

           Sincerely yours
           American International Cargo Service Inc.
           Henry Marshall
           Henry Marshall
           Manager, Sales Department
           HM/hs/mlm
           CC Mr. Harry Bush

1.4 USEFUL TERMS AND EXPRESSIONS

1. letterhead	信头
2. inside name and address	信封内姓名地址
3. courtesy title	尊称

Unit 1 Introduction to Business Communication

4. complimentary closing	结尾客套语
5. attention line	收信人提示栏
6. subject line	事由栏
7. reference initials	经办人代号
8. postscript	附笔
9. enclosure	附件
10. carbon copy	抄送
11. full-blocked style	全齐头式
12. blocked style	齐头式
13. semi-blocked style	混合式
14. limited liability company (LLC)	有限责任公司
15. company limited (Co., Ltd.)	有限公司
16. joint stock company limited	股份有限公司
17. group	集团
18. holdings limited (Ltd.)	控股有限公司
19. holdings Inc.	控股有限公司
20. NV	有限责任公司(荷兰)
21. AG	有限责任公司(德国)
22. PLC (public limited company, in UK or Ireland)	(上市)公开有限公司
23. PPP (Public-Private Partnership)	政府和社会资本合作

1.5 COMMUNICATION LABORATORY

Application Exercises

A. Correct the errors in the following letter parts.

1. Dear Madam or Sir:
   Best regards
2. sh/HKShelly
3. Titanic Cement Inc.
   200 Lincoln Ave.
   New York, N.Y. 10009
   Subject: L/C No.: ND308

Dear Mr. McDonald:

B. Write the salutation and complimentary closing for each of the following.

1. A letter to a business friend, John Bush, who was recently promoted to an important post.
2. A letter to a state councilor, Adam Wang, asking support for an investigation into the serious air pollution in your local community.

Case Study

Read the following case and then think over one situation in your daily life where communication fails. Discuss with your classmates barriers there to effective communication.

The Communication Process

Although all of us have been communicating with others since our infancy, the process of transmitting information from an individual (or group) to another is a very complex process with many sources of potential error.

Consider the simple example:

> Terry: I won't make it to work again tomorrow; this pregnancy keeps me nauseous and my doctor says I should probably be reduced to part time.
> Boss: Terry, this is the third day you've missed and your appointments keep backing up; we have to cover for you and this is messing all of us up.

In any communication at least some of the "meaning" is lost in simple transmission of a message from the sender to the receiver. In many situations a lot of the true message is lost and the message that is heard is often far different than the one intended. This is most obvious in cross-cultural situations where language is an issue. But it is also common among people of the same culture.

Look at the example. Terry had what appeared to be a simple message to convey she won't make it to work today because of nausea. But she had to translate the thoughts into words and this is the first potential source of error. Was she just trying to convey that she would be late? Was she trying to convey anything else? It turned out she was. She was upset because she perceived that her co-workers weren't as sympathetic to her situation as they should be. Her co-workers, however, were really being pressured by Terry's continued absences, and her late calls. They wished she would just take a leave of absence, but Terry refused because she would have to take it without pay.

Thus what appears to be a simple communication is, in reality, quite complex. Terry was communicating far more than that she would miss work; she was conveying a number of complex emotions, complicated by her own complex feelings about pregnancy, work, and her future.

She sent a message but the message was more than the words; it included the tone, the timing of the call, and the way she expressed herself.

Similarly, the boss went through a complex communication process in "hearing" the message. The message that Terry sent had to be decoded and given meaning. There are many ways to decode the simple message that Terry gave and the way the message is heard will influence the response to Terry.

In this case the boss heard far more than a simple message that "Terry won't be at work today". The boss "heard" hostility from Terry, indifference, lack of consideration, among other emotions. Terry may not have meant this, but this is what the boss heard.

Communication is so difficult because at each step in the process there is a major potential for error. By the time a message gets from a sender to a receiver there are four basic places where transmission errors can take place and at each place, there are a multitude of potential sources of error. Thus it is no surprise that social psychologists estimate that there is usually a 40%–60% loss of meaning in the transmission of messages from the sender to the receiver.

It is critical to understand this process, understand and be aware of the potential sources of errors and constantly counteract these tendencies by making a conscientious effort to make sure there is a minimal loss of meaning in our conversation.

It is also very important to understand that a majority of communication is non-verbal. This means that when we attribute meaning to what someone else is saying, the verbal part of the message actually means less than the non-verbal part.

Unit 2 Establishing Business Relations

2.1 INTRODUCTION

Establishing business relations to a company is what matters to a person. In order to guarantee the sustainable development and secure its place in the competitive business field, it seems that a company, be it a newly established one or an old one, has no other choice but to form business relations with other firms or companies.

Usually there are two ways to establish business relations. The first is to send business representatives to do research on other markets or in other countries to establish direct business relations with the new customers, while the second way is to write letters to new firms or customers. Compared with the former one, which demands more money input, the latter is a common practice in business communication. Therefore, a company should seize every opportunity to search information of other firms and to get access to its potential partners or customers. Generally speaking, such information is obtainable through the following channels:

- Trade directory;
- Commercial counselor's office;
- Commercial attache;
- Market investigation;
- Advertisements;
- Introduction (from other business firms or friends known to both parties) or self introduction;
- Bank;
- Chamber of commerce both at home and abroad;
- Internet;
- Mutual visits by trade delegations and representatives;
- Attendance at the fairs and exhibitions at home and abroad;
- Business association of the same trade.

Nowadays two channels, namely, the Internet and attendance at the fairs and exhibitions at home and abroad, are the most popular in the world. With the rapid development of science and technology, the Internet has become an indispensable tool to our life. There exist many useful websites where you can gather commercial information of various kinds, one of which is Alibaba.com—the famous B2B brand, which is made up of three related websites, namely china.alibaba.com for the Chinese market, www.alibaba.com for the global businessmen and japan.alibaba.com for the Japanese market. Another website which is worth mentioning is Made-in-China.com, which organizes and provides the most complete, accurate and valid information of Chinese products and Chinese suppliers. Nowadays, Made-in-China.com has already become a leading B2B portal especially in assisting global buyers and Chinese manufacturers to make contact and conduct international trade. And every year many fairs and exhibitions on various levels and in varied fields are held such as Canton Fair, Expo Riva Schuh, PIEDRA, South Africa International Building and Construction Exhibition, MICAM, Footwear UK and Heimtextil, to name just a few.

2.2 CREDIT ENQUIRIES

After the information of the would-be customer or partner is obtained from the above-mentioned channels, the next step is to set about investigating the finance and credit status of the new customer so as to reduce the possible risks in business transactions, which, if not handled properly, will inflict heavy losses on your company. As a usual practice, this type of investigation includes the following:
- Capital, financial condition (registered capital; financial ratio analysis; claim and liabilities; capital asserts);
- Business capacity, activity (section layout; person in charge; turnover; quality of the products);
- Business credit (performance of a contract; payment practice);
- Political stand (the political background and attitude of the person who is in charge of the company).

Business credit is the focus of the enquiry, which is indispensable to the successful deal in the future and can be conducted through many channels, the chamber of commerce, bank, sales representative, consultative companies, old customers, to name just a few. You can also entrust it to a trustworthy credit agency. However, a bank will not give information directly to an unknown trader. Therefore, you have to ask your own bank to do the investigation for you. Generally speaking, in doing the first business transaction, the buyer would provide his own bank and some trading partners as the credit references for the seller to make enquiries.

Credit enquiry letters follow the same format in some large companies and should be generally headed "Confidential" or "Private and Confidential". These words should be written on the envelope.

In writing this kind of letter, you should make sure to raise specific questions and use polite and appreciative terms. And when you receive the corresponding information, be it favorable or unfavorable, you should send an appropriate letter of acknowledgement and thanks.

2.3 INFORMATION TO BE CONTAINED

After an analysis of the data you have collected, you may begin to send a letter, which is called "First Enquiry", to the new customer if you suppose that the customer enjoys a good finance and credit status and are determined to establish business relations with the company. Generally speaking, such kind of letters should include the following information:

- State clearly the source of your information (from where and whom you get the company's name and address, etc.);
- Make a brief self-introduction of your company (the business scope of your company, its branches and liaison offices, your financial standing and integrity);
- Make clear your intention of writing this letter (what kind of business relations you want to establish with the other party: to sell your own products, to purchase their products or cooperate with them. Sometimes the terms of sales or purchases can be mentioned and catalogues, price lists and other details enclosed for reference or requests for samples, price lists, booklets, catalogues, credit reference can be made);
- Express your hope of close cooperation, developing business relations with mutual benefit and your desire of receiving the early reply.

This kind of letters should be clear, concise and polite. You should be sincere and courteous in the writing so as to leave a good impression on the reader. Make sure that the letter is written according to the standard format, neatly typed and error-free.

On the other hand, if you receive this type of letter, please answer it with courtesy and without any possible delay, which will turn out to be very rewarding.

2.4 SAMPLE LETTERS

Sample Letter 2 (1)

Dear Sir or Madam,

We owe your name and address to Mr. Ye, the general manager of Optim, who has informed us that your corporation deals in steel and tempered glass furniture and is the largest in this field.

We are the leading importers of furniture in Europe and have been in this line for twenty years. Your latest product invites our attention with its appealing design. Therefore, we wish to establish friendly business relations with you to enjoy a share of mutually profitable business. Would you please give us a complete set of your latest catalogue?

Your prompt reply is appreciated.

Yours faithfully

Sample Letter 2 (2)

Dear Sir or Madam,

We are much indebted to the Commercial Counsel's Office of our Embassy in your country for name and address of your company and are pleased to learn that you are one of the main importers of food in America. We now avail ourselves of this opportunity to write to you with a view to entering into business relations with you.

Our company specializes in the manufacturing and sales in the overseas markets for foods. Our products involve varieties of seasoning products, canned foods, dehydrated foods, and noodles, vermicelli, etc. We have been in this line for 20 years and our products are up to the ISO and HACCP standards; therefore, you can be rest-assured about the quality of our products. We enclose a copy of our catalogue for your reference.

We are looking forward to hearing from you soon.

Sincerely yours

Sample Letter 2 (3)

Dear Sir or Madam,

We thank you for your letter of the ninth this month and are willing to enter into business relations with you. We have been exporting all kinds of art and craft goods for more than 35 years and have many customers and friends in over 60 countries and regions.

As requested, we are sending you by air the latest catalogue and price list of our products for your reference. We are certain that business can be consummated between us. If any of the items listed in the catalogue meets your interest, please let us have your specific enquiry, and our quotation will be forwarded to you without delay.

We look forward to your favorable reply.

Sincerely yours

Sample Letter 2 (4)

Dear Sirs,

Recently we have received a rather large order from a new customer. We should be much obliged if you could give us some information on their financial and credit standing. Their correspondence bank is the Bank of America.

Any information you may obtain for us will be treated in strict confidence and without any liability on your part.

Thank you in advance.

Yours faithfully

2.5 USEFUL TERMS AND EXPRESSIONS

1. Commercial Counselor's Office	商务参赞处
2. B2B (business-to-business)	企业间的电子商务模式
3. Canton Fair	广交会
4. Expo Riva Schuh	意大利加达春/秋季国际鞋展
5. PIEDRA	西班牙马德里国际石材展览会
6. MICAM	意大利米兰国际鞋展
7. Footwear UK	英国伯明翰国际鞋展
8. Heimtextil	法兰克福家用纺织品贸易博览会
9. HACCP (Hazard Analysis Critical Control Point)	危害分析关键控制点
10. counter sample	相对样本，对等货样
11. textiles products and garments	纺织服装类商品
12. apparel	成衣
13. backless dress	露背装
14. knitted or crocheted fabrics	针织物及钩编织物
15. blouse	女装衬衫
16. briefs	三角裤；短内裤
17. impregnated, coated textile fabrics	浸渍、涂布纺织物
18. denim	牛仔
19. dinner jacket	晚礼服
20. dress coat	燕尾服,礼服

Unit 2 Establishing Business Relations

21. evening gown set	晚睡袍
22. wool, fine or coarse animal hair	羊毛、动物细毛或粗毛
23. high-waisted skirt	高腰裙
24. leisure style	休闲款式
25. leisure wear	休闲服
26. one-piece dress	连衣裙
27. twine, cordage, ropes and cables and articles thereof	线、绳、索、缆及其制品
28. swimsuit/bathing suit	游泳衣
29. fitness wear	女式紧身衣(分上衣、裤子)
30. owe one's name and address to	承蒙……告知名称和地址
31. avail oneself of	利用
32. through the courtesy of	承蒙……的好意;蒙……允许
33. enter into	加入,参加;缔结(契约等)
34. as per	按照
35. in compliance with	遵从;依从
36. be in the market for	想要购买
37. consummate	完成;结束
38. standing	在社会或职业中的地位、名声或身份;尊严
39. cover	包括;涉及
40. line	行业;产品的类型

2.6 COMMUNICATION LABORATORY

Application Exercises

A. Translate the following sentences into Chinese.

1. The commodities we are handling consist of the manufactures of the first rate tractor plants of this country, and so we are in a good position to serve your customers with the most reliable quality of the line you suggest.

2. We invite you to send us details and prices, possibly samples, of such goods as you would be interested in selling. We shall gladly study the sales possibilities in our

market.
3. As a state-operated corporation we specialize in light industrial goods and are willing to establish business relationship with you.
4. We are very well connected with all the major dealers here of furniture, and feel sure we can sell large quantities of Chinese goods if we get your offers at competitive prices.
5. We are very sensible of your friendly services on our behalf, for which please accept our sincere thanks.
6. As to our financial standing, we refer you to American City Bank, who, we feel sure will be glad to furnish you with any information you require.
7. In order to give you some idea of various qualities of printers we carry, we have pleasure in forwarding you by airmail one catalogue and a few sample books for your reference.
8. We are one of the well-organized and experienced firms in the export trade throughout the world, and for your full information, we are enclosing a list showing our import and export items for your perusal.
9. The foregoing information is given in confidence and for your private use only.
10. Established in 1984, the company has a sound business standing with an excellent business turnover.

B. Translate the following sentences into English.
1. 我们旭日牌电器和电子产品已经荣获国家金奖,并在国内外市场上赢得了巨大的声誉。(win great popularity)
2. 由于这种商品属于我们的经营范围,我们将很高兴地尽早与你们建立直接的业务关系。(fall within the scope of)
3. 我们专营纺织品的进口业务,希望在这一行业与你方合作。(specialize in)
4. 交易会上展出的服装很吸引人,特别是时尚的款式令参观者非常感兴趣。(interest)
5. 贵方若能及早告知你方准备提供的条款和条件,本公司则深感荣幸。(at your earliest convenience)
6. 我公司经营进出口业务已达30多年,在中国华北地区建立了广泛的业务关系。(have extensive contacts)
7. 如果你方信誉良好,要取得这笔贷款就没有什么问题了。(credit)
8. 这个建议是照顾各有关方面的利益而提出的。(interest of all parties)
9. 我们相信在双方的共同努力下,我们的业务会朝着互惠互利的方向发展。(joint efforts)
10. 考虑到对方的资信情况,本公司认为贵方避免和那家公司来往是相当明智的。(refrain from)

C. Write a favorable reply to Sample Letter 2 (2).

Case Study

Please read the following introductions to Huawei and Nokia and find differences, if any, between them in presenting themselves.

Who Is Huawei?

Founded in 1987, Huawei is a leading global provider of information and communications technology (ICT) infrastructure and smart devices. We are committed to bringing digital to every person, home and organization for a fully connected, intelligent world. We have nearly 194,000 employees, and we operate in more than 170 countries and regions, serving more than three billion people around the world.

Huawei's end-to-end portfolio of products, solutions and services are both competitive and secure. Through open collaboration with ecosystem partners, we create lasting value for our customers, working to empower people, enrich home life, and inspire innovation in organizations of all shapes and sizes. At Huawei, innovation focuses on customer needs. We invest heavily in basic research, concentrating on technological breakthroughs that drive the world forward.

Who Owns Huawei?

Huawei is a private company wholly owned by its employees. Through the Union of Huawei Investment & Holding Co., Ltd., we implement an Employee Shareholding Scheme that involves 96,768 employee shareholders. This scheme is limited to employees. No government agency or outside organization holds shares in Huawei.

Who Controls and Manages Huawei?

Huawei has a sound and effective corporate governance system. Shareholding employees elect 115 representatives to form the Representatives' Commission. This Representatives' Commission elects the Chairman of the Board and the remaining 16 board directors. The Board of Directors elects four deputy chairs and three executive directors. Three deputy chairs take turns serving as the company's rotating chairman.

The rotating chairman leads the Board of Directors and its Executive Committee while in office. The board exercises decision-making authority for corporate strategy and operations management, and is the highest body responsible for corporate strategy, operations management, and customer satisfaction.

Meanwhile, the Chairman of the Board chairs the Representatives' Commission. As Huawei's highest decision-making body, the Representatives' Commission makes decisions on important company matters, like profit distribution, capital increases, and the elections of members of the Board of Directors and the Supervisory Board.

Who Does Huawei Work with?

Externally, we rely on our customers. They are at the center of everything we do, and we create value for them with innovative products. Internally, we rely on our dedicated employees. Dedication is a core part of our work ethic. At Huawei, those who contribute more get more.

We work with stakeholders including suppliers, partners, industry organizations, open source communities, standards organizations, universities, and research institutes all over the world to cultivate a broader ecosystem that thrives on shared success. In this way we can help drive advancements in technology and grow the industry as a whole.

We create local employment opportunities, pay our taxes, and comply with all applicable laws and regulations in the countries where we operate. We help local industries go digital, and we openly engage with governments and the media.

What Do We Offer the World?

We create value for our customers. Together with our partners, we provide innovative and secure network equipment to telecom carriers. We provide our industry customers with open, flexible, and secure ICT infrastructure products. In addition, we provide customers with stable, secure, and trustworthy cloud services that evolve with their needs. With our smartphones and other smart devices, we are improving people's digital experiences in work, life, and entertainment.

We ensure secure and stable network operations. We have made cyber security and privacy protection our top priorities since 2018. Over the past three decades, we have worked closely with our carrier customers to build over 1,500 networks in more than 170 countries and regions. Together, we have connected more than three billion people around the world, and we have maintained a solid track record in security throughout.

We promote industry development. Huawei advocates openness, collaboration, and shared success. Through joint innovation with our customers and partners, we are expanding the value of ICT to develop a more robust and symbiotic industry ecosystem. Huawei is an active member of more than 400 standards organizations, industry alliances, and open source communities, where we work with our peers to develop mainstream standards and lay the foundation for shared success. Together, we are driving the industry forward. We enable sustainable development.

Huawei has contributed significantly to bridging the digital divide and promoting digital inclusion, helping to connect places as remote as Mount Everest and the Arctic Circle. We are keenly aware of the importance of telecommunications in emergency situations. Having faced Ebola in West Africa, nuclear contamination triggered by the tsunami in Japan, and the massive earthquake that struck Sichuan, China, our people hold fast in disaster zones to restore communications networks and ensure the reliable operation of essential telecoms equipment. To further promote sustainability, we prioritize a low-carbon footprint and environmental protection. We are also supporting the development of the next generation of local ICT talent to boost the digital economy.

We provide dedicated people with a strong growth platform. Inspiring dedication is one of Huawei's core values, and it manifests itself in many ways. We assess employees and select managers based on their contribution, as well as the extent of their responsibilities. We provide our teams with a global development platform, giving young team members the opportunity to shoulder greater responsibilities and accelerate their careers. In this way, we have enabled over 100,000 Huawei people to yield ample returns and gain memorable life experience.

What Do We Stand for?

For the past 30 years we have maintained an unwavering focus, rejecting shortcuts and easy opportunities that don't align with our core business. With a practical approach to everything we do, we concentrate our efforts and invest patiently to drive technological breakthroughs. This strategic focus is a reflection of our core values: staying customer-centric, inspiring dedication, persevering, and growing by reflection.

The digital era has been generous. We will make the most of this historic opportunity, and boldly forge ahead to build a fully connected, intelligent world.

Corporate Highlights

Employees	194,000
Joint Innovation Centers	36
R&D Institutes & Centers/Offices	14

Our Vision

Huawei's vision is to bring digital to every person, home and organization for a fully connected, intelligent world. To this end, we will:

- Provide ubiquitous connectivity to give everyone equal access to connections;
- Provide pervasive intelligence to drive businesses forward;
- Build digital platforms to help all industries and organizations become more agile, efficient, and vibrant;
- Deliver a personalized experience to all, respecting the unique character of everyone, and enabling the full potential of every person to be realized.

Core Value

Openness, Collaboration, and Shared Success

Executives

The Shareholders' Meeting is the company's authoritative body, making decisions on major issues such as the company's capital increase, profit distribution, and selection of the members of the Board of Directors/Supervisory Board.

The Board of Directors (BOD) is the highest body responsible for corporate strategy, operations management, and customer satisfaction. The BOD's mission is to lead the company forward. It exercises decision-making authority for corporate strategy and operations management, and ensures the protection of customer and shareholder interests.

The BOD and its Executive Committee will be led by rotating chairmen. During their terms, the rotating chairmen will serve as the foremost leader of the company.

The key responsibilities of the Supervisory Board include overseeing the responsibility fulfillment of BOD members and senior management, monitoring the company's operational and financial status, and supervising internal control and legal compliance.

Liang Hua, Chairman

Born in 1964, Mr. Liang holds a doctorate degree from Wuhan University of Technology. Mr. Liang joined Huawei in 1995 and has served as President of Supply Chain, CFO of Huawei, President of the Business Process & IT Mgmt Dept, President of the Global Technical Service Dept, Chief Supply Chain Officer, Chairman of the Audit Committee, and Chairman of the Supervisory Board. Mr. Liang is now Chairman of Huawei's Board of Directors.

Sustainability

ICT Sustainable Development Goals Benchmark

The United Nations Sustainable Development Goals (SDGs), also known as Global Goals, offer a pathway to end poverty, fight inequality, and tackle climate change, while ensuring that no one is left behind.

Huawei believes that the SDGs provide an opportunity for long-term growth. ICT infrastructure will be crucial to help the world achieve these goals. Thus, there is a positive correlation between Huawei's vision of Building a Better Connected World and society's ability to achieve the goals.

We believe that ICT is a critical enabler to achieve the SDGs at the scale and speed necessary to fulfill the 2030 Agenda for Sustainable Development.

Corporate Governance

By staying customer-centric and inspiring dedication, we have sustained long-term growth through continuous improvement of our corporate governance structure, organizations, processes, and appraisal systems.

The Shareholders' Meeting is the company's authoritative body, making decisions on making decisions on major issues such as the company's capital increase, profit distribution, and selection of the members of the Board of Directors/Supervisory Board.

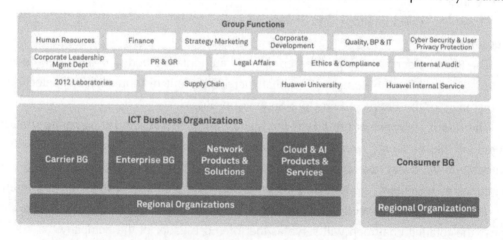

The Board of Directors (BOD) is the highest body responsible for corporate strategy, operations management, and customer satisfaction. The BOD's mission is to lead the company forward. It exercises decision-making authority for corporate strategy and operations management, and ensures the protection of customer and shareholder interests.

The BOD and its Executive Committee will be led by rotating chairmen. During their terms, the rotating chairmen will serve as the foremost leader of the company.

The key responsibilities of the Supervisory Board include overseeing the responsibility fulfillment of BOD members and senior management, monitoring the company's operational and financial status, and supervising internal control and legal compliance.

KPMG has been Huawei's independent auditor since 2000. The independent auditor is responsible for auditing a company's annual financial statements. In accordance with applicable accounting standards and audit procedures, the independent auditor expresses an opinion as to whether the financial statements are true and fair.

To strengthen end-to-end operations management of our ICT infrastructure business, the company set up the ICT Infrastructure Managing Board, which is the primary owner of our business strategy, operations management, and customer satisfaction for ICT infrastructure business.

Group Leadership Team

Our Group Leadership team is responsible for the operative management of Nokia. The Chair and members of the Group Leadership Team are appointed by the Board. The Group Leadership Team is chaired by the President and CEO. The President and CEO's rights and responsibilities include those allotted to the President under Finnish law.

Rajeev Suri, President and Chief Executive Officer (CEO)

Since April 2014, as Chief Executive Officer of Nokia, Rajeev has been the driving force behind Nokia's recent transformation, including its acquisition of Alcatel-Lucent, its successful expansion into enterprise vertical markets, the creation of a standalone software business, and the return of the Nokia brand to mobile phones. In his previous role as CEO of Nokia Solutions and Networks he also delivered a complete turnaround, increasing the value of the company from approximately 1 billion to more than 10 billion.

In his 30 years of international experience Rajeev has developed deep expertise across a range of technology areas that will be critical in the onset of the Fourth Industrial Revolution, including telecommunication networks and devices, the Internet of Things, virtual reality, digital health, big data analytics, cloud computing, artificial intelligence, enterprise digitalization, and internet business models. He has held senior business roles leading major Nokia accounts and various business units and regions. He has rich business experience working across a range of functions including strategy, mergers and acquisitions, product marketing, sales, account leadership, and regional and business unit leadership. As a successful global leader, he has lived in the Middle East, Asia, Africa, and Europe.

With broad global experience, Rajeev is a commissioner of the United Nations Broadband Commission, as well as a member of the Digital Communications Industry steering committee and the stewardship board of the Health and Healthcare System Initiative at the World Economic Forum.

Rajeev holds a bachelor's degree in Engineering (Electronics and Communications) from Manipal Institute of Technology, India. Rajeev was born in India in 1967, went on to become a Singaporean citizen, and is based in Espoo, Finland.

- CEO, Nokia Solutions and Networks (previously Nokia Siemens Networks) 2009—2014
- Head of Services, Nokia Siemens Networks 2007—2009
- Head of Asia Pacific, Nokia Siemens Networks April 2007—August 2007
- Senior Vice President, Asia Pacific, Nokia Networks 2005—2007
- Vice President, Hutchison Customer Business Team, Nokia Networks 2004—2005
- General Manager, Business Development, Asia Pacific, Nokia Networks 2003
- Sales Director-BT, O2, and Hutchison Global Customers, Nokia Networks 2002
- Director, Technology and Applications, BT Global Customer, Nokia Networks 2000—2001
- Head of Global Competitive Intelligence, Nokia Networks 1999—2000
- Head of Product Competence Center, South Asia, Nokia Networks 1997—1999
- System Marketing Manager, Cellular Transmission, India, Nokia Networks 1995—1997
- Head of Group Procurement, Imports/Special Projects, Churchgate Group, Nigeria 1993—1995
- National Account Manager, Strategic Planning, ICL India (ICIM) 1990—1993
- Production Engineer, Calcom Electronics 1989
- Commissioner of the United Nations Broadband Commission.
- Member of the Digital Communications Industry steering committee and the stewardship board of the Health and Healthcare System Initiative at the World Economic Forum.
- Named Finland's "Business Leader of the Year 2017" by Kauppalehti.
- Included in the "2016 All-Europe Executive Team-Best CEOs" by Institutional Investor.
- Recipient of the Marco Polo Award in China in recognition of Nokia's friendship with China.
- Holds an honorary doctorate from Manipal University, India.

What We Do

We create the technology to connect the world.

We develop and deliver the industry's only end-to-end portfolio of network equipment, software, services and licensing that is available globally.

Our customers include service providers whose combined networks support 6.1 billion subscriptions, as well as enterprises in the private and public sector that use our network portfolio to increase productivity and enrich lives. We also serve consumers with technology and devices.

Through our research teams, including the world-renowned Nokia Bell Labs, we are leading the world to adopt end-to-end 5G networks that are faster, more secure and capable of revolutionizing lives, economies and societies. Nokia adheres to the highest ethical business standards as we create technology with social purpose, quality and integrity.

Our History

Nokia has been adapting to the needs of an ever-changing world for over 150 years.

From its humble beginning in 1865 as a single paper mill operation, Nokia has found and nurtured success over the years in a range of industrial sectors including cable, paper products, rubber boots, tires, televisions and mobile phones.

Nokia's transition to a primary focus on telecommunications began in the 1990s. The first GSM call was made in 1991 using Nokia equipment. Rapid success in the mobile phone sector allowed Nokia to become by 1998, the best-selling mobile phone brand in the world. In 2003 Nokia introduced the first camera phone. In 2011, to address increasing competition from iOS and Android operating systems, Nokia entered into a strategic partnership with Microsoft. In 2014 Nokia sold its mobile and devices division to Microsoft.

The creation of Nokia Networks, following the buy-out of joint-venture partner Siemens in 2013, laid the foundation for Nokia's transformation into primarily a network hardware and software provider. The 2015 acquisition of Franco-American telecommunications equipment provider Alcatel-Lucent greatly broadened the scope of Nokia's portfolio and customer base. Additional acquisitions have positioned Nokia to be an industry leader in the transition to 5G wireless technology by offering the only end-to-end 5G network portfolio available on a global basis.

In 2016 Nokia re-entered the mobile handset business with a licensing agreement with HMD Global allowing them to offer phones under the Nokia brand.

Our Awards

We are recognized by our customers and the industry for our leadership in shaping the future of technology.

- Oct, 2019

    Nokia Deepfield awarded best secured network initiative at 2019 Broadband World Forum

- Sep, 2019

  Nokia named one of the world's most reputable companies for corporate responsibility in 2019
- Mar, 2019

  GSMA MWC-19 Global Mobile Award for 5G Leadership
- Nov, 2018

  Telecom Asia Wireless Home Technology of the Year Award
- Oct, 2018

  Metro Ethernet Forum (MEF) Awards
- Oct, 2018

  Broadband Award 2018: Best Fixed Access Solution
- Dec, 2017

  "Are You Well" wins 2017 Finnish Security Innovation Award
- Nov, 2017

  TelecomAsia Readers' Choice & Innovation Awards: CEM Innovation of the Year
- Nov, 2017

  Telco Data Analytic Awards

Security and Privacy

Security and privacy are part of everything we do. By design through delivery, and without compromise, we ensure your network is seamlessly secure.

Customers can trust Nokia when it comes to security and protecting their information and interests. We provide the assurance that you, as a customer, require through our five security promises.

1. We protect your information as rigorously as we protect our own;
2. We are transparent in our security practices;
3. We embed security into all our products and services;
4. We will inform you promptly of any serious product or service issues that affect you;
5. We independently validate our security practices.

Sustainability

We can achieve the greatest positive impact and help accelerate achievement of the United Nations Sustainable Development Goals by creating the technology that connects people and things. Our technology improves lives by providing access to education, information, better healthcare, and economic opportunity, and can enable a safer, smarter and healthier planet. The technology we provide can help create a more equitable society by connecting the unconnected.

Corporate Governance

Nokia's corporate governance practices comply with Finnish laws and regulations, Nokia's Articles of Association, the Finnish Corporate Governance Code 2015, and

Unit 2　Establishing Business Relations

corporate governance standards of the following stock exchanges: Nasdaq Helsinki and the New York Stock Exchange ("NYSE").

Unit 3 Enquiries and Replies

3.1 GENERAL INTRODUCTION TO ENQUIRIES AND REPLIES

3.1.1 Definition and Classification of Enquiries

An enquiry is a kind of questioning made by a buyer or sometimes a seller asking information about a certain commodity or a kind of service, with the purpose of obtaining answers to these questions within a reasonable period of time. Questions of enquiries include those on the availability of goods or services, prices, specifications, quality or even quantity, terms, catalogues, samples, etc. Enquiries are very commonly used during the first stage of business as an invitation to offer, and therefore they are often regarded as the real beginning of business negotiations.

Enquiries can be divided into different categories in various ways.

- The most common classification is to divide them into general and specific. A general enquiry refers to those aiming at gaining information about some goods or services rather than doing business right away, and thus only prices, catalogues or samples are required; on the other hand, a specific enquiry refers to those aiming at doing business right away if the offer is acceptable, and therefore it usually includes all of the trade terms of a specific commodity or service.
- Based on types of questions made in enquiries, enquiries can be further classified into enquiries about availability, enquiries about quality, quantity or specifications, enquiries about prices, enquiries about payment, enquiries about shipment, enquiries about packing, enquiries about insurance, etc.
- Besides, based on delivery methods, enquiries can be classified into written enquiries, i.e., enquiries sent by letter, telegram, telex or fax, and oral enquiries, i.e., enquiries delivered by telephone or even through face-to-face talk.
- Based on whether an enquiry is sent to some supplier for the first time, enquiries can also be divided into first enquiries and non-first enquiries.

3.1.2 Definition and Classification of Replies to Enquiries

On the basis of the definition of enquiries given above, a reply to an enquiry can be defined as the answering to questions usually raised up by a seller or sometimes a buyer, the supply of information and/or materials, as well as the attempt to satisfy the needs of those who make the requests.

Based on the classification of enquiries, replies, in turn, can be divided into those replied to general enquiries and those to specific enquiries, written replies and oral replies, or replies to first enquiries and those to non-first enquiries.

3.2 BASIC PRINCIPLES FOR SENDING ENQUIRIES AND REPLIES

3.2.1 Basic Principles for Sending Enquiries

As we have stated above, an enquiry is usually regarded as the first step in business negotiations, and therefore it is very important to leave a good first impression on the recipient. In order to make effective and efficient enquiries, we should pay attention to the following writing principles.

The contents should be concise and clear. Since the purpose of an enquiry is to ask for information, the enquiry sender has every obligation to make the enquiry as simple as possible, so as to save the time of the recipient and make it easy for them to make judgment. The enquiry sender should consider clearly what he/she wants to contain in the enquiry beforehand. Questions should be phrased in the way that the reader will know immediately the type of information to be sought, the reason for seeking the information, and how the information is to be used. If possible, it is better to put the questions in a numbered list that is restricted to a minimum so that the recipient can understand the questions as fast as possible and therefore can answer them in the corresponding sequence and none of them will be easily skipped over.

The attitude of the enquiry should be reasonable. This means that the enquiry sender should state clearly where he/she got the information about the recipient when the enquiry was conducted for the first time between them to avoid abruptness; questions related to business secrets should be avoided so that awkwardness will not be caused.

The tone should be courteous and sincere. The requests or questions should be made in a courteous way as usually the sender is asking for information and nobody will offer any help if the enquiry is made in a mandatory way. A return envelop with a stamp and the address of the sender can usually indicate the sincerity of the enquiry sender and can improve the chances of getting a reply. However, courtesy and sincerity does not mean blarney or self-debasement. It should always be remembered that the enquiry sender and the recipient are equal in a business relationship and therefore any blarney or self-debasement will cause damage to the relationship in the future.

What is more, although enquiries can be sent to different companies, they should not be sent out randomly as confidential information such as the need of the enquiry sender will be leaked along the enquiries.

3.2.2 Basic Principles for Sending Replies

As far as replies to enquiries are concerned, there are several principles to follow.

The importance of enquiries should be realized and therefore promptness and carefulness are required when making replies. Usually one of the measurements of the successfulness of a company is the quality and quantity of enquiry letters it receives as an enquiry usually indicates the greatest recognition and respect to the recipient. Few or almost no enquiries indicate non-promising development of the company. Therefore, non-action or ignorance to enquiries indicates the shortsightedness of the company. On the other hand, enquiries can always bring business opportunities to enquiry recipients, such as helping them make more money or save money, the potential of building good business relationship or network, the gaining of new information and acquaintance of the market trend, etc. Thus a bright and prudent company always welcomes enquiries, and usually organizes a group of experts to make analysis and assessment on the enquiries and send the replies in a prompt way.

A reply should either indicate a pleasant acceptance or a polite decline. Always be polite and show the eagerness of cooperation if possible. Even when there is no possibility of cooperation at the moment, always be polite and offer to provide further information if needed.

A reply should also be clear and helpful. It should cover all the information asked for in the enquiry. Better to organize it in the same number-listed way as the enquiry. It should be as concise and as direct as possible.

Besides, the reply sender should also pay attention to the "selling" of itself so as to make it prominent in all of the replies the enquiry sender can receive.

3.3 STRUCTURES OF ENQUIRIES AND REPLIES

3.3.1 Structures of Enquiries

An enquiry, written or oral, often includes the following parts:
- The opening:
—A brief introduction to the company and products and/or services of the enquiry sender.

> e.g. We are one of the leading companies dealing in the line of ... in ... market. We note you from the advertisement you put in (name of the newspaper) and are very much interested in your (name of products).

—Statement of the purpose of the enquiry.

> e.g. We are particularly interested in / We have a great interest in ... / We are very much keen on ... / We are in the market for / in need of ...

- The body:
—Expectation towards the reader or listener.

> e.g. Will you please send us by ... (things required)?

—An exact description or specification of the wanted product or service, including the weight, material, quantity, delivery, size, etc. (only for a specific enquiry)

> e.g. When replying, please state ...

—Clarification on terms, methods of payment, shipment, expected discount, etc. (only for a specific enquiry)

> e.g. We would like to know whether you are able to allow us ... (a special discount)

—Potential opportunities for or benefits of the reader or listener.

> e.g. If we find ... at your end satisfactory, we will place regular orders with you.

- The closing:
—Demonstration of optimism and request of an early reply.

> e.g. We are looking forward to your reply. Your prompt attention to this matter will be much appreciated.

However, if the enquiry is made between the potential buyer and seller for the first time, it should usually state at first its information source, i.e., how the company name of the enquiry recipient (the reader or listener of the enquiry) is acquired. Sample sentence frames can be as follows:

> You name was given to us by ... who has been our regular customer for some years. We understand that you are one of the largest manufacturers of ... in your country, and we want to avail this opportunity to express our hope of entering into business relations with you.
> We are told (by ... that) you are potential buyers / experienced importers of ...

Besides, a first enquiry should put stress on the potential opportunities for or benefits of the recipient if the deal is made so as to motivate the recipient to respond as soon as possible. A description of future cooperation opportunities is usually helpful. A sample sentence frame could be:

> We are large dealers in (field of business) and believe there is a promising market in our area for moderately priced goods of the kind mentioned.

3.3.2 Basic Contents of Replies to Enquiries

Generally speaking, there are usually two cases of replies, i. e., affirmative replies indicating potential cooperation opportunities and negative replies indicating no cooperative possibility at the moment.

An affirmative reply usually contains the following:
- The opening:
—Notification of the reception of the enquiry, appreciation of the interest demonstrated by the enquiry sender and confirmation on the possibility of cooperation.

> e. g. Thank you for your letter of ... regarding / concerning / in connection with ... We have (reviewed our available stock) / checked / looked into / investigated (the possible approaches) ...

- The body:
—Reference to the enclosing of the required catalogue or price list.

> e. g. As requested, we enclose ... and ... with details of ... We are also posting ... separately.

—Statement of the competitiveness and advantages of the product or service, including the discount the counterpart can get if there is any.

> e. g. On regular purchases in quantities of not less than ... of individual items, we would allow you a discount of

—Statement of the possible methods of payment, shipment, etc.

> e. g. Payment is to be made by (methods of payment).

—Indication of the product range and achievements of the reply sender and their significance.

> e. g. We invite your attention to our other products such as ... details of which you will find in the catalogue.

- The closing:
—Demonstration of optimism and request of an early reply.
Structural sentence frames:

> e. g. If you require any further information, please do not hesitate to contact us. / Do contact us on ... if you need further information. / We should appreciate a prompt reply. / Look forward to receiving your ...

A negative reply can be organized as follows:
- The opening:

—Notification of receipt of the enquiry, appreciation of the interest demonstrated by the enquiry sender and confirmation on the impossibility of cooperation at the moment.

> e. g. We thank you for your enquiry of (date of enquiry) for our (product). We regret that we have no (product) at present and we will get new source of (product) (time) / our requirements have already been filled in full / we have fully covered our demand for the time being / we have placed our order elsewhere / there is no demand for this item at the moment.

- The body:
—Reasons for impossibility of cooperation at the moment.

> e. g. The supply has run out. / The goods are in short supply. / Large number of enquiries is pouring in. The supply position is rather tight.

—Introduction to the reply sender's company and product range, especially those within the scope of or similar to the requiry sender's interest.

> e. g. We invite your attention to our other products such as ... details of which you will find in the catalogue.

- The closing:
—Demonstration of optimism and wish for future cooperation.

> e. g. If there is any need for the goods, we will be sure to let you know. / We look forward to doing business with your company in the future ... / We shall let you know when ... / We will keep your requirements in mind ...

3.4 SAMPLE LETTERS

Sample Letter 3 (1)

> Dear Sir or Madam,
> We learn from the Commercial Counselor of our Embassy in your country that you manufacture and export a variety of handicraft articles. We are the leading dealer in art craft products in San Francisco where Chinese hand-made art and craft items are especially popular. As there is a high demand of high quality brocade handbags recently and we are in short of stock, we would like you to send us as soon as possible the following items:
> 1. Two illustrated catalogues of your rectangle-shaped small-size (less than 0.3 m * 0.2 m) brocade handbags;
> 2. Samples of the above mentioned handbags;

3. Prices, terms of payment, the earliest shipment and quantity available of the above mentioned handbags;
4. Discounts you would allow on purchases of quantities of no less than 500 of individual items.

If the products are of the standards we require, we will place a substantial order with you.

Your early reply will be very much appreciated.

Yours faithfully

Sample Letter 3 (2)

Dear Mr. Crane,

Thank you for your enquiry of May 23 about our brocade handbags. We are thankful for your interest in our products and we wish this will help us enter a longtime business relation in the future. As requested, I would like to provide you with the following information:

1. As requested, we enclose two copies of the illustrated catalogue and price list of our rectangle-shaped small-and-medium-sized (smaller than 0.3 m * 0.2 m) brocade handbags. We also enclose another copy of illustrated catalogue and price list of our square-shaped small-and-medium-sized (smaller than 0.3 m * 0.3 m), which might be of interest to you as well since they are sold very well in Canada and more fashionable currently;
2. We are also posting the samples of the required handbags separately;
3. It is to be understood that unless otherwise stated, all prices quoted are on the basis of CIF terms without any commission. Besides, we always deal on payment by sight L/C and shipment is to be made within 45 days of receipt of order and payment. What is more, since we are the largest manufacturer of such handbags in our area, we always have sufficient goods in stock and we can ensure production of 100,000 pieces per day in case of large quantity of order.
4. We can offer you the quantity discount you asked for which would be 5% off net prices for orders over $10,000.

If there is any further information you require, please contact us.

Yours faithfully

Sample Letter 3 (3)

Dear Mr. Wong,

<u>Re: Enquiry for Batteries</u>

Thank you for your letter of Friday, May 25, 2021 regarding making copies of the sample battery you sent us.

We have investigated the situation and found that your specifications are exactly the same as the design of a proprietary camera battery manufactured by a large Japanese electronics company.

We feel that it would not be in our interests to supply this type of battery. However, we would like to thank you for considering our company as your supplier.

Look forward to doing business with your company in the future.

Sincerely yours

3.5 USEFUL TERMS AND EXPRESSIONS

1.	enquiry	询盘
2.	general enquiry	一般询盘
3.	specific enquiry	具体询盘
4.	first enquiry	首次询盘
5.	commission	佣金
6.	catalogue	目录
7.	price list	价目表
8.	discount	折扣
9.	sample	样品
10.	separately	另寄
11.	light industrial products	轻工业商品
12.	general merchandise	日用百货
13.	plastic articles	塑料制品
14.	suitcase, bags and leather products	箱包及皮件
15.	footwears	鞋
16.	clock & watch	钟表

17.	household utensils	家用器具
18.	household electric appliance	家用电器
19.	furniture	家具
20.	kitchenware	厨具
21.	building materials	建筑材料
22.	glassware	玻璃器皿
23.	Western musical instruments	西洋乐器
24.	Chinese musical instruments	中国民族乐器
25.	toys	玩具
26.	photographic and cinematic graphic supplies	照相及电影器材
27.	deal	做买卖(with); 经营(in)
28.	place	发出(订单)
29.	appreciate	感激
30.	competitive	竞争性的
31.	illustrate	给……作插图说明(或装饰)
32.	enclose	包含, 封入

3.6 COMMUNICATION LABORATORY

Application Exercises

A. Translate the following sentences into Chinese.

1. We have obtained your name and address from the New York Federated Chamber of Commerce.
2. Enclosed please find a price list for our new product line.
3. We look forward to receiving a full range of samples at your earliest convenience.
4. It would be appreciated if samples could be forwarded to us.
5. We enclose the catalogue of typewriters for which you ask in your letter of March 9.
6. Will you please send me a copy of your catalogue and price list of watches, and copies of any descriptive leaflets that I could pass to prospective customers?
7. Your firm has been recommended to us by IDEE Co. of US, with whom we have done business for many years.
8. We are interested in electronic products and shall be glad if you will send us a copy of your catalogue and current price list.
9. There is an increasing demand for the cotton textiles. We suggest that you quote us

competitive prices and give us favorable terms because our order will be very large.

10. Please say whether you could supply the goods from stock as we need them urgently.

B. Translate the following sentences into English.

1. 请详告价格、质量、可供量和其他有关情况。（as to）
2. 请寄贵方厨房用品目录，并注明付款条件及能给的最大折扣。（allow a discount of）
3. 如果贵方年总购买量超过 2 万美元，我方愿给予 5% 的折扣。（annual total purchase）
4. 贵方如能保证定期供应，我方将向贵方大量订购。（assure regular supplies）
5. 我们相信我方的皮革产品的质量完全适合你方市场。（be suitable for）
6. 我们是经营轻工业产品的国有公司。（handle）
7. 如果你方价格可行，我们的客户将有意订货。（workable）
8. 随函附上我方最近一季度产品新目录一份，介绍多种新品种以及上季度颇受欢迎的货物，请贵方研究新目录并提出你方下一季度的需求以便我方调整对其他客户的供货。（adjust supply）
9. 有关贵方关于我方红茶的询盘，我们愿做如下答复。（with regard to）
10. 我方对贵公司的罐头食品有兴趣，希望能收到产品目录。（take interest in）

C. Write a reply to Sample Letter 3（1）.

Case Study

Website for Enquiry

Nowadays, some companies provide specific websites to handle enquiries and replies will be sent back automatically or manually to enquiry senders according to the nature of the enquiries.

Please study the following website of Panasonic for enquiry carefully and then create a similar enquiry website for the brocade handbag company in Sample Letter 3（2）.

This Enquiries Site ...

... is for exclusive use by partners who trade in the OEM products described on "industrial.panasonic.com", customer production facilities, and all related businesses.

Our Products

Batteries, power supplies Optics, sensors, I/O Processing technology & materials OEM storage（drivers, supplies） Motors, fans, compressors Passive & electromechanical components Factory automation	Semiconductors （Microcontroller, transistor, diode LED, IC, LSI, CCD, MOS FET, IPD, MMIC, GaAs, Hall IC, photo interrupter, photo coupler） [MN-, AN-, MA-, MIP-, 2S-, MTM-, MSG-, MW-, NP-, UN-, UP-, XN-, XP-, CN-, LN-, PN-, HUL-]

Our Sites

● Industry group production sites	● Industry group sales bases

Enquiries that cannot be handled:
National Panasonic personal and office products
Panasonic household appliance repair: ● Go here
Construction, architectural, and design-related products
Enquiries regarding Panasonic PCs and peripheral devices
    For general Matsushita enquiries, go to:
        ● http://panasonic.net/corporate/global_network

[1] **Enquiry Details Entered**

ID (e-mail address) entered / password chosen, and other customer information entered.
Note: Replies may not be received by e-mail addresses with limited character numbers.

[2] **Receipt Confirmation E-mail Sent**

Note 1:	Sent from typical address.
Note 2:	If the confirmation e-mail is not received within 30 minutes: There may have been a problem when the customer information was entered. In particular, check that there are no errors in the e-mail address (which is used as ID).

[3] **Reply from Supervisor**

Note: Sent from typical address.

[4] **Repost Enquiry (If Problem Is the Same)**

Enter data to the enquiry system from the personal URL described in the reply.
Note: The details handled last time will be carried over.

[5] **New Enquiry (at a Later Date)**

Use the ID and password used in [1] above.
Note: Customer information does not need to be reentered.

Further, the typical address is send-only from the system.
Note that replies to this address will not be answered.

Scope of Enquiries and Replies

On your first visit, register customer information and organizational affiliation so that we can supply better-tailored advice on customer design and development.

Your personal information will never be divulged outside of the relevant industry group.

Go here for relevant scope:	● Industry group production sites
	● Industry group sales bases
Go here also:	● Personal privacy and this site

Replies are valid only for the customer and company concerned.

Passing the replies in whole or in part to a third party or for secondary use is strictly prohibited by copyright.

Company Close

We will be closed from April 28, 2007 to May 6, for holiday in Japan.

We will resume our regular operation from May 7, 2007.

Sorry for inconvenience, but we will appreciate your understanding.

Thank you ...

Read the above conditions carefully, and if you agree, select the Agree checkbox and then click the Next button to proceed.
(Also go here if you have forgotten your password.)
☐ Agree

● Checking and changing your details	● Deleting your details

[Cancel Your Enquiry]

Unit 4 Quotations, Offers and Counteroffers

4.1 GENERAL INTRODUCTION TO QUOTATIONS, OFFERS AND COUNTEROFFERS

4.1.1 Definition of Quotations

When a seller receives an enquiry for the goods that he is in a position to supply, it is expected of him to send an immediate reply to the enquirer in which the requested information should be included. As enquiries often concern the prices of goods, most replies contain a quotation or offer.

A quotation is a written form in response to an enquiry, informing the enquirer of the price and other terms of transaction. A quotation is different from an offer, though these two words are sometimes confused in use, the difference of which will be illustrated in the later part.

4.1.2 Definition and Classification of Offers

According to the *UN Convention of Contracts for the International Sale of Goods*, a proposal for concluding a contract addressed to one or more specific persons constitutes an offer if it is sufficiently definite and indicates the intention of the offeror to be bound in case of acceptance. A proposal other than one addressed to one or more specific persons is to be considered merely as an invitation to make offers, unless the contrary is clearly indicated by the person making the proposal. Making an offer is an important step in negotiating a transaction. The person making the offer is called the offeror and the person to whom the offer is made is called the offeree. It expresses the wishes of the offeror to enter into a contract with the offeree under certain terms. An offer must be made and accepted before a contract can exist. It can refer to trading terms put forward by offerors to offerees, which mainly include name of commodity, brand, specification, quantity, price, packing and shipment.

An offer may be made in reply to an enquiry or made voluntarily with a view to expanding business. Usually it is sent from sellers to buyers. However, sometimes buyers send an offer to sellers, which is called *bid*.

An offer falls into two types: firm offer and non-firm offer.

A firm offer or offer with engagement is a definite expression from the offeror that he is ready to sell goods at a stated price within a stipulated time. Once a firm offer is made, the offeror is in no position to withdraw the offer within its validity to make any amendments to the contents of the offer. To put it another way, a firm offer is irrevocable and unchanging and is binding on the offeror. Once the offer is accepted, business is done. On the other hand, the moment the terms of validity end, the offer lapses. Thereupon the offeror is no longer responsible to what is stipulated in the offer. Even now the offeree expresses his wish to accept what is offered, the offeror has his right to refuse it.

A firm offer is to satisfy the following two requirements. First, the terms put forward should be complete, clear, definite and without reservations. The contents must be as clear as possible covering quality, quantity, packing, shipment, payment, insurance and validity. Such ambiguous diction as "about", "reference price" should be avoided. And no reservation, such as "subject to our final confirmation" should exist. Second, time of validity must be specified. There are several ways to indicate the validity.

(1) Indicating the deadline

- We offer you firm subject to reply by 17:30, (before) ... our time, October 30.
- The offer is subject to your acceptance by ninth September.

(2) Specifying a period of time for acceptance

- The offer is subject to your reply in nine days.
- We offer you firm subject to your reply (acceptance) reaching us within 3 days from today.

(3) Indicating the non-specific time

- We look forward to your early reply.
- Our offer is subject to your acceptance as soon as possible.

Here, in the first example, since no specific date is set, the offeree should reply within a reasonable time. However, as to the terms "a reasonable time" and "as soon as possible" there is no universal understanding. Therefore, to avoid disputes in the future, it is preferred to fix the validity in a specific way.

A non-firm offer is a non-undertaking expression of the offeror. It just displays the intention of the offeror and thus is not binding on the offeror. The content of a non-firm offer is not so complete and clear as that of a firm one. It has no term of validity and is more flexible to the offeror as he can make changes according to the economic context. A non-firm offer is with reservation. If any of the following appears, the offer should undoubtedly be a non-firm one.

- Subject to our final confirmation
- Subject to prior sale
- Subject to change without notice

- Subject to the goods being unsold
- Subject to fluctuations of the market
- Without engagement (obligation)

4.1.3 Definition of Counteroffer

A reply to an offer which purports to be an acceptance but contains additions, limitations or other modifications is a rejection of the offer and constitutes a counteroffer. It is virtually a new offer of the buyer or offeree. The buyer may disagree to any of the terms listed in the offer, such as the price, packing and shipment, to name just a few, and put forward his own terms instead.

Once a counteroffer is made, the offer lapses. If the buyer wants to accept the previous offer later because of the appearance of some favorable elements, the seller has every right to decide whether he will accept it or not, even it is within the time of validity of the previous offer. The counteroffer enables the previous offeree to be the offeror and the previous offeror the offeree, who enjoys the full right of acceptance or refusal. When receiving a counteroffer, the seller may make a re-offer considering the current situation. Sometimes business can be finalized without counteroffers; sometimes many rounds of counteroffers occur before a contract is reached or before the business is called off.

4.2 DIFFERENCE BETWEEN QUOTATIONS AND OFFERS

Despite the misusage of them, a quotation is actually different from an offer. A quotation is usually about a unit price with delivery terms. It is just an indication of price, which is subject to change without previous notice. An offer can be divided into two types: firm offer and non-firm offer. As far as the content is concerned, an offer is more complete, clear, and definite than a quotation. An offer contains not only price but also quantity, shipment, payment, the time of validity, etc. What is more, from the legal point of view, an offer, when it is made firm, can not be withdrawn or revoked within its validity time; while, void of these characteristics, a quotation is more flexible. And quotations with certain qualifying words can sometimes play the function of firm offers.

4.3 GUIDELINES FOR OFFERS

4.3.1 Points for Attention

In making offers, you should first make it clear that it is a firm offer or a non-firm offer. Generally speaking, there are four principles to follow in the writing of a firm offer.

(1) The offer must be definite, clearly expressing your intention to make a contract with the other party.

(2) The offer must be complete, clear and specific, including all the main terms of transaction, such as price, quantity, delivery, insurance, payment, packing, etc.

(3) The offer must be final, not open. As soon as it is accepted by the offeree within the time of validity, the offer is irrevocable and cannot be withdrawn. Next step for both parties is to enter into a contract upon the terms stated in the offer.

(4) The term of validity must be stated clearly.

4.3.2 Basic Contents of Offers

In business transaction as a usual practice, a satisfactory offer should include the following:

- To express thanks for receiving the enquiry, if any;
- To make favorable comments on the goods needed, if necessary;
- To properly introduce the market quotation and the marketability of the goods concerned so as to arouse the desire of the prospective buyer to buy them;
- To supply detailed information concerning the contract, such as names of commodities, quality, quantity, specifications, prices, discounts, shipment or delivery, terms of payment, packing conditions. Make a statement or clear indication of what the prices cover (e.g. packing, freight and insurance);
- To show validity of the offer;
- (If the goods are not available) To suppose the commodities can not be supplied now for certain reasons, inform the enquirer when they will be available and also recommend other suitable substitutes or introduce other kinds of products. Make sure that you leave no impression of forcing the enquirer to buy your products or making decisions for them;
- To express the hope that the offer can be accepted or an order will be placed.

In order to illustrate the products more vividly, an offer with pictures is a better choice. The reader can get a direct image from the picture and know more about the products. A proper picture may win agreeable comments from the readers and leave a favorable impression on them.

4.4 GUIDELINES FOR COUNTEROFFERS

4.4.1 Basic Contents of Counteroffers

In order to persuade the offeror into accepting your proposal, you should draft your counteroffer letter with great care and tact. Try to convince the offeror that your request is justifiable, make reasonable explanations and persuade him with facts. In writing a counteroffer, you should state your opinions and the terms most explicitly and make sure to use words carefully so as to avoid ambiguity or misunderstanding. A counteroffer usually covers the following points:

- To express thanks to the seller for his offer. Make a friendly start and put the reader in a good mood;
- To show your regret for not being able to accept the offer. Assure the seller that his

offer has been under serious consideration and your response is made after careful thought;
- To state the reasons for not being able to accept the offer. Provide a factual explanation and make sure that your reasons hold water. Write in an objective way and sincere tone. Do not argue or accuse others;
- An indirect approach is preferred, that is, you should state your reasons first and put your positions second;
- To indicate clearly your own idea, including the altered terms and conditions acceptable;
- To express your hope for a favorable reply and your interest in doing business.

4.4.2 Replies to Counteroffers

Upon receipt of a counteroffer, a prompt reply is needed. If the seller agrees to the counteroffer, he should present clearly his reasons and try to be on good terms with the buyer. If the seller turns down the counteroffer, he should explain the reason with caution and express the hope for the possibilities of future cooperation. Politeness is needed here and the "going straight to the point" approach is not recommended. The seller partly agrees to the counteroffer and makes another counteroffer, which may bring about a series of counteroffers before the business is concluded.

As far as simple response, acceptance or refusal is concerned, replies to counteroffers usually include the following:
- To tell the reader that you have known his intention and show your regret;
- To express your acceptance or regret that the counteroffer can not be accepted;
- To explain the reasons for accepting or declining the counteroffer;
- To express your wish to establish business relations.

4.5 SAMPLE LETTERS

Sample Letter 4 (1): Quotation

Dear Sir or Madam,

We are pleased to learn from your letter of fourth June that you are interested in our silicone bracelets. We are glad to take advantage of this chance to introduce to you our various products available. We are sending separately a copy of our catalogue and price list with sample pictures for your reference.

We are the leading producers in this area and enjoy good reputation in the trade. We are sure that our different types of products, being cheap and excellent, will meet your requirements.

We look forward to receiving your order soon.

Yours faithfully

Sample Letter 4 (2): Reply to a Quotation

Dear Sir or Madam,

Thank you for your quotation for Men's Shirts and the samples sent us on sixth May. We have approached a number of our customers in this area and many of them take an interest in "Lion" brand shirts. We, therefore, ask you to make us your best offer on C&F Rangoon basis for 6,000 Men's Shirts (No. G-4). We believe we may secure some orders for you.

We, however, would like to point out that unless your quotation is attractive to the buyers, it would be difficult to push the sale of your shirts successfully. We shall appreciate your offer in the form of a proforma invoice.

Yours faithfully

Sample Letter 4 (3): A Firm Offer

Dear Sir or Madam,

We acknowledge with thanks receipt of your letter dated first September. As quested, we are airmailing you separately, our latest catalogue. We hope it will reach you in due course.

In reply, we have pleasure in making the following offer, subject to your reply reaching us by the end of this month.

Name of Commodity: Cylindrical Lock (3871PB-FT)

Specifications: Cylindrical construction with different kinds of keyways: KW1, SC1, YALE, C4, Sega;

Entranced with fixed or adjustable latch 2 3/8 inches or 2 3/4 inches; For doors with 1 3/8-inch to 1 3/4-inch thickness

Packing: in boxes and blisters

Price: at STG £ 6 per piece FOB Shanghai

Shipment: Within one month after receipt of your TT or L/C

Minimum Order: 300 to 400 pieces

Payment: by TT or irrevocable L/C at sight

Cylindrical Lock

We look forward to the pleasure of receiving an order from you soon.

Sincerely yours

Sample Letter 4 (4): A Non-Firm Offer

Dear Sir or Madam,

We thank you for your letter of eighth May asking for garbage bags. As requested, we are pleased to make an offer for 400 dozen of garbage bags (WT 02) at the price of USD144 per dozen. Shipment will be effected within 15 days after receipt of your L/C.

The offer above is subject to our final confirmation. We have also airmailed you separately a brochure of our products. We hope some of them may interest you.

We look forward to receiving a trial order from you.

Yours faithfully

Sample Letter 4 (5): A Counteroffer

Dear Sir or Madam,

Thank you for offer of eleventh March for washing machine (style TD-KB).

We appreciate the good quality of your goods, but we regret to tell you that we are not in a position to accept the offer on your terms. Your price appears to be on the high side, which will leave us with only a small profit on our sales. We can obtain goods of the same quality from our usual suppliers at lower prices.

May we suggest that you make some allowance on your quoted prices, say 6%. If you can do so, we believe that we can establish long-term relations with each other.

We look forward to your favorable reply.

Yours faithfully

4.6 USEFUL TERMS AND EXPRESSIONS

1.	quotation	报价
2.	offer	发盘
3.	offeror	报盘人
4.	offeree	受盘人
5.	firm offer	实盘
6.	non-firm offer	虚盘
7.	combined offer	搭配报盘

Unit 4 Quotations, Offers and Counteroffers

8.	lump offer	综合报盘
9.	bid	递盘
10.	terms and conditions	条款
11.	machinery and equipment	机械设备类商品
12.	machines tools	机床
13.	power machines and equipment	动力机械及设备
14.	machinery for light industry and textile industry	轻纺机械
15.	petro-chemical machinery	石油化工机械
16.	machinery for printing industry	印刷机械
17.	cereals processing machines	粮食加工机械
18.	foodstuff making machines	食品加工机械
19.	complete industrial equipment (plant)	成套工业设备
20.	transport machinery	运输机械
21.	tractors and auxiliary equipment	拖拉机及辅助设备
22.	other agricultural machines	其他农业机械
23.	tools and agricultural implements	工具和农具
24.	miscellaneous machinery	杂项机械
25.	stipulate	按合约的条件规定；按合同要求
26.	irrevocable	不能撤回的；不可废止的
27.	lapse	失效的,不再有效的；期满的
28.	validity	(法律上)有效；合法(性) 合逻辑；正确(性)
29.	engagement	正式的承诺或保证
30.	allowance	折价,折扣
31.	be subject to	以……为条件
32.	on the high/low/small/heavy side	偏高/低/小/重
33.	literature	小册子；传单

4.7 COMMUNICATION LABORATORY

Application Exercises

A. Translate the following sentences into Chinese.

1. While we do not doubt whatever you said, we are of the opinion that the quality of the Brazilian goods is far from being comparable to ours.
2. We make this allowance because we should like to do business with you if possible, but we must stress that it is the lowest price we can accept.
3. To push the sales of this new-concept bicycle, they have no choice but to make a concession in certain respects.
4. We are much interested in your curtains but because your minimum limit for order is too big for this market, we have difficulty in inducing buyers to place trial orders for your products.
5. Since we are preparing for the summer seasoning sale in June and July, your offer for June shipment may be somewhat late for the sale.
6. If you could increase the quantity you require to 100 dozen, we may consider to allow you a 10% reduction, but this does not imply that we would give you such a reduction for separate orders totaling 100 dozen.
7. As we want to expand our turnover with you, we have quoted you very low prices. We shall be unable to repeat these when our present stock is exhausted.
8. Through lengthy and on-and-off negotiations, we now finally reached agreement and concluded business.
9. We have the pleasure of sending you separately our latest catalogue of the complete line of our sporting goods with their price list.
10. Please send us one of these models by air immediately. We are enclosing a check to cover the amount.

B. Translate the following sentences into English.

1. 如果你方价格有竞争性，我们有意大量订购这种型号的计算机。(competitive)
2. 请贵方注意，我方的报盘是以随信附上的先售条件为准。(prior condition)
3. 由于贵方价格比我们地区的批发价还高，我们不可能接受贵方报价。(wholesale)
4. 复你方7月9日信，我们乐意向你方报盘如下，以北京时间7月20日前复到为有效。(subject to)
5. 如果你方可以安排较早的装运期，我们相信这必将有助于促进业务。(shipment)
6. 请报最优惠盘，并注明原产地、包装、详细规格、可供数量及最早装期。(favourable)
7. 本报盘已于10月21日失效，我们已不受此盘约束。(free from)
8. 请寄厨房用品目录，并注明你方付款条件及能给予的最大折扣。(discount)
9. 除非另有说明或约定，价格一律没有折扣。(agree upon)
10. 我公司的装运部门准备依从贵公司对运输路线的特殊要求，特此通知。(comply with)

C. Cloze

Dear Sir or Madam,

    We a _____ receipt of both your offer of seventh May and the sample of Men's Shirts, and thank you for these.

    While a _____ the good q _____ of your shirts, we find your price is rather too high for the m _____ we wish to s _____.

    We have also to point out that the Men's Shirts are a _____ in our market from several European m _____, all of them are at prices from 15% to 20% b _____ yours.

    Such being the case, we have to ask you to consider if you can make r _____ in your price, say 10%. As our order would be worth around $50,000, you may think it worthwhile to make a c _____.

    We await with keen interest your immediate reply.

                                               Yours faithfully

Case study

Please write two different replies, an acceptance and a rejection, to the following letter.

Dear Sir or Madam,

    We have received your letter dated March 22, and regret to note that you find our price for Art. No. 125 is on the high side. As you may know, our goods are very popular in many countries. Despite a limited supply at present, demand is on the rise. If you make a comparison between our goods and other makes, we trust you will agree that our price is workable. As a matter of fact, we have already cut our price to the minimum and concluded substantial business with other buyers at this level.

    However, if you agree to increase your order to 7,000 cases, we'd be willing to reduce our previous quotation by another 2%. This is the best we can do, and we hope it's acceptable to you. We would appreciate your early reply.

                                               Sincerely yours

Unit 5 Orders and Their Execution

5.1 GENERAL INTRODUCTION TO ORDERS

An order is a formal request from a buyer to supply a certain quantity of specified goods at a certain price within a certain period of time. To put it simply, it is an offer to buy. An order may come into existence through the following two ways:

- Through offer or counteroffer, the buyer eventually accepts the offer and places an order accordingly.
- The buyer makes a direct order for specific goods according to the catalogue, price list or sample forwarded by the seller beforehand.

An order can be sent by letter or memorandum, a printed order form, a fax or e-mail message or orally at a meeting, etc. However, it is a common practice to make orders or to confirm them in writing in international business so as to avoid misunderstanding and disputes in the future. Nowadays a printed order form/sheet is employed by many companies, as this method displays the following advantages:

- The sheet is pre-numbered and therefore easy to inquire about in the future, if need be, which brings great convenience.
- Important details will not easily be overlooked and thus negligence or errors can be avoided.
- The general conditions under which orders are placed can be printed on the back. But if these conditions are referred to, they should be put in the front, because otherwise they have no sanction against the seller.

As a result of these, in placing orders, the only thing needed to be done is to fill in the sheets and send them out with letters.

An order must have the following two essential qualities: accuracy and clarity. To put it another way, it should be specific and complete. A detailed description should be provided so that misunderstanding and troubles can be avoided. The information must be presented explicitly and no ambiguous and vague expressions are allowed. If you have several items to go in one order, you had better put them in a listed form.

The buyer's order is not legally binding unless it is an acceptance of the firm offer from the seller. However, when the order is accepted or confirmed by the seller, business is concluded and both parties, the buyer and the seller, are legally bound to honor their

agreement. They should bear their responsibilities respectively. It is required by law of the buyer to do the following:
- To accept the goods, provided they comply with the terms of order;
- To pay for them according to the terms agreed upon;
- To check the goods as soon as possible (failure to give prompt notice of faults or discrepancies to the seller will be taken as acceptance of the goods, which will bring you a lot of trouble).

The following are the seller's obligations:
- To deliver goods exactly of the kind ordered, and at the agreed time;
- To guarantee that the goods to be free from faults, which the buyer could not be aware of at the time of purchase.

If the seller cannot supply goods promptly, he should send a letter immediately to the buyer, in which he should make an apology first, then explain reasons for the delay, hope that it will not bring too much inconvenience or cause heavy losses to the buyer and if possible make clear when the goods can be delivered.

If faulty goods are delivered, the buyer is in every position to demand either a reduction in price, or replacement of goods, or cancellation of the order. The buyer has every right to make complaints and claims on the seller for the losses inflicted on him.

5.2 BASIC CONTENTS OF ORDERS

You can never be too clear in making an order. An order, therefore, should include the following:
- An accurate and full description of goods required: name of commodity, a catalogue or model number, size, color, shade or whatever other data necessary to identify the merchandise;
- All the trading terms: quality, quantity, price per item, total price, discount (if for resale, or if you are given a discount because you are paying promptly), terms of payment agreed upon, packing (by case, carton or bag, etc.), place to which goods are to be shipped, date and method of shipment, marking requirements, insurance, and other necessary details;
- Purchase order number, date of order, signature of person authorized to order;
- All documents required;
- The hope of being given prompt and careful attention to the order.

Any success depends upon previous preparation. Thereby, in placing an order, make sure that every detail has been taken care of beforehand, which will sure save you a lot of trouble in the future. The more thorough the information provided is, the more smooth the transaction will be.

5.3 REPLIES TO ORDERS

5.3.1 Acceptance of Orders

Upon receipt of an order, be it an initial order or not, which is an order placed according to the seller's quotation, price lists and samples, a letter of acknowledgement should be written as soon as possible. Generally speaking, this kind of letter should include the following contents:

- An expression of pleasure at and thanks for receiving the order;
- A favorable comment on the goods to be supplied;
- Restatement of some important terms agreed upon;
- An assurance of prompt and careful execution of the order;
- Drawing attention to other products likely to be of interest to the buyer;
- Hope for future orders.

In addition, a Sales Contract or Sales Confirmation in duplicate is enclosed for counter-signature according to usual practice, one copy of which is to be returned for the seller's file.

5.3.2 Rejection to Orders

If for certain reasons, the seller cannot accept the buyer's order, a rejection letter should be provided in time or a counteroffer be made. Such kind of letters should be written with the utmost care. You should be polite, try not to hurt the other party's feelings and make it clear that there stands likelihood for future business. It is recommended that the following points be included in a rejection letter:

- To acknowledge receipt of the order with thanks;
- To express regret of inability to accept the order;
- To provide justified reasons for why you cannot meet the buyer's requirement;
- To recommend other items as a replacement or presentation of a counteroffer;
- To show your appreciation of the buyer's confidence in your company and express your wish for future cooperation.

5.4 SAMPLE LETTERS

Sample Letter 5 (1)

> Dear Sir or Madam,
>
> Thank you for your letter of May 16 with your latest catalogue and price list of Speed Brand Electric Scooter. The latest model HL-E18 impresses us greatly with its satisfying quality and original appearance.

We are very glad to place the following order with you.

Article: Speed Brand Electric Scooter HL-E18

Quantity: 80 sets

Color: red, green, blue, sliver (please supply 20 for each color)

Unit Price: at US $400 per set FOB Shanghai

Amount: US $3,200.00

Shipment: during June 2021

Our usual terms of payment are cash against documents, which we hope will be acceptable to you.

If this order turns out to be satisfactory, we will place larger orders with you in the near future.

Yours faithfully

Sample Letter 5 (2)

Dear Sir or Madam,

We are glad to receive your Order No. 1210 for 50 Tempered Glass Coffee Table Sets (T608).

We appreciate your interest in our products which are of good quality and best prices. We will ship your ordered goods as soon as possible. We enclose our latest catalog, and if you are interested in some other items, please inform us.

We hope to cooperate with you again in the future.

Yours faithfully

Sample Letter 5 (3)

Dear Sir or Madam,

We acknowledge receipt of your order No. 1315 for 200 air-conditioners. Much to our regret, we cannot at present entertain your order owing to shortage of stocks.

In the meantime because of the fluctuation of the price of raw materials, we are now adjusting our price list. We will, however, send you quotations as soon as your ordered goods are available and the price list is settled. We sincerely regret any inconvenience you may have experienced. You can rely on our best attention at all times.

Yours faithfully

5.5 USEFUL TERMS AND EXPRESSIONS

1.	trail order	试购订单
2.	repeat order	续订订单
3.	order sheet/form	订货单
4.	duplicate order	复制订单
5.	sample order / order by sample	订购样品,凭样订购
6.	initial/ first order	第一次订购
7.	limited order	有限订单
8.	market order	按行情订购
9.	back order	未能按时交货订单
10.	additional order	追加订货,补充订货
11.	split order	分批订单
12.	official order	正式订单
13.	export order	出口订单
14.	import order	进口订单
15.	mail order	邮购
16.	cable order / telegraphic order	电报订单
17.	verbal order	口头订单
18.	provisional order	临时订单
19.	day order	当天有效的订单
20.	regular order	定期订单,经常订货
21.	pressing order	紧急订单
22.	advance order	预订单
23.	fill an order	按订单供应
24.	confirm an order	确认订单
25.	execute an order	履行订单
26.	dispatch an order	发货

27. place on order in blank	寄空白订单
28. pass with an order	不订货
29. transmit an order to	给……传送订单
30. carriage forward	运费到付
31. claim damages	索赔损失赔偿金
32. sales confirmation	销售确认书
33. general conditions	一般条件
34. order with conditions attached	附条件订购
35. advice note	通知单
36. proforma invoice	形式发票
37. native products and animal by-products	土产品和畜副产品
38. olive oil	橄榄油
39. aquatic products	水产品
40. PU leather	皮革原料
41. cassava slice	木薯干
42. frozen chicken	冻鸡
43. raw material for fur dressing	裘皮原料
44. canola	菜籽油（芥子酸含量很低的）
45. animal casing	肠衣
46. eel infant	鳗鱼苗
47. pistachio	开心果
48. sweet almond	甜杏仁
49. bitter almond	苦杏仁
50. cashew	腰果
51. rosin	松香
52. macadamia nut	夏威夷果
53. white kidney bean	白芸豆
54. walnut	核桃

55.	Chinese cinnamon	桂皮
56.	Himenmatsutake	姬松茸
57.	capsicum	辣椒
58.	sanction	使人们不违背法律、规定等的因素或约束力
59.	countersign	副署,会签
60.	duplicate	使重复;复制 复制的 复制品

5.6 COMMUNICATION LABORATORY

Application Exercises

A. Translate the following sentences into Chinese.

1. We regret that we have to notify you of so many orders being cancelled at the same time.
2. The Order No. 107 is so urgently required that we have to ask you to speed up shipment.
3. We thank you for your quotation of May 29 and are pleased to place a trial order for your electrical product.
4. Enclosed is our Sales Contract No. 968 in duplicate. If you find everything in order, please sign and return one copy for our file.
5. According to our records, it has been a long time since we last had the pleasure of serving you, and we are wondering whether something has "gone wrong".
6. We are sorry to say that the quantity of cotton at the market just now is very small and prices consequently have advanced. It is, therefore, out of our power to execute your order.
7. We regret it as much as you do, but circumstances make it unavoidable in this case.
8. Thank you for your quotation for bicycles, but we regret that we have to place our orders elsewhere as your prices are too high for this market.
9. To our regret, we are unable to accept your order, since our profit margin does not allow us any concession by way of discount of prices.
10. We have received your Order No. 745 and it will be executed to your satisfaction.

Unit 5　Orders and Their Execution

B. **Translate the following sentences into English.**
  1. 很抱歉由于我公司在今后一段时间内,所有货物已完全够用,因此,不得不取消此次订货,敬请谅解。(cover)
  2. 本公司已收到贵公司订单,致感欣慰。贵方所需的各项产品,均以现货供应,特此奉告。(in stock)
  3. 价格表已收到,请尽可能迅速以水路货运下列商品,当不胜感激。(by water)
  4. 感谢您7月8日的订单,本月已经履约,特此奉告。(execute)
  5. 我正安排通过中国银行镇江分行开立相关的信用证。(covering)
  6. 请按照贵公司提供的样品,供应我50吨煤炭,谢谢。(in accordance with)
  7. 对于这批订货,我方客户已经同意分批装运,这样可以使你方从9月到11月分批装运。(partial shipment)
  8. 由于工资和原材料价格大幅度上涨,很抱歉无法按我方半年前所报价格接受订单。(in a position)
  9. 希望第一批到货能证明与你方提供的样品一致,以便今后建立定期业务。(in line with)
  10. 如贵方停止发货,不胜感激,但在今后的业务中定会作出补偿。(abstain from)

C. **Cloze**

Dear Sir or Madam,
　　As a result of our recent e _____ of faxes, we c _____ having sold to you 2,000 tons of goods on the following terms and conditions.
　　Price: at USD 89 per ton CFR Genoa
　　Packing: in 6 ply kraft-paper bags for about 50 kg n _____ each
　　Shipment: in one or two lots to be shipped from Shanghai to Genoa before May 2005, t _____ not allowed.
　　Insurance: to be c _____ by the buyers
　　Payment: by a confirmed, irrevocable letter of credit payable by draft at sight
　　We are sending you herewith our S/C No. 3465 in d _____, please c _____ and return one copy to us for our file. You are kindly asked to open a letter of credit in our f _____ immediately, and stipulations in it should strictly conform to the terms of the S/C to avoid any subsequent a _____.
　　We are looking forward to future e _____ of trade to our mutual benefit.
　　　　　　　　　　　　　　　　　　　　　　　　Yours faithfully

Case Study

Please write a letter to decline the following order.

Dear Sir or Madam,

Many thanks for your quotation of November 7 and the samples of Women's Nylon Garments.

We are satisfied with both the quality and the prices, and are ready to place the following order according to your terms and conditions.

Commodity	Size	Unit Price (per dz. CIF London)	Quantity (dz.)
Women's Nylon Garments	Small	USD 80.00	5
Women's Nylon Garments	Middle	USD 120.00	7
Women's Nylon Garments	Large	USD 160.00	4

The above is subject to your goods arriving at this end before Dec. 15. Our company will reserve the right to cancel this order or reject the goods for any late arrival.

For your information, our usual payment terms are by D/P 60 days. Please kindly let us have your confirmation.

Sincerely yours

Unit 6 Payment

6.1 PAYMENT METHODS FOR INTERNATIONAL TRADE

There are many ways to make and receive payment in international trade. Owing to the physical distances between the importer and the exporter, and the fact that the transaction may have taken place without the two parties actually meeting, minimizing exposure to risk is on the minds of both parties. The importer wants to make sure they receive their order in acceptable condition and on time, and the exporter needs to know they will get paid for it.

An experienced exporting firm extends credit cautiously. It evaluates new customers with care and continuously monitors older accounts. Such a firm may wisely decide to decline a customer's request for open account credit if the risk is too great and propose instead payment on delivery terms through a documentary sight draft or irrevocable confirmed letter of credit or even payment in advance. On the other hand, for a fully creditworthy customer, the experienced exporter may decide to allow a month or two to pay, perhaps even on open account.

Other good credit practices include being aware of any unfavorable changes in your customers' payment patterns, refraining from going beyond normal commercial terms, and consulting with your international banker on how to cope with unusual circumstances or in difficult markets. It is always advisable to check a buyer's credit (even if the safest payment methods are employed).

Listed in order from the most secure for the exporter to the least secure, the basic methods of payment in international trade are:

- Cash in advance;
- Documentary letter of credit;
- Documentary collection or draft;
- Open account;
- Other payment mechanisms, such as consignment sales.

Each of the above-mentioned methods of international payment provides you with a different level of protection and cost. Your choice will depend upon your relationship with your trading partner, the level of risk in the transaction, and, in some cases, the regulatory requirements of foreign countries. Below is a table of the most popular payment methods for international trade.

TABLE 6.1 Popular Payment Methods for International Trade

Payment Method	Details	Allocation of Risk
T/T or Cash Advance	T/T is the easiest payment form and is typically used for new relationships or for small transactions of samples. Shipping happens only after money is safely in the seller's bank account.	100% Buyer Risk
Letter of Credit(L/C)	Letter of Credit means any arrangement, however named or described, that is irrevocable and thereby constitutes a definite undertaking of the issuing bank to honor a complying presentation: to pay at sight if the credit is available by sight payment, or to incur a deferred payment undertaking and pay at maturity if the credit is available by deferred payment, or to accept a bill of exchange ("draft") drawn by the beneficiary and pay at maturity if the credit is available by acceptance (for more details, refer to the Uniform Customs and Practice for Documentary Credits, UCP 600).	Evenly Shared
Documentary Collections	The exporter ships the goods, and then gives the documents (including the bill of lading necessary to claim the goods at the foreign port) to his bank, which will forward them to a bank in the buyer's country, along with instructions on how to collect the money from the buyer. When the foreign bank receives the documents, they will contact the buyer and provide documents to the buyer only when the buyer pays (D/P) or accepts (D/A).	Mainly with Supplier
Open Account	The buyer pays the seller subsequent to receipt of an invoice, normally after goods are received and inspected.	100% Seller Risk

6.2 EXAMPLES OF TERMS OF PAYMENT IN CONTRACTS

(1) T/T Remittance

Terms of Payment: The buyers shall pay 100% of the sales proceeds in advance by T/T to reach the seller's account with the Bank of China not later than December 8, 2008.

(2) Documentary Collection

Terms of Payment: The buyer shall duly accept the documentary draft drawn by the seller at XXX days sight upon first presentation and make payment on its maturity. The documents are to be delivered against acceptance.

Terms of Payment: The buyer shall pay, upon first presentation, the documentary draft drawn by the seller at sight upon first presentation and make payment on its maturity. The shipping documents are to be delivered against payment only.

(3) Documentary Letter of Credit

Terms of Payment: The buyer shall open through a bank acceptable to the seller an irrevocable L/C at 60 days sight to reach the seller not later than December 8, 2008, remaining valid for negotiation in China until the 15th day after the time of shipment.

6.3 LETTER OF CREDIT

6.3.1 Establishment of an L/C

Typical steps of an irrevocable letter of credit are as follows:

- After the exporter and buyer agree on the terms of a sale, the buyer arranges for its bank to open a letter of credit that specifies the documents needed for payment. The buyer determines which documents will be required.
- The buyer's bank issues, or opens, its irrevocable letter of credit including all instructions to the seller relating to the shipment.
- The buyer's bank sends its irrevocable letter of credit to a bank in the exporter's country.
- The exporter reviews carefully all conditions in the letter of credit. The exporter's freight forwarder is contacted to make sure that the shipping date can be met. If the exporter cannot comply with one or more of the conditions, he will ask the applicant to instruct its bank to have the letter of credit amended.
- The exporter arranges with the freight forwarder to deliver the goods to the appropriate port or airport.
- When the goods are loaded, the freight forwarder completes the necessary documentation.
- The exporter presents the documents, evidencing full compliance with the letter of credit terms, to the bank.
- The bank reviews the documents. If they are in order, the documents are sent to the buyer's bank for review and then transmitted to the buyer.
- The buyer (or the buyer's agent) uses the documents to claim the goods.
- A draft, which accompanies the letter of credit, is paid by the buyer's bank at the time specified or, if a time draft, may be discounted to the exporter's bank at an earlier date.

The example of an irrevocable letter of credit here illustrates the various parts of a typical letter of credit.

FORM OF DOC. CREDIT	*40A:	IRREVOCABLE
DOC CREDIT NUMBER	*20:	AD1202587DF012
DATE OF ISSUE	31C:	190826
EXPRIRY	*31D:	DATE 191126 PLACE BENEFICIARY COUNTRY
APPLICANT	*50:	KIM INTERNATIONAL TRADING CO., LTD
		NAEDANG-DONG SEOUL
		KOREA
BENEFICIARY	*59:	JIANG FOREIGN TRADE GROUP
		208 ZHONGSHAN ROAD, XUZHOU
		JIANGSU, P. R. CHINA
AMOUNT	*32B:	CURRENCY USD AMOUNT 72,000.00
AVAILABLE WITH/BY	*41D:	ANY BANK
		BY NEGOTIATION
DRAFTS AT	42C:	AT SIGHT
DRAWEE	42A:	*NATIONAL AGRICULTURAL BANK
		*SEOUL
PARTIAL SHIPMENTS	43P:	ALLOWED
TRANSSHIPMENT	43T:	PROHIBITED
LOADING IN CHARGE	44A:	SHANGHAI PORT, CHINA
FOR TRANSPORT TO	44B:	BUSAN PORT, KOREA
LATEST DATE OF SHIP	44C:	191110

DESCRIPTION OF GOODS   45A:

GOODS DESCRIPTION	QUANTITY	UNIT PRICE	AMOUNT
MEN'S CORODUROY PANTS	30,000PCS	USD2.40/PC	USD72,000.00
TOTAL	30,000PCS	USD72,000.00	

ORIGIN CHINA
FOB SHANGHAI

DOCUMENTS REQUIRED   46A:
 + FULL SET OF CLEAN ON BOARD OCEAN BILLS OF LADING MADE OUT TO ORDER MARKED FREIGHT COLLECT AND NOTIFY ACCOUNTEE.
 +SIGNED COMMERCIAL INVOICE IN QUINTUPLICATE
 +PACKING LIST IN TRIPLICATE

ADDITIONAL COND   47A:
 + DISCREPANCY FEE OF USD40.00 OR EQUIVALENT WILL BE DEDUCTED FROM THE PROCEEDS OF EACH PRESENTATION OF DOCUMENTS WITH DISCREPANCY FOR PAYMENT / REIMBURSEMENT UNDER THIS LETTER OF CREDIT
 + THE COPY OF APPLICANT'S CERTIFICATE TO HAVE RECEIVED ALL THE SHIPPING DOCUMENTS BY FAX WITHIN 3 DAYS AFTER THE DATE OF SHIPMENT MUST BE SUBMITTED ALONG WITH OTHER DOCUMENTS FOR NEGOTIANTION

```
DETAILS OF CHARGES      71B: ALL BANKING CHARGES INCLUDING
    REIMBURSEMENT CHARGES OUTSIDE KOREA ARE FOR ACCOUNT OF BENEFICIARY
PRESENTATION PERIOD     48: WITHIN 21 DAYS AFTER THE DATE OF
    ISSUNACE OF THE SHIPPING DOCUMENT(S) BUT WITHIN THE VALIDITY OF THE CREDIT
CONFIRMATION            *49: WITHOUT
INSTRUCTIONS            78: ALL DOCUMENTS SHOULD BE FORWARDED
    TO THE NATIONAL AGRICULTURAL BANK BANKING DEPARTMENT 75, 1-KA, CHUNGJEONG-
    TO, JUNG-KU, SEOUL, KOREA IN TWO CONSECUTIVE LOTS BY REGISTERED AIRMAIL OR AIR-
    COURIER
    ADVISE THROUGH      57D: BANK OF CHINA, XUZHOU BRANCH
    THIS LETTER OF CREDIT IS SUBJECT TO THE UNIFORM CUSTOMS AND PRACTICE FOR
DOCUMENTARY CREDITS (2007 REVISION), INTERNATIONAL CHAMBER OF COMMERCE
PUBLICATION NO. 600.
```

There may be circumstances where the buyer fails to establish the L/C in time, or the L/C does not reach the seller in time. Then a letter (or a fax, etc.) has to be sent to the buyer to urge him to open the L/C as soon as possible or to ascertain its whereabouts.

Messages urging establishment of an L/C must be written with tact. It is not advisable to start off too strongly by blaming the buyer for non-performance of his obligation under the contract to establish the L/C in time.

6.3.2 Amendment to an L/C

All the documents related to the L/C must reflect the details as exactly contained in the L/C itself. Hence the L/C must be checked very minutely prior to acceptance so as to ensure that no unacceptable conditions have been placed in the L/C which will make shipment difficult. Upon receipt of the L/C, the beneficiary should check:

- Name and address of the beneficiary to see if they are correctly spelt;
- The description of the item, the unit price and payment terms as per the contract;
- The total value of the L/C to ensure that it is sufficient to cover the quantity ordered and any additional costs that may be incurred;
- The validity of the L/C to ensure that it allows sufficient time for the shipment of cargo and negotiation of documents;
- The details of insurance required to ensure that they are clearly spelt out and can be met by the seller;
- The documents required to ensure that it is able to provide all the stipulated shipping and other documents in the specified forms and number;
- Inclusion of any restriction on vessel selection.

If unacceptable terms are found in the L/C, the beneficiary (seller) should ask the applicant (buyer) to instruct his bank to make necessary amendments to the covering L/C without delay.

Letters concerning L/C amendment should be written with courtesy because a mere amendment costs time and money, which is always an annoying thing to the buyer. Such letters can be planned as follows:

- Begin the letter by acknowledging receipt of the covering L/C;
- Carefully list all the discrepancies (unacceptable terms) in the L/C;
- Ask the buyer to instruct its bank to make necessary amendments to the L/C and let you have the amendment advice before a certain date;
- End the letter by expressing your thanks in advance for the buyer's cooperation.

6.4 SAMPLE LETTERS

Sample Letter 6 (1)

Dear President Smith,

Thank you for your letter of August 17 in which you ask for an extension of our payment terms.

In consideration of the very pleasant business relationship we have had with you for more than twenty years, we have decided to agree to your suggestion. We shall, therefore, in future draw on you at 90 days, documents against payment, and trust that these terms will suit your requirements.

It is hoped that our concession will greatly facilitate your efforts in sales and result in a considerable increase of your orders. You may rest assured that we shall always endeavor to execute them to your complete satisfaction.

Sincerely yours

Sample Letter 6 (2)

Dear Sir or Madam,

With reference to the goods under Sales Contract No. NJ5687, we'd like to inform you that they have been ready for shipment for quite some time.

According to the above-mentioned contract, shipment is to be made not later than November 26. The date of delivery is approaching, but we have not yet received the covering L/C to date.

Please do your utmost to expedite establishment of the L/C in our favor, available at sight in respect of 1,000 men's 26-inch bicycles and 600 women's 20-inch bicycles. The required documents are Bills of Lading(2), Commercial Invoices(3), Insurance Policy and Certificate of Origin.

We hope to hear favorably from you soon.

Yours faithfully

Sample Letter 6 (3)

Dear Sir or Madam,

<u>L/C CB2310</u>

We have received the captioned L/C for US$80,000 covering Sales Contract No. NJ5687 for 1,000 men's 26-inch bicycles and 600 women's 20-inch bicycles.

It appears that the amount in your L/C is insufficient, as the total CFR value of the contract comes to US$80,800, instead of US$80,000, the difference being US$800.

As stipulated in Sales Contract No. NJ5687, shipment could be made not later than November 26 provided your L/C reached us before October 9. However, we received your L/C only today. In such circumstances, we regret to have to ask you to extend the above L/C to December 15 and December 30 for shipment and negotiation respectively, with the amendment advice to reach us by October 25 to enable early shipment.

We look forward to receiving the relevant amendment and thank you in advance.

Sincerely yours

6.5 USEFUL TERMS AND EXPRESSIONS

1.	Uniform Customs and Practice for Documentary Credits	跟单信用证统一惯例
2.	cash in advance	现金预付
3.	payment in advance	预付款
4.	documentary letter of credit	跟单信用证
5.	documentary collection	跟单托收
6.	remittance	汇款
7.	T/T (telegraphic transfer)	电汇
8.	D/A (documents against acceptance)	承兑交单
9.	D/P (documents against payment)	付款交单
10.	D/P at sight	即期付款交单
11.	D/P after sight	远期付款交单
12.	documentary draft	跟单汇票
13.	clean draft	光票
14.	sight draft	即期汇票

15. time draft	远期汇票
16. banker's bill	银行汇票
17. commercial bill	商业汇票
18. open account	赊账
19. consignment sales	寄售
20. confirmed L/C	保兑信用证
21. irrevocable L/C	不可撤销信用证
22. transferable credit	可转让信用证
23. standby letter of credit	备用信用证
24. issuing bank	开证行
25. advising bank	通知行
26. confirming bank	保兑行
27. reimbursing bank	偿付行
28. drawee bank	付款银行
29. applicant	开证申请人
30. beneficiary	受益人
31. drawer	出票人
32. bona fide holder	善意持有人
33. teletransmitted credit	电开信用证
34. allowances in credit amount	信用证金额幅度
35. sight payment	即期付款
36. deferred payment	延期付款
37. installment drawings	分期支款
38. assignment of proceeds	款项的过户
39. acceptance	承兑
40. negotiation	议付
41. revocation of a credit	信用证的撤销
42. amendment	修改

43.	advice of amendment	修改通知书
44.	expiry date and place	到期日及地点
45.	validity	有效期
46.	extension	延期
47.	presentation of documents	交单
48.	presentation period	交单期
49.	examination of documents	审单
50.	discrepant documents	瑕疵单据
51.	bid bond	投标担保
52.	performance bond	履约担保
53.	letter of guarantee	银行保函
54.	account payable	应付款
55.	account receivable	应收款
56.	draw	开出（汇票）
57.	facilitate	使容易；便于
58.	expedite	迅速处理

6.6 COMMUNICATION LABORATORY

Application Exercises

A. Translate the following into Chinese.

1. Our terms of payment are by irrevocable letter of credit in our favor, available by draft at sight, reaching us one month ahead of shipment, remaining valid for negotiation in China for another 21 days after the prescribed time of shipment, and allowing transshipment and partial shipments.
2. We regret we cannot accept "cash against documents on arrival of goods at destination".
3. In compliance with your request, we exceptionally accept delivery against D/P at sight, but this should not be regarded as a precedent.
4. We have today instructed our bank to remit the amount due by T/T. Please acknowledge receipt.
5. Your invoice was filed incorrectly and, therefore, was not paid.

6. Much to our surprise, our draft on you dated May 12 and due July 1 was returned dishonored yesterday.

7. If you fail to make your payment, we shall be compelled to enforce payment through the hands of attorney. If we do not hear from you favorably by August 15, we shall have to take legal means for collection.

8. The Uniform Customs and Practice for Documentary Credits, 2007 Revision, ICC Publication No. 600 ("UCP") are rules that apply to any documentary credit ("credit") (including, to the extent to which they may be applicable, any standby letter of credit) when the text of the credit expressly indicates that it is subject to these rules. They are binding on all parties thereto unless expressly modified or excluded by the credit.

B. **Translate the following sentences into English.**

1. 由于资金被许多业务占用,我们不得不要求放宽付款条件。(tie up)
2. 请在扣除你方应收手续费后,将货款贷记我方账户。(credit)
3. 鉴于这笔交易金额甚微,我们准备以付款交单方式办理装运。(be prepared to)
4. 由于你方没有按照第 FT156 号合同要求及时开立信用证,我们不得不撤销该合同,并要求你方负担由此而产生的一切费用。(rescind)
5. 我们感到有必要明确今后的交易以即期信用证付款。(future business dealings)

C. **Cloze**

We have received your letter dated October 5. As already pointed out in our p_____ letter, we had made arrangements with our manufacturers to make delivery as p_____ as possible in future. We shall see to it that your interest is well taken care of at all times.

R_____ the terms of payment, while we have every c_____ in your integrity and ability, we wish to r_____ that our usual terms of payment by L/C remain unchanged in all ordinary cases. For the time being, therefore, we regret our i_____ to accept D/A terms in all transactions with our buyers abroad.

For future shipments, however, we shall do our best to f_____ your orders within the time stipulated, if, by any chance, it is impossible for us to do so, we will effect shipment on a D/P b_____ in order to avoid putting you to so much trouble in the extension of letter of credit. We trust you will a_____ our cooperation.

Case study

Check the terms set forth in the sample L/C in this unit with the contents of the under-mentioned S/C No. FU 5078 to see what discrepancies between them exist and then write a letter in English requesting the buyer to instruct his bank to make necessary amendments to the L/C.

Sales Confirmation No. JU5078

Date: May 5, 2021

The Seller: Jiang Foreign-Trade Group
　　　　　　208 Zhongshan Road, Xuzhou
　　　　　　Jiangsu, P. R. China

The Buyer: Kim International Trading Co., Ltd
　　　　　　Naedang-Dong Seoul
　　　　　　Korea

This sales confirmation is made by and between the seller and the buyer, whereby the seller agrees to sell and the buyer agrees to buy the under-mentioned goods according to the terms and conditions stipulated below:

Name of Commodity: Men's Coroduroy Pants
Quantity: 31,000pcs
Unit Price: at USD2.40 per piece FOB Shanghai
Amount: USD74,400.00
Shipment: on or before December 26, 2021
Insurance: to be effected by the buyer
Payment: 100% by irrevocable L/C at sight

Unit 7 Packing

7.1 GENERAL INTRODUCTION TO PACKING

In international trade, packing means the covering, wrapping or sealing as well as proper marking of goods with certain containers, materials, accessories, etc. based on specific techniques to protect the goods, make storage and transportation convenient, or promote sales. And packing procedures usually include the choosing of packing materials or containers as well as marking.

Generally speaking, there are usually two kinds of packing—outer packing and inner packing. The former is also called transport packing, which serves as a form of protection against damage or proliferation during transportation; the latter is called packaging or sales packing, which is regarded as a decisive selling aid, especially for household consumer goods or similar goods. There is also another kind of packing, i. e., neutral packing, which indicates no production country or manufacturer and is often used under request of the buyer.

Packing is very important for both the seller and buyer in international trade. For the seller, it is necessary to put the goods into a nice and compact shape that can stay the rough journey, while the buyer usually expect his goods can arrive in perfect condition. Thus there are some requirements on both the outer packing and inner packing of international cargos.

Outer Packing. For outer packing, a balance between durability and minimum size and weight should be reached. In international trade, goods usually need to travel long distance, sometimes even across continents and there are a lot of things needed to be considered, such as accidents, bad weather, loading and unloading, etc. Therefore, good outer packing should be strong enough to stand rough handling or rough weather on the way, and sometimes it needs to be reinforced with strong materials such as nylon straps, plastic straps or even iron bands. On the other hand, since freight is calculated on the basis of size and weight of the cargo, outer packing should also be as light and as small as possible to reduce freight costs.

Inner Packing. Packing is an art. Therefore, attention should also be paid to the creation of good inner packing since it is gaining increasing importance in the marketing of goods in international trade. Sometimes, it can even decide whether the deal can be reached or not. Thus good inner packing should be novel, beautiful and attractive to help push sales.

Since packing has so much significance in international trade, large export companies pay great attention to the expertise of packing. They usually have a special department for export packing, which is also devoted to the development of new packing materials and new methods. Many companies may also hire some specialist export packer or forwarding agent to handle packing in international trade.

Besides, there are some other issues to be taken into consideration for packing:
- The value of goods can determine whether packing will be cheap or expensive.
- Nature of the goods and means of transportation can determine the form of packing and packing materials.
- Cost of packing is usually included in the export price of goods unless otherwise stated in the contract; however, if the buyer requires particular packing for the goods ordered, details on the specific packing and way of payment should be stated clearly in the contract.
- Insurance companies generally shoulder no responsibility for damages or losses caused by improper packing by the seller.
- Some kinds of materials for packing are prohibited by some countries and attention should be paid in such cases.

7.2 PACKING CONTAINERS USED IN INTERNATIONAL TRADE

Packing form differs with the nature of goods. And thus there are a variety of packing containers used in international trade, including packing containers for single piece transportation and those for unitization transportation. The outer packing of the former can be further divided into three types: (1) those especially used for bulk cargos; (2) those used for general cargos; (3) those used for liquids.

(1) Packing Containers Used for Bulk Cargos or Soft Goods
- Bag (Bg/Bgs): made of strong paper, linen, canvas, rubber, plastics, etc.; used for bulk cargos such as cement and fertilizers;
- Sack (Sx/Sxs): a large bag made of jute; used for cereals.

(2) Packing Containers for General Cargos
- Carton (Ctn/Ctns): made of light but strong cardboard or fiberboard with double lids and bottoms, fixed by glue, adhesive tapes, metal bands, wire or staples; sometimes several of them are made up into one package, tightened up by metal bands;
- Case (C/Cs): a strong container made of wood or sometimes made of thinner wood with metal bands or wires around; may have a batten for extra strength with the inside maybe lined with various materials such as damp resisting paper, tin foil, etc., to prevent damage by water, air or insects; used especially for dry goods;

- Crate (Crt/CrtsP): a case not fully enclosed with a bottom and a frame and sometimes open on the top; often used for particular things such as machinery;
- Bale (Bl/Bls): a package tightly pressed together and wrapped in a protective material; used for soft goods such as cotton, wool, sheepskin; usually with the size of 30 *15 *15 inches; can be strengthened with metal bands.

(3) Packing Containers Used for Liquids

- Drum (Drm/Drms): a cylinder-shaped container; usually made of metal; used for liquids including chemicals and paints;
- Carboy: a large container protected in a metal or wicker cage with soft packing between the glass and the cage; usually used for corrosive liquids such as sulfuric acid.

Inner packing containers usually include the following:

- Box (Bx/Bxs): a small case made of wood, cardboard or metal with a folding (hinged) lid;
- Can/Tin (Cn/Cns // Tn/Tns): a small metal container; used for small quantities of paint, oil or certain foodstuffs;
- Paper packet: a small packet made of paper;
- Bottle.

In unitization transportation, a number of single piece transportation packing is put into a much larger package to make loading and unloading of goods more efficient and cheaper. Containers used for unitization packing include:

- Bundle: miscellaneous goods packed without a container; made of a number of small cartons, etc., fixed together;
- Container: a strongly built very large metal rectangle-shaped case; used for holding non-standardized goods in separate packing for transportation; can be used repeatedly; with standard dimensions of 8 *8 *40 (30 / 20) feet; the most efficient and important way of transportation in international trade today;
- Pallet: a large tray or platform made of wood or metal; used for moving loads (by means of slings, etc.).

Among the above mentioned, containerization revolutionized cargo shipping and it is used most often nowadays. Today, approximately 90% of cargo moves by containers stacked on transport ships. Over 200 million containers per year are now moved between international ports.

7.3 MARKS

Packing must be marked before shipment. Marks are printed on transportation packing for recognition of goods in transportation, storage, commodity inspection and customs declaration to secure safe delivery. There are mainly three categories of marks, i.e., shipping marks, indicative marks and warning marks.

(1) Shipping Marks

Shipping marks are used for easy recognition of goods during transportation so as to avoid wrong delivery. Shipping marks consist of the following four elements:

- The consignor's or consignee's distinctive mark, i.e., the code name of the consignor or the consignee, which is usually put inside or outside of a geometric figure;
- The port mark, i.e., mark that indicates the port of destination;
- The case number / package number, i.e., the serial number of the cases;
- Official marks required by authorities, usually include the country of origin of the goods, the contract number and sometimes weight and dimensions.

An example of shipping marks:

AB & C: The consignee's distinctive mark
San Francisco: The port mark
Nos1-20: The case number, the first piece of the overall 20 cases
Made in China: country of origin

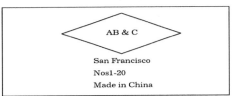

(2) Indicative Marks

Indicative marks, also known as directive marks, are usually marks put on packages using simple and striking figures and words to suggest specific items of attention during transportation, loading and unloading as well as storage.

Examples of directive marks:

Sometimes, only words are used:

handle with care	perishable
this side/end up	guard against damp (wet)
with care	no smoking
no hook (use no hook)	keep flat (stow level)
keep cool (keep in cool place)	not to be thrown down

keep dry
keep/store away from boiler
fragile
fusible
glass with care
open here
sling here
to be kept upright
keep away from heat

(3) Warning Marks

Warning marks are marks printed clearly on packing of hazardous or dangerous goods such as inflammable, explosive, poisonous, corrosive and radioactive articles. For packing of such goods, each country has specialized principles and regulations, which should be observed strictly. Exporters are encouraged to use the "universally recognized cautionary marks" as those stated in the UN Warning Marks.

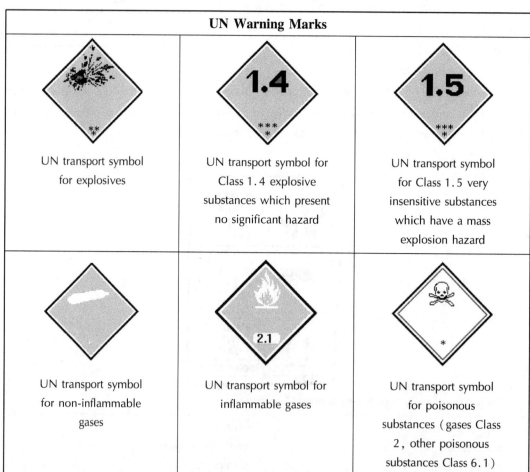

UN Warning Marks		
UN transport symbol for explosives	UN transport symbol for Class 1.4 explosive substances which present no significant hazard	UN transport symbol for Class 1.5 very insensitive substances which have a mass explosion hazard
UN transport symbol for non-inflammable gases	UN transport symbol for inflammable gases	UN transport symbol for poisonous substances (gases Class 2, other poisonous substances Class 6.1)

UN Warning Marks

 UN transport symbol for inflammable gases (Class 2) or liquids (Class 3)	 UN transport symbol for inflammable solids (Class 4)	 UN transport symbol for substances liable to spontaneous combustion
 UN transport symbol for substances which, in contact with water, emit inflammable gases	 UN transport symbol for oxidizing substances and for organic peroxides	 UN transport symbol for infectious substances
 UN transport symbol for radioactive substances, Category Ⅰ	 UN transport symbol for radioactive substances, Category Ⅱ	 UN transport symbol for radioactive substances, Category Ⅲ
 UN transport symbol for radioactive substances	 UN transport symbol for corrosive substances	 UN location of serial number: ＊＊

7.4 EXAMPLES OF TERMS OF PACKING IN CONTRACTS

- In wooden cases of about 38 kg net each.
- In cartons, each containing 6 dozen.
- Folding chairs are packed 2 pieces to a carton.
- Pens are packed 12 pieces to a box and 200 boxes to a carton.
- Each Christmas stocking is to be packed in a polybag, a dozen pieces to a box and 12 boxes to a carton lined with waterproof paper and reinforced with 2 iron straps outside.

7.5 PACKING LIST

One of the important documents in international shipping is packing list, also called "specification of contents" or "packing specification", which is a commercial document prepared by the exporter to record various contents of a specific bunch of goods and serving as a supplementary document to the invoice. In packing lists, usually description, quantity for each item, weight and values should be indicated.

Here is an example of packing list.

			PACKING LIST			
Messers & Address:			Invoice No.: GECMHK070599-7-3W		Date: APR. 26, 2021	
TO WHOM IT MAY CONCERN			Vessel:			
Shipping Mark: GW030165/07			Port of Loading: SHANGHAI, CHINA		Date:	
HONG KONG MADE IN CHINA NO.1 -78			Port of Destination: HONG KONG			
Container/ Seal No.	Total Pallets	Reams/ Pallet	Description		Net Weight (MT)	Gross Weight (MT)
					Total	Total
			C2S ART PAPER			
CRXU15 35237/06 3562	1	22	95GSM	889MMX1194MM	1.109225	1.137000
	2	22	95GSM	889MMX1194MM	2.218450	2.275000
	15	13	157GSM	787MMX1092MM	13.155300	13.480000
	2	13	157GSM	787MMX1092MM	1.754040	1.797000

Code			GSM	Dimensions		
HAHU2 013890/063558	24	24	95GSM	635MMX889MM	15.445056	15.849000
			MATT ART PAPER			
	3	19	105GSM	787MMX1092MM	2.571750	2.636000
			C2S ART PAPER			
HALU32 15976/063555	15	24	95GSM	635MMX965MM	10.478400	10.751000
	7	22	95GSM	889MMX1194MM	7.764575	7.963000
TOTAL	69				54.496796	55.888000

7.6 LETTERS ON PACKING

Generally speaking, letters about packing issues should be concise and explicit since packing has so much importance in international trade. Letters on packing can be grouped into the following three categories: (1) enquiries/suggestions on packing, (2) clarification/requirements on packing, and (3) complaints on improper packing.

(1) Enquiries/Suggestions on Packing

Enquiries/suggestions on packing usually follow such a pattern:

- The opening: reference to the former letters concerning the goods and statement of the need for enquiries or suggestions on packing.
- The body: enquiries/suggestions on packing, including types of packing containers (both outer packing and inner packing if necessary), way of packing, marks, etc. A specific enquiry on outer packing or inner packing or even packing marks is also possible.
- The closing: expectation of replies or a packing list.

(2) Clarification/Information on Packing

Clarification or information on packing is usually the response to letters of the former group and the general structure can be as follows:

- The opening: reference to the former letters concerning the enquiries on packing.
- The body: clarification or information on packing, including types of packing containers (both outer packing and inner packing if necessary), way of packing, marks, etc. A specific response to enquiry on outer packing or inner packing or even marks is also possible.
- The closing: expectation of replies.

(3) Complaints on Improper Packing

Complaints on improper packing usually include suggestions for future packing if the improper packing does not result in huge damage and if the buyer still wants to do business

with the seller in the future. A general pattern can be as follows:
- The opening: notification of the shipment of the goods and the statement of the flaws of packing after inspection.
- Clarification or requirements on future packing, including types of packing containers(both outer packing and inner packing if necessary), way of packing, marks, etc.
- Expectation of consideration of the matter and future improvement.

7.7 SAMPLE LETTERS

Sample Letter 7 (1)

Dear Mr. Bao Feng,

Packing of Maoshan Tea

We would refer to our order No. 23398 of 15 September for your Maoshan Tea.

Please now dispatch the first part of this order by sea as stated in our S/C No. 90SP-23398. We suggest that the packing of the tea should be in accordance with the following:

1. We recommend the usage of international tea boxes, 20 boxes on a pallet, and 10 pallets in an FCL container.
2. For the outer packing, please mark our initials MST in a triangle, under which the port of destination and our order number should be stenciled.
3. Besides, warning marks including KEEP DRY, USE NO HOOK and TO BE KEPT COLD should also be included.

We should be obliged if you would send us by airmail a copy of the packing lists included in container to be sent by sea and also duplicates of the Certificate of Origin and the Commercial Invoice. This will enable us to arrange speedy passage through Customs upon arrival of the consignment.

Sincerely yours

Sample Letter 7(2)

Dear Sir or Madam,

Re: Packing of Maoshan Tea

Thank you for your letter of September 21 with your proposal of the packing of the Maoshan Tea of your Order No. 23398, the first part of which will be ready for dispatch by October 2 as stated in our S/C No. 90SP-23398.

For your information, the Maoshan Tea is packed as follows:

1. It is wrapped in plastic bags before being packed in its individual tea boxes of

international standard to better protect the contents from moisture. The boxes are then packed by 24 on a pallet, since it is more compact and up to the international standard, and 10 such pallets are then put in an FCL container.
2. On one side of each container, your initials MST are marked in a triangle, under which SHANGHAI and the Order No. 23398 as well as the weight and dimension of each container are stenciled.
3. Warning marks including KEEP DRY, USE NO HOOK and TO BE KEPT COLD are stenciled on the opposite side.

We state the above for your reference. If we do not hear from you to the contrary before September 25, we shall pack the captioned goods in containers as stated above and a copy of the packing lists included in container to be sent by sea and duplicates of the Certificate of Origin and the Commercial Invoice will be sent to you by airmail for your convenience.

Sincerely yours

Sample Letter 7 (3)

Dear Sir or Madam,

We regret to inform you that of the ten bundles of steel bars you shipped to New York on 12 January, eight bundles of different grades were found in a scattered and mixed condition because the iron hoops on them were not strong enough and most of them are damaged. The difficult assortment of their grade caused us a lot of inconveniences and losses. Thus we feel it necessary to stress the importance of trustworthy export packing for your future deliveries to us.

As steel bars are susceptible to shock, they must be wrapped in soft materials first and then firmly packed in bundles with extra strong iron hoops. Besides, marks on different grades of the steel bars are required on each bundle to make assortment easy.

We trust that you can meet the above requirements and thank you in advance for your cooperation.

Yours faithfully

7.8 USEFUL TERMS AND EXPRESSIONS

1.	packing	包装
2.	package	包裹, 包, 包件
3.	outer packing	外包装

4. inner packing	内包装
5. packing charges/expenses	包装费用
6. packing container	包装容器
7. packing instruction	包装要求
8. packing marks	包装唛头
9. packing list	装箱单
10. packing method	包装方式
11. bag（Bg/Bgs）	袋
12. sack（Sx/Sxs）	麻袋
13. carton（Ctn/Ctns）	硬纸箱
14. case（C/Cs）	箱
15. crate（Crt/CrtsP）	板条箱
16. bale（Bl/Bls）	包
17. drum（Drm/Drms）	桶,鼓桶
18. carboy	大玻璃瓶
19. box（Bx/Bxs）	盒
20. can/tin（Cn/Cns//Tn/Tns）	罐
21. paper packet	纸包
22. bottle	瓶
23. bundle	集装包,捆
24. container	集装箱
25. pallet	托盘
26. country of origin	原产地国
27. consignee	收货人
28. consigner/consignor	发货人
29. dimension	尺寸
30. gross weight	毛重
31. net weight	净重

32.	trade mark	商标
33.	port mark	港口标志,卸货港标志
34.	shipping mark	运输标志
35.	directive mark	指示性标志
36.	warning mark	警告性标志
37.	case number/package number	件号
38.	handle with care	小心轻放
39.	this side/end up	此面向上
40.	with care	小心搬运
41.	no hook (use no hook)	请勿用钩
42.	keep cool (keep in cool place)	放置冷处
43.	keep dry	保持干燥
44.	keep/store away from boiler	远离锅炉
45.	fragile	当心破碎
46.	glass with care	小心玻璃
47.	open here	由此开启
48.	sling here	此处吊索
49.	to be kept upright	竖立安放
50.	keep away from heat	隔离热气
51.	perishable	易坏货物
52.	guard against damp (wet)	勿使受潮
53.	no smoking	严禁烟火
54.	keep flat (stow level)	注意平放
55.	not to be thrown down	不可抛掷
56.	inflammable	易燃货物
57.	explosive	易爆货物
58.	poisonous	小心有毒
59.	corrosive	腐蚀性货物
60.	radioactive	放射性货物

61.	metals & minerals	五金矿产
62.	non-metallic minerals & products	非金属矿产品和制品
63.	building hardware & metal product	建筑五金及制品
64.	refractory material	耐火材料
65.	cast iron product	铸铁制品
66.	non-metallic building material	非金属建筑材料
67.	brass, copper & aluminum product	铜、铝制品
68.	non-ferrous metal	有色金属
69.	assure	保证

7.9 COMMUNICATION LABORATORY

Application Exercises

A. Translate the following sentences into Chinese.

1. Please ensure that these goods are carefully packed and protected against damage during transportation.
2. As the goods will probably be subject to a thorough customs examination, the cases should be of a type which can easily be fastened again after being opened.
3. We have already taken steps to improve our packing and are confident that our future shipments will give you complete satisfaction.
4. We pack our shirts in plastic-lined, waterproof cartons, reinforced with metal traps.
5. We require that you supply your products with our brand, not only in the label but also on the package and the box in which the individual packages are placed.
6. The outer packing for exports is chiefly for safe transportation while the inner packing must suit the tastes of customers abroad. Therefore, commodities with attractive and tasty inner packing will enjoy a good sale.
7. This is to apply to all orders unless otherwise specified.
8. Packing in cartons prevents skillful pilferage. As the trace of pilferage will be more in evidence, the insurance company will be made to pay the necessary compensation for such losses.
9. Our detergent Art. No. F258 is in loose packing of 10 kilos per carton instead of in bags and then packed in cartons. Thus it is more suitable for use in launderettes, hospitals and restaurants.
10. In view of the fragile nature of the goods, buyers usually place great importance on proper packing.

B. **Translate the following sentences into English.**
1. 为了把运输中的损坏减少到最低程度,我们坚持用坚固的木箱包装货物。(insist on)
2. 请注意,纸箱外面要刷上"易碎品"和"小心轻放"的标志。(fragile/handle with care)
3. 请在包上刷上我公司名称的缩写 ABC。(initials)
4. 绿豆可以散装供应,也可以用麻袋装,使用何种方式由买方来决定。(at the discretion of)
5. 我方出口商品,其外包装上的标志,除收货人的区别标志及毛重、净重和皮重外,还须印上"中华人民共和国制造"字样。(stencil)
6. 油每罐净重20千克,每板条箱装两罐。(crate)
7. 由于所有的货物已按售货合同装入箱内,即使我们同意,现在再来改变包装也太晚了。(be cased up)
8. 包装和标志由买方决定。(be at somebody's option)
9. 纸板箱很适合海运。我们运往其他口岸的货物都广泛地使用纸板箱而让客户完全满意。(to the satisfaction of)
10. 兹欣然奉告,你方所订购的货物将用特制的板条箱装运。包装费包括在价格里,不必返回板条箱。(packing charge)

C. **Cloze**

Dear Sirs,

　　The 12,000 bicycles you ordered will be ready for d_____ by December 17. Since you require them for onward s_____ to Bahrain, Kuwait, Oman and Qatar, we are arranging for them to be packed in seaworthy c_____.

　　Each bicycle is enclosed in a corrugated c_____ pack, and 20 are bundled together and wrapped in sheet plastic. A container holds 240 cycles; the whole cargo would therefore comprise 50 containers, each w_____ 8 tons. Dispatch can be made from our works by r_____ to be forwarded from Shanghai harbor. The f_____ charges from works to Shanghai are US $80 per container, totally US $4,000 for this c_____, excluding container hire, which will be charged to your account.

　　Please let us have your d_____ instruction.

　　　　　　　　　　　　　　　　　　　　　　　Yours faithfully

Case Study

　　Study carefully the section of packing list and create a packing list based on Sample Letter 7 (2).

Unit 8 Shipment

8.1 TRAMP AND LINER

Over 90% of world trade is carried by the international shipping industry. Without shipping the import and export of goods on the scale necessary for the modern world would not be possible. There are around 50,000 merchant ships trading internationally, transporting every kind of cargo. The world fleet is registered in over 150 nations, and manned by over a million seafarers of virtually every nationality.

The world's cargoes are transported using one of two main methods: tramp or liner. A tramp is a freight-carrying vessel which has no regular route or schedule of sailings. A liner, on the other hand, is a vessel with regular sailings and arrivals on a stated schedule between specified ports.

Tramp shipping is synonymous with calling a taxi. It is transport on demand going from wherever the cargo originates to wherever the customer wants it transported. Generally speaking, tramp shipping is used for whole ship loads of cargo as it would be difficult to accommodate without compromise the demands of two different customers. In the days prior to about 1850, ships were generally tramps although liner services did exist.

As trade flourished and the industrial revolution of the 1800's expanded, steam ships began to dominate the shipping scene and the liner services were strengthened by the dependability of steam over sail.

Liner services are scheduled sailings from pre-arranged ports to pre-arranged destinations. Most of the international sea lanes are served by liner ships which include container vessels.

8.2 TRANSPORT DOCUMENTS

The bill of lading (in ocean transport), waybill or consignment note (in air, road, rail or sea transport), and receipt (in postal or courier delivery) are collectively known as the transport documents.

The bill of lading (B/L) serves as a receipt for goods, an evidence of the contract of carriage, and a document of title to the goods. The carrier issues the B/L according to the information in a dock receipt.

The B/L must indicate that the goods have been loaded on board or shipped on a named vessel, and it must be signed or authenticated by the carrier or the master, or the agent on behalf of the carrier or the master.

The signature or authentication must be identified as the carrier or the master, and in the case of agent signing or authenticating, the name and capacity of the carrier or the master on whose behalf such agent signs or authenticates must be indicated.

8.2.1 The Date of B/L

In cases where the bill of lading (B/L) has pre-printed wording indicating that the goods have been loaded on board or shipped on a named vessel, the issuance date of such B/L is considered to be the date of loading on board or the date of shipment. In cases where the B/L does not have pre-printed wording indicating that the goods have been loaded on board or shipped on a named vessel, the loading on board a named vessel is evidenced by the on board notation (e.g. "on board", "laden on board" or "shipped on board") on the B/L, which must be initialed and dated by the carrier or its agent. The date of the on board notation is considered to be the date of shipment.

8.2.2 Full Set and Number of Original B(s)/L

Full set means all the originals as so issued by the carrier or its agent. A set contains at least two originals. In practice, a set of three originals is the most common.

The number of original bills of lading (Bs/L) may be expressed as 3/3 (read as "three of three") or 2/2 (read as "two of two"). If the L/C stipulates "Full Set 3/3", which means that it requires a full set B/L containing three originals. If the L/C did not contain the expression "Full Set 3/3", then the number of original bills of lading required would depend on the number as so issued by the carrier. It can be a sole original B/L, that is, one original only.

The originals are marked as "original" on their face and all have equal value, that is, all have the same validity. The purpose of issuing more than one original is to ensure that the port of destination will receive the original when dispatched separately. The original Bs/L are proof of ownership of goods, one of which must be surrendered to the carrier at destination, duly endorsed by the title holder in the goods. When one of the originals is surrendered to the carrier, the others become invalid.

8.2.3 Two (2) Non-negotiable Copies of B/L

The non-negotiable copy of bill of lading (B/L) should not be confused with the non-negotiable bill of lading or straight bill of lading.

The non-negotiable copy of B/L simply means the unsigned copy of the B/L, which is for information purposes. The copies are marked as "non-negotiable". The copies of the B/L can be of any number. The number depends on the requirements of the importer, importing country, shipper, carrier, Chamber of Commerce (if the L/C calls for certification of the B/L), and Consulate (if the L/C calls for consular legalization of the B/L).

8.2.4 Shipper

Unless otherwise stipulated in the letter of credit (L/C), the bill of lading may indicate as the shipper (the consignor) of the goods a party other than the beneficiary of the L/C.

8.2.5 The Notify Party

The notify party is the party that the carrier must notify when the goods arrive at the port of destination.

The notify party depends on the L/C requirement; it can be the importer, freight forwarder or bank. If the letter of credit stipulates "notify the above accountee", in other words the notify party is the applicant or importer.

If the notify party and the consignee are the same party, then enter the word "SAME" or "CONSIGNEE" in the "Notify Party" field in the bill of lading (B/L).

8.2.6 Clean versus Foul Bills of Lading

The bill of lading (B/L) is made out according to the information contained in the dock receipt. If a dock receipt is clean, the B/L will be clean; otherwise the B/L will be foul. The bank will reject a foul bill of lading, unless stipulated otherwise in the letter of credit (L/C).

The clean bill of lading bears an indication that the goods were received without damages, irregularities or short shipment, usually the words "in apparent good order and condition", "clean on board" or the like are indicated on the B/L.

The foul bill of lading—unclean bill of lading, dirty bill of lading or claused bill of lading—is the opposite of the clean bill of lading. It bears an indication that the goods were received with damages, irregularities or short shipment, usually the words "unclean on board" or the like are indicated on the B/L, for example, "insufficient packing", "missing safety seal" and "one carton short".

8.2.7 Short Form versus Long Form Bills of Lading

In a short form bill of lading, the terms and conditions of carriage on the reverse (back) of the bill of lading (B/L) are omitted, instead they are listed on a document other than the B/L. Unless otherwise stipulated in the letter of credit (L/C), a short form bill of lading is acceptable. The short form B/L saves the cost of printing (i.e., no printing on the back of the B/L) and if the terms and conditions of carriage change, there is no need to reprint the B/L form.

In a long form bill of lading the terms and conditions of carriage are printed on the reverse (back) of the bill of lading. The long form bill of lading is commonly used in international shipping.

8.2.8 Straight versus Order Bills of Lading

In a straight bill of lading—non-negotiable bill of lading—the title to the goods is conferred directly to a party named in the letter of credit (the importer usually), as such the title to the goods is not transferable to another party by endorsement. In other words, the bill of lading is not negotiable. The letter of credit calls for a straight bill of lading usually by using such words as "consigned to [the named party]" or "issued in the name of [the named party]". The named party can obtain the goods directly from the carrier at destination. Therefore, unless the cash payment has been received by the exporter or the buyer's integrity is unquestionable, the use of a straight bill of lading is risky.

In an order bill of lading—negotiable bill of lading—the title to the goods is conferred to the order of shipper or to the order of a named party in the letter of credit (the issuing bank usually). The purpose of an order bill of lading is to protect the interest of the shipper or the named party to the title to the goods.

The title to the goods is transferable to another party by endorsement, usually on the reverse (back) of the bill of lading (B/L) by the title holder of the B/L. If the endorsement of B/L is required in the letter of credit (L/C), all the originals must be endorsed.

The letter of credit may call for an order bill of lading that is: (1) to order blank endorsed or to order of shipper and blank endorsed, (2) to order of shipper and endorsed to order of [the named party], or (3) to order of [the named party (other than the shipper)].

8.2.9 Place of Receipt

If the place of receipt (or taking in charge) is different from the port of loading, as in the case of multimodal transport, the on board notation or the pre-printed wording must include the letter of credit (L/C) stipulated port of loading and the name of vessel on which the goods have been loaded.

8.2.10 Shipper's Load and Count

The carrier marks this phrase on the B/L if it does not supervise the loading or unloading of the cargo, which is the typical case in a full container load shipment. Hence, the carrier will not be held accountable for the number of units reported on the B/L. The carrier often adds the words "said to contain" or "said by shipper to contain" before the number of units of a commodity, for example, "3 40-FT. CONTAINERS SAID TO CONTAIN 4,095 CARTONS LEATHER SHOES".

8.2.11 Through Bill of Lading

The through bill of lading—combined transport bill of lading—is used to cover at least two different modes of transportation, known as multimodal transport, or different means of conveyance. The format of a through bill of lading is closely similar to the ocean bill of lading, except the words "Through Bill of Lading", "Combined Transport Bill of Lading", or "Combined Transportation" or the like usually are printed on the bill of lading.

8.2.12 Charter Party Bill of Lading

The charter party bill of lading is issued by the carrier or its agent in the charter shipping. The documentary requirements in a charter party bill of lading are similar to the ocean (marine) bill of lading. Unless otherwise authorized in the letter of credit (L/C), the charter party bill of lading is not acceptable in the L/C negotiation.

8.3 SHIPPING ADVICE

The shipping advice is a notice to the importer on summary of the shipment. Foreign importer may arrange the cargo insurance on time based on the shipping advice (if the buyer is to arrange the insurance). Moreover, the importer may know when to receive the goods and arrange with a customs broker for the cargo clearance.

The shipping advice is particularly important in short-sea trades, for example within the Asian countries where the goods may arrive at the port of destination before the shipping documents, and in the ports of destination where theft and pilferage of the imported goods is rampant.

Example: Shipping Advice

ZHONGSHAN IMPORT AND EXPORT CORPORATION

28 Spring Road, Shanghai, China

TEL: 86-21-84567321   FAX: 86-21-84567326

SHIPPING ADVICE

July 26, 2021

American Garment Inc.
124 Sweeten Creek Road
Asheville, NC 28803
USA

Dear Sir or Madam,

Re: Invoice No: SA568 L/C No. LKGR23589

We hereby inform you that the goods under the above-mentioned credit have been shipped. The details of the shipment are as stated below.

Name of Commodity: Men's Shirts

　Quantity: 260 Cartons

　Amount: USD56,522.20

　Ocean Vessel: East Wind V. 5689SA

　Bill of Lading No.: COSCO1352

　E.T.D.: On or about August 29, 2021

　Port of Loading: Shanghai

　Port of Destination: New York

Please arrange insurance on the shipment.

Sincerely yours

Zhongshan Import and Export Corporation

8.4 TERMS OF SHIPMENT IN CONTRACTS

8.4.1 General Expressions as to Date for Shipment

UOS, the expression "shipment" used in stipulating an earliest and/or a latest date for shipment will be understood to include expressions such as, "loading on board", "dispatch", "accepted for carriage", "date of post receipt", "date of pick-up", and in the case of a credit calling for a multimodal transport document the expression "taking in charge".

Expressions such as "prompt", "immediately", "as soon as possible" and the like should not be used. If they are used, banks will disregard them.

If the expression "on or about" or similar expressions are used, banks will interpret them as a stipulation that shipment is to be made during the period from five days before to five days after the specified date, both end days included.

8.4.2 Date Terminology for Periods of Shipment

"To", "until", "till", "from" shall be understood to include the date mentioned.

"After" shall be understood to exclude the date mentioned.

"First half", "second half of a month" shall be construed respectively as the 1st to the 15th, and the 16th to the last day of such month, all dates inclusive.

"Beginning", "middle" or "end of a month" shall be construed respectively as the 1st to the 10th, the 11th to the 20th, and the 21st to the last day of such month, all dates included.

8.4.3 Allowances in Quantity

UOS, the quantity of the goods specified must not be exceeded or reduced, a tolerance of 5% more or less will be permissible, always provided that the amount of the drawings does not exceed the amount of the credit. This tolerance does not apply when the credit stipulates the quantity in terms of a stated number of packing units of individual items.

8.4.4 Examples of Terms of Shipment in Contracts

Shipment: on or before June 20, 2021

Shipment: during February/March 2021

Shipment: within 45 days after receipt of L/C, allowing partial shipments and transshipment

Shipment: during January/February 2021 in two equal monthly lots (in two equal monthly shipments)

Shipment: during March/April/May 2021 in three monthly shipments

        during March 500 metric tons

        during April 750 metric tons

        during May 1,000 metric tons

8.5 SAMPLE LETTERS

Sample Letter 8 (1)

Dear Sirs,

Contract No. 6389

Referring to our previous letters and faxes, we wish to invite your attention to the fact that up to the present moment no news has come from you about the shipment under the captioned contract.

As you have been informed in one of our faxes, the end-users are in urgent need of the goods contracted and are in fact pressing us for assurance of timely delivery.

Under the circumstances, it is obviously impossible for us to extend our L/C No. 8963, which expires on November 20, 2021 and we are obliged to remind you of this matter once again.

As your prompt attention to shipment is most desirable to all parties concerned, we hope you will let us have your shipping advice soon without fail.

Yours faithfully

Sample Letter 8 (2)

Gentlemen,

Referring to our Order No. ST5689 for 6,500 Electric Sewing Machines, we wish to remind you that the time for shipment has long been overdue.

When we placed the order with you we pointed out that punctual shipment was of utmost importance because this order was secured from the largest dealers here and we had given them a definite assurance that we could supply the goods by the end of October.

Your delay has caused us much inconvenience and we must now ask you to do your utmost to despatch the first 2,000 sets by air under this order as the goods are urgently required by our customers.

We suggest the use of cartons to facilitate opening for customs examination. You will no doubt proceed with your arrangements for the shipment of the remaining 4,500 sets of the consignments by sea without further delay.

We would be obliged if you would send us by air a copy of the packing list for the shipment to be despatched by sea, and also duplicates of the insurance policy and commercial invoice. This will enable us to arrange speedy passage through customs on arrival of the consignment.

Sincerely yours

Sample Letter 8 (3)

Dear Sirs,

<u>Re: S/C No. JY 10236</u>

We have received your letter dated September 20 in connection with the subject above.

In reply, we have the pleasure of informing you that the irrevocable L/C No. DO36781 amounting to USD12,560 has been opened this morning with the Chartered Bank, London. Upon receipt of the same, please arrange shipment of the goods ordered by us without the least delay. We are informed by the local shipping company that s. s. "East Wind" is due to sail from your city to our port on or about October 10 and, if possible, please try your best to ship by that steamer.

If this trial order proves satisfactory to our customers, we can assure you that repeat orders in increased quantities will be placed.

Your close cooperation in this respect will be highly appreciated. In the meantime we await your shipping advice by facsimile.

Yours faithfully

Sample Letter 8 (4)

Gentlemen,

<u>M. V. "Aegis Bravery"</u>

Subject vessel loaded a full cargo of bulk wheat at Kalama, Washington, for account of Garner Grain Co. As a requirement of the National Cargo Bureau, trimming was found necessary in certain hatches. Also, to ensure statutory stability, No. 4 Hatch had to be strapped secure.

These two items a) trimming and b) securing gave rise to costs that had been unforeseen by charterer's stevedores. These extra costs were subsequently billed to us as being for your account.

On receiving invoices, we faxed the stevedoring company advising that these costs under terms of the C. P. were for charterer's account. A copy of that fax was sent to you and a further copy is now enclosed. We have now received further notice from Jones Oregon Stevedoring Co. advising that although the charterers have paid the cost of trimming, they still insist that securing costs should not be for their account. Jones Oregon have therefore again presented us with billing for US$2,689 covering the cost of labour and material involved. A copy of their letter and billing of October 20, 2021 is enclosed for your guidance.

Again we have faxed Jones Oregon Stevedoring Co. denying responsibility for the costs, but in an effort to conclude this matter, we now bring it more fully to your attention. We would add that Jones Oregon performed their duties on this vessel, and now find themselves in the unfortunate position of being unable to collect for out-of-pocket expenditure.

However, we refer to Jones Oregon's letter of October 15, 2019, wherein they quote Garner Grain as stating "this is for ship's account because it is required by the vessel's maritime authority for the safety of the ship and comes under the charter requirements that the vessel be in every way fitted for the voyage and loads under the National Cargo Bureau Inspection at her expense and to comply with their rules."

Our reading and interpretation of the charter party does not in our opinion, make you responsible for strapping and securing No. 4 Hatch because:

- The term "in every way fitted for the voyage" has often been confused as referring to grain fittings and then clearly interpreted as meaning suitable for the voyage.
- The expenses referred to in the term "loads under N. C. B. Inspection at her expense", we believe, refers solely to the National Cargo Bureau expenses, that is, survey expenses. These were paid by us in this case.
- The freight rate quoted was clearly f. i. o. s. (free in and out, stowed) terms, and in this case we view the stowage not to have been finished until the strapped securing was completed. Proper stowage on this vessel included the necessary securing of No. 4 Hatch.

We bring these points to your notice as our view and reading of the Charter Party. Direct approach to the charterer has not been made by us, nor have the charterers contacted us on the subject.

As there might be some other conditions during negotiations of which we are unaware, we ask you to review this case, giving us your opinion and instructions.

We look forward to your reply.

Yours very truly

8.6 USEFUL TERMS AND EXPRESSIONS

1. shipping company	船舶公司
2. shipping instructions	装船须知
3. shipping advice	装船通知
4. shipping space	舱位

5.	shipping port	装运港
6.	loading port	装货港
7.	port of shipment	装运港
8.	port of destination	目的港
9.	port of discharge	卸货港
10.	tramp	不定期船
11.	liner	班轮
12.	sailing schedule	航期
13.	shipper	托运人
14.	carrier	承运人
15.	shipping order	装货单
16.	dock receipt	码头收据
17.	mate's receipt	大副收据
18.	receipt for goods	货物收据
19.	contract of carriage	运输契约
20.	document of title	所有权凭证
21.	on board notation	装船注记
22.	order bill of lading	指示提单
23.	straight bill of lading	记名提单
24.	non-negotiable bill of lading	不可流动转让提单
25.	consignor	发货人
26.	consignee	收货人
27.	notify party	通知人
28.	clean bill of lading	清洁提单
29.	foul bill of lading	不清洁提单
30.	short form bill of lading	简式提单
31.	long form bill of lading	全式提单
32.	through bill of lading	转运提单

33.	charter bill of lading	租船提单
34.	accepted for carriage	受妥待运
35.	date of post receipt	邮局收据日期
36.	date of pick-up	收货日期
37.	taking in charge	接受监管
38.	partial shipments	分批装运
39.	instalment shipments	分期装运
40.	despatch money	速遣费
41.	demurrage	滞期费
42.	estimated time of arrival	预计到达时间
43.	estimated time of departure	预计离港时间
44.	airway bill of lading	空运单
45.	bulk cargo	散装货
46.	light cargo	轻泡货
47.	trimming charges	平舱费
48.	tally charges	理货费
49.	dead freight	空舱费
50.	laydays	停泊期
51.	ice-free port	不冻港
52.	seasonal port	季节港
53.	EMP (European Main Ports)	欧洲主要港口
54.	port of call	停靠港口
55.	Amsterdam	阿姆斯特丹(荷兰)
56.	Antwerp	安特卫普(比利时)
57.	Auckland	奥克兰(新西兰)
58.	Baltimore	巴尔的摩(美国)
59.	Bangkok	曼谷(泰国)
60.	Barcelona	巴塞罗那(西班牙)

61.	Bremen	不来梅（德国）
62.	Calcutta	加尔各答（印度）
63.	Colombo	科伦坡（斯里兰卡）
64.	Genoa	热那亚（意大利）
65.	Glasgow	格拉斯哥（英国）
66.	Hamburg	汉堡（德国）
67.	Kobe	神户（日本）
68.	Jeddah	吉达（沙特阿拉伯）
69.	Lisbon	里斯本（葡萄牙）
70.	Liverpool	利物浦（英国）
71.	London	伦敦（英国）
72.	Los Angeles	洛杉矶（美国）
73.	Manila	马尼拉（菲律宾）
74.	Marseilles	马赛（法国）
75.	Melbourne	墨尔本（澳大利亚）
76.	Montreal	蒙特利尔（加拿大）
77.	Nagoya	名古屋（日本）
78.	Naples	那不勒斯（意大利）
79.	New Orleans	新奥尔良（美国）
80.	New York	纽约（美国）
81.	Osaka	大阪（日本）
82.	Philadelphia	费城（美国）
83.	Rotterdam	鹿特丹（荷兰）
84.	San Francisco	旧金山（美国）
85.	Singapore	新加坡（新加坡）
86.	Southampton	南安普顿（英国）
87.	Stockholm	斯德哥尔摩（瑞典）
88.	Sydney	悉尼（澳大利亚）

89. Tokyo	东京(日本)
90. Vancouver	温哥华(加拿大)
91. Venice	威尼斯(意大利)
92. Wellington	惠灵顿(新西兰)
93. Yokohama	横滨(日本)
94. bulk wheat	散装小麦
95. out-of-pocket expenditure	实际开支
96. FIO (free in and out)	船方不负责装卸费
97. charter party	租船契约
98. punctual shipment	按时发运
99. dispatch	(迅速)发送

8.7 COMMUNICATION LABORATORY

Application Exercises

A. Translate the following into Chinese.

1. In the absence of any indication on the transport document as to the numbers issued, banks will accept the transport document(s) presented as constituting a full set. Banks will accept as original(s) the transport document(s) whether marked as original(s) or not.

2. We have pleasure in informing you that the shipment of Chemical Fertilizer under Contract No. ZU2368 will be effected by s. s. "East Wind" which is scheduled to leave Shanghai Port on May 16. Please arrange insurance for this cargo.

3. The goods have been packed and marked exactly as directed so that they may be shipped by the first steamer available toward the end of this month.

4. We trust you will see to it that the order is shipped within the stipulated time, as any delay would cause us no little inconvenience and financial loss.

5. We are pleased to inform you that we have booked freight space for your Order No. 5689 of cement on s. s. "Taishan" with ETA June 20. For delivery instructions, please contact Messrs. Lombard Bros. Co., London.

6. As requested, we are sending you separately two copies of our Invoice No. 897, two copies of Insurance Policy No. 5632 and one copy of Non-negotiable B/L No. 8496 covering 500 cartons of leather shoes for your Order No. 8544 under our Contract No. 9898.

7. We fear that half-month delay in shipment may seriously affect the quality. In the event that some deterioration of the quality is found on arrival, we shall have to hold you responsible for the defective goods and request you for necessary adjustment or replacement by the perfect goods.
8. FCA is the most used Incoterm (about 40% of the international trade operations are carried out with this Incoterm) since it is very versatile and allows the delivery of goods in different places (seller's address, land transport terminal, port, airport, etc.)
9. The new Incoterm would be denominated as CNI (Cost and Insurance) and would cover a gap between FCA and CFR/CIF. As in the other Incoterms in "C", this new Incoterm would be an "arrival Incoterm", i.e., the risk of transport would be transmitted from the seller to the buyer at the port of departure.
10. The Incoterms 2020 Drafting Committee is considering creating two Incoterms based on DDP: DTP (Delivered at Terminal Paid) and DPP (Delivered at Place Paid).

B. Translate the following sentences into English.
1. 一万吨大豆因舱位不够，无法提前全部在12月份装船，请修改信用证，允许分批装运。(advance)
2. 大豆信用证已照改，请尽量赶装11月16日起航的"红星"号轮和12月10日起航的"东风"号轮。(catch)
3. 如让我们代你办理装运及报关手续，你们既可以节省时间又可以节省开支。(handle ... formalities)
4. 请告在途运输时间有多长，班轮航次有多少，货舱是否要预订。(book)
5. 请即处理此事，务使交货不再推迟。(take the matter up)

C. Cloze

We learn from your shipping advice that the antique potteries and porcelain-ware we ordered have been shipped by s.s. "Morning Star". According to the shipping s_____, it is expected to arrive in a day or two. H_____, after several contacts with the local forwarding agent, we are surprisingly told that the s_____ vessel has not yet at all arrived at Shanghai, let alone finished loading and set s_____ for Kobe. The duplicate copies of the bill of lading you sent us were i_____ and dated in advance. As a matter of fact, the goods are still lying at the dock in Shanghai waiting for shipment. These copies will not do you any good; on the contrary, they will prove your d_____ manner in handling this transaction.

You may recall that we have time and again emphasized the vital importance of p_____ shipment because these antique potteries and porcelain-ware are for display at an international exhibition to be held in Osaka. We think it absurd to d_____ with you over the delay in shipment on the present occasion when time is so pressing. The only r_____ for avoiding non-performance of the contract we signed with the exhibition administration is to send the goods by air at once and at any cost.

To be fair, we are prepared to pay for the air f_____, while you should be responsible for the other expenses such as shifting the goods from the dock to the airport.

Case Study

Read the sample L/C in Unit 6 and make out a B/L on behalf of the carrier.

Unit 9 Insurance

9.1 INTRODUCTION

Insurance is generally defined as a financial arrangement where one party agrees to compensate another for a loss if it results from the occurrence of a specified event, and it is more technically defined as a device for reducing risk by combining a sufficient number of exposure units to make their individual losses collectively predictable. The predictable loss is then shared by or distributed proportionately among all units in the combination. The fundamental objective of insurance is to provide a means for offsetting the burden of financial losses. The often repeated sayings, "Ignorance is bliss" and "What you don't know won't hurt you", do not apply to insurance.

It is true to say that insurance provides a pool or fund into which the many contribute and out of which the few who suffer losses are compensated. Insurers frequently re-insure a portion of the "risk" they have accepted. The insurance of large "risks" is spread directly or indirectly over a large number of insurance or re-insurance companies or underwriters.

Insurance has become a vast subject and now enters into almost every activity of man. The idea of insurance is to obtain some indemnity in the event of any happenings that cause loss of money; insurance is against risk. It is possible in these days to insure against almost any eventuality that may cause loss of one kind or another.

In insurance no one desires the event to occur; if it does so, the insured person receives an indemnity for the loss sustained.

Fire, accident, life and marine are the chief branches of insurance.

9.1.1 Insurance in International Trade

It is customary to insure goods sold for export against the perils of the journey. In international trade, the transportation of goods from the seller to the buyer generally covers a long distance by air, by land or by sea and has to go through the procedures of loading, unloading and storing. During this process it is quite possible that the goods will encounter various kinds of perils and sometimes suffer losses. In order to protect the goods against possible loss in case of such perils, the buyer or seller before the transportation of the goods usually applies to an insurance company for insurance covering the goods in transit.

The transportation insurance covering goods in import and export trade means:

- The insured or assured (either the exporter or importer) applies to an insurance

- company for insurance to cover a lot or several or several lots of goods to be transported by declaring the sum to be insured, the kinds of insurance cover and by paying the insurance premium.
- The insurance company, after agreeing to cover the insurance, will pay the assured any financial loss eventually suffered by the goods during transportation according to the terms of the insurance agreement, which is called an insurance policy or certificate.

The term "marine insurance" is somewhat misleading because the contract of marine insurance can, by agreement of the parties or custom of the trade, be extended so as to protect the insured against losses on inland waters or land which are incidental to the sea voyage. In the export trade it is usual to arrange an extended marine insurance under the "warehouse to warehouse" clause in order to cover the transportation of goods from the warehouse of the seller to the port of dispatch, and from the port of arrival to the warehouse of the overseas buyer.

China is fast becoming one of the world's most important economies. Although its financial services sector is still small compared to the US, Europe, or Japan, its rapid growth rates and huge potential size make it a critical arena for expansion for insurers. Since 2000, the Chinese insurance market has tripled in size to about US$60 billion in premium. Major non-life insurance companies in China are PICC P&C, China Pacific Property Insurance, China United Property Insurance, China Continent Insurance, Hua Tai Insurance and Sinosafe General Insurance.

9.1.2 Classifications of Perils and Losses

Goods during transportation on sea and in the course of loading and unloading might encounter various kinds of perils and the goods might suffer losses of some kind.

In marine insurance, perils are generally of two kinds:

(1) Perils of the Sea
- Natural Calamities: such as vile weather, thunder and lightning, tidal wave, earthquake, floods, etc.
- Fortuitous Accidents: such as ship stranded, striking upon the rocks, ship sinking, ship collision, colliding with icebergs or other objects, fire, explosion, etc.

(2) Extraneous Risks: such as theft, rain, shortage, leakage, breakage, dampness, etc. They may also include special risks, such as war risks, strikes, non-delivery of cargo, refusal to receive cargo, etc.

The term "Perils of the Sea" does not include the possible perils caused by ordinary action of the winds and waves.

Furthermore, such losses caused by natural deterioration or deficiency in the quality of the goods, are generally not accounted as perils in marine insurance.

Losses fall into two main categories: Total Loss and Partial Loss. Both are again subdivided.

(1) Total loss can either be Actual Total Loss where vessel or cargo are totally and irretrievably lost, or Constructive Total Loss in a case where the ship or the goods have been abandoned because the cost of salvage or recovery would have been out of proportion to the value.

(2) Partial loss means that the loss to the goods is only partial.

In case of a partial loss a fine distinction is drawn between Particular Average and General Average. In marine insurance Average has an entirely different meaning from its normal usage and it means loss or damage to the goods in the course of sea transportation due to natural calamities and accidents and extraneous risks.

If a particular cargo is damaged by any cause the damage is called particular average and the loss must be borne by the owner of this individual consignment. If the owner estimates the possibility of this risk as very small he may think it unnecessary to insure against it and take out a policy Free of Particular Average (F. P. A.) and thus obtain a slightly lower premium.

General average is of an entirely different character. It applies to a loss intentionally incurred in the general interest of the ship owner and the owners of the various cargoes. For example, a ship may have run aground and all efforts to re-float it have failed. In order to save the ship from breaking up the master may decide to jettison (i. e., to throw overboard) part of the cargo to lighten the ship. This loss is borne by all concerned in proportion. The same applies to additional expenses incurred in the common interest, i.e., the cost of using a tug to tow a damaged vessel into port; all parties have to contribute in proportion to their interests. A merchant can, and usually will insure against this liability.

9.1.3 Insurance Cover

According to the regulations and stipulations of the People's Insurance Company of China, the following basic insurance covers are available in marine insurance:

Free of (from) Particular Average (F. P. A.) Insurance. The insurance company will be responsible to pay claims for total or constructive total losses suffered by the whole lot of cargoes during transportation due to such natural calamities as vile weather, thunder and lightning, tidal wave, earthquake, and floods, or for total or partial losses due to the ship or carrier being on fire, stranded, sinking, colliding or encountering other fortuitous accidents.

The insurance company will also be responsible, when losses are incurred in the course of loading or unloading, for instance, when one or several whole parcels of the goods are dropped into the sea and are considered lost, or when general average is incurred, i. e., when losses or expenses are incurred in the common interest.

With Particular Average (W. P. A.) Insurance or With Average (W. A.) Insurance. The cover under this insurance is more extensive. The insurer is liable also for the partial losses of the insured goods due to the risks caused by natural calamities mentioned under

F. P. A. insurance.

All Risks Insurance. Among the three kinds of basic insurance, under an "all risks" policy the goods are insured against all risks, e. g. from natural calamities, fortuitous accidents at sea, or general extraneous risks, irrespective of percentage of loss, total or partial. A natural deterioration of perishable goods, delay, loss or damage caused by inherent vice or nature of the subject matter are not covered.

Insurance Covers of Additional/Extra Risks. Risks that are not covered under the basic insurance covers F. P. A. and W. P. A. mentioned above may be insured against under separate declarations by the insured. These risks may be general extra risks such as Theft, Pilferage & Non-delivery Risks (T. P. N. D.), Fresh and/or Rain Water Damage Risks, Shortage Risk, Inter-mixture & Contamination Risks, Leakage Risk, Clash & Breakage Risks, Taint of Odor Risk, Sweating & Heating Risks, Hook Damage Risk, Rust Risk, Breakage of Packing Risk. These risks are covered under All Risks insurance. Or they may be special extra risks such as Failure to Deliver Risk, Import Duty Risk, On Deck Risk, Rejection Risk, War Risk, etc.

The distinction between the clauses F. P. A. (free from particular average) and W. A. (with average) or W. P. A. (with particular average) is of great practical significance. Policies embodying a clause of the former type can be obtained at a cheaper rate of premium than those embodying a W. A. (W. P. A.) clause, but do not provide such comprehensive insurance cover as the latter. The exporter has to decide in each particular case whether F. P. A. terms are sufficient or a W. A. (W. P. A.) insurance is required; he should, if in doubt, exercise his discretion in favor of a W. A. (W. P. A.) insurance notwithstanding the higher rates of premium. Where fragile or delicate goods are shipped, for example glassware or textiles, a W. A. (W. P. A) policy is generally apposite even if the goods are expertly packed. When rough cargoes are shipped, for example sheet-iron or coal, an F. P. A. policy is sufficient.

9.1.4 The Warehouse to Warehouse Clause

The "warehouse to warehouse" clause, by which marine insurance cover is extended to land risks incidental to the sea voyage and which is very common in export transaction, is stipulated by the People's Insurance Company of China. It naturally covers port risks and the risk of craft to and from the ship. The warehouse to warehouse clause, which does not apply to war risk insurance, provides complete protection; it covers the landing risks in the port of destination as part of the transit from the warehouse of the seller to that of the buyer.

In other words, by the warehouse to warehouse clause, the liability of the insurer is extended to cover pre-shipment and post-shipment risks. The insured goods are covered from the time when they leave the warehouse at the place named in the policy for the commencement of the transit and continue to be covered until they are delivered to the final warehouse of the destination named in the policy, but the policy provides an overriding time limit of sixty days after the completion of discharge overside the oversea vessel at the final port of discharge; on the expiration of that time limit of sixty days the cover ceases to protect the goods even though they have not reached the final warehouse.

9.1.5 Insurable Value

Insurable value is generally calculated as: cost of goods + amount of freight + insurance premium + percentage of the total sum to represent a reasonable profit for the buyer. The buyer's anticipated profits are normally included in the value declared by adding a percentage, say 10 or 15 percent, to the invoice value and the incidental shipping and insurance charges of the goods, but the additional percentage should not be more than 30 percent. Insurable value is the maximum amount payable by the insurance company in case of loss and premium is calculated and paid on the basis of this amount. Insurance companies will not accept additional percentage of more than 30%.

9.1.6 Insurance Policy or Certificate

In an export transaction, the terms of the contract of sale provide normally whether the costs of marine insurance shall be borne by the seller or by the buyer. If the goods are sold on F. O. B. terms these costs have to be paid by the buyer and that is even true if the F. O. B. seller, by request of the buyer, has taken out the policy on behalf of the buyer. If the goods are sold on C. I. F. terms, it is the duty of the seller to take out the policy and pay the costs of insurance.

Where goods are sold C. I. F. the seller is obliged to take out a marine insurance policy which provides cover against the risks customarily covered in the particular trade in respect of the cargo and voyage in question, but he is not required to do more. He need not take out an all risks policy unless the parties have agreed thereon and it is demanded by the custom of the trade.

The marine insurance policy or certificate forms part of the shipping documents. As marine insurance is very old, its documents and practice are very much a legacy of the past. It is able to meet present-day needs by means of constant improvisation. We find, therefore, the standard forms of a marine insurance policy in foreign countries using old phraseology but the clauses and provisions, which govern the policy, are constantly revised and kept up to date.

The risks against which the insurer undertakes to hold the insured covered are stated in standardized clauses, some to be found in the body of the policy itself, and others, so-called clauses or Institute Clauses, normally attached to the policy on separate slips of paper.

The parties to a contract of marine insurance are known as the insured and the insurer. The insured is the party who will receive the benefit of the insurance in case of loss. Insurers are the marine insurance companies.

In the normal course of business the exporter in Britain, for instance, does not approach the insurer directly and instructs an insurance broker to effect the insurance on his behalf.

When the risk is covered, the broker sends the insured a memorandum of the insurance effected which is conveniently executed on a duplicate form of the instructions. According to the nature of insurance which the broker was instructed to obtain, the memorandum assumes the form of a closed or open cover note. A closed cover note is sent if the insured, in his instructions, has given full particulars as to cargo and shipment and the insurance has, thus, been made definite. An open cover note is sent if the instructions of the insured are so general and indefinite that further instructions are required from him to define the voyage and cargo shipped under the insurance; this happens where the insured requires a "floating policy" or an "open cover" or where he reserves the right to give "closing instructions".

In the meantime the broker arranges with the insurer to have the insurance policy (or certificate) issued. The insurance policy is a very important instrument because it forms part of the shipping documents, which are sent to the consignee either direct or, more usually, through a bank.

9.1.7 Floating Policy or Open Cover (Policy)

This type of policy is of great importance for export trade; it is, in fact, a convenient method of insuring goods where a number of similar export transactions are intended, e.g. where the insured has to supply an overseas importer under an exclusive sales agreement or maintains permanent sales representatives or subsidiary companies abroad. A floating policy covers the shipments, as soon as they are made, under previous arrangement between the insured and the insurance company and particulars of the shipment may be supplied to the insurance company later on. An open cover is similar to a floating policy. While a floating policy is usually limited to 12 months, the open cover may be limited in time or may be permanent. Where the open cover is perpetual in character ("always open"), a clause is inserted enabling both parties to give notice of cancellation of the cover within a stated time, e.g. thirty days or three months.

9.1.8 Blanket Policy

In the case of a floating policy or open cover the insured has normally to make declarations of the individual shipments falling under these insurances to the insurer. This is inconvenient to the exporter and requires an excessive amount of labor and costs where the various consignments are of small value or the voyage is of short duration. In these cases the insured will take out a "blanket policy" which usually provides that he need not advise the insurer of the individual shipments and that a lump sum premium—instead of a premium at several rates—shall cover all shipments.

9.1.9 Claims

If the insured learns, even unofficially, that the goods might possibly be lost or damaged in transit he should forthwith inform his insurance broker and act on his advice. It is customary to employ brokers not only for the conclusion of a contract of insurance but also for the settlement of claims. If the consignee is informed that the goods have arrived damaged, he should immediately notify the insurer's agent at the port of discharge who will survey the goods and issue a survey report. He, then, could claim indemnity from the insurer by producing the insurance policy, survey report and other necessary documents.

9.2 WRITING GUIDE

9.2.1 Inquiries for Insurance Rates

Insurance is an important part in business affairs, especially in international business affairs, for a qualified businessperson should know how to protect his/her or his/her company's interests by trying to reduce the possible risks, perils, misfortunes and losses and at the same time, how to claim for his/her compensation when misfortunes of any kind do happen to him/her. As insurance of risks, and especially of marine risks calls for specialized knowledge, it is quite necessary for the businessperson, whether a seller or a buyer, to forward a letter to a certified insurance company asking for the rates, or he/she can ask a broker to do it on his/her behalf.

The following points must be specified when writing an inquiry for insurance.
- The name of the goods to be insured;
- The value of the goods to be insured;
- The port of discharge and the name of the vessel to be used;
- The destination to which the goods are scheduled to be shipped;
- The kind of insurance you are inquiring about.

9.2.2 Application for Insurance

When you are informed of the rates for the insurance you have requested, you are supposed to write an application for insurance.

The following points are suggested to be specified when writing an application for insurance.
- The name of the goods to be insured;
- The total value of the goods to be insured;
- The port of discharge and the name of the vessel to be used;
- The destination to which the goods are scheduled to be shipped;
- The kind of insurance you want to apply for.

9.3 SAMPLE LETTERS

Sample Letter 9 (1): Inquiry for Insurance Rate

Dear Sir or Madam,

Knowing that your company is the largest insurance company in China with branches and sub-branches throughout the country and survey and claim settling agents in major ports of the world, China Arts & Crafts Import and Export Corporation wishes to insure with your company a shipment of Chinese porcelain valued at USD780,000 on board the vessel "Oriental Star" against all risks, bound from Shanghai to Vancouver sailing on May 4.

We shall highly appreciate it if the goods could be insured at a favorable rate.

Yours faithfully

Sample Letter 9 (2): Inquiry for Insurance Rate

Dear Sir or Madam,

We enclose a list of goods of our company to you for your kind verification.

We shall be glad to be informed of your rates for insuring the listed goods at an early date.

Yours faithfully

Sample Letter 9 (3): Inquiry for Insurance Rate

Dear Sir or Madam,

We shall shortly have a consignment of silk scarves, valued at US $5,000 CIF New York, to be shipped from Shanghai by a vessel of Victor Co., Ltd. We'd like to cover the consignment against all risks for our warehouse at 80 King Street to the port of New York. Will you please quote your rate for the cover?

Yours faithfully

Sample Letter 9 (4): Inquiry for Insurance Rate

Dear Mr. Smith,

We ship consignments, on a regular basis, of bottled mineral water to Singapore by cargo liners of the Oriental Shipping Line. Will you please inform us whether you can insure an all-risks policy for these shipments and, if so, on what terms? And in particular, may we have the knowledge whether you can issue a preferential rate in return for the promise of regular monthly shipments.

Yours faithfully

Sample Letter 9 (5): Application for Insurance

Dear Sir or Madam,

We wish to insure the following consignment against all risks for the sum of US＄25,000 for 8,000 men's T-shirts.

These goods are now lying at Dock 5, Hong Kong, waiting to be shipped by SS "Oriental Star" and due to leave for New York on Friday, May 4. We require immediate cover as far as New York and shall be glad if you will let us have the policy as soon as it is ready. In the meantime, please confirm that you hold the consignment covered.

Yours faithfully

Sample Letter 9 (6): Application for Insurance

Dear Sir or Madam,

We wish to insure the following consignment against all risks for the sum of US＄30,000 for motorcycles of Chinese make.

These goods are now lying at Dock 8, Shanghai, waiting to be shipped by SS "Oriental Star" and due to leave for Liverpool on Friday, May 4. We require immediate cover as far as Liverpool and shall be glad if you will let us have the policy as soon as it is ready. In the meantime, please confirm that you hold the consignment covered.

Yours faithfully

Sample Letter 9 (7): Application for Insurance

Dear Sir or Madam,

Thank you very much for your letter dated May 10 quoting rates for insurance cover of stock already in our warehouse at the address as specified above. The total value of the stock held may vary with the market, but does not, in any case, normally exceed US＄20,000 at any time. Please arrange cover in this sum for all the risks mentioned in your letter and on the terms quoted, namely 275 annum, as from June 1.

Yours faithfully

Sample Letter 9 (8): Application for Insurance

Dear Sirs,

Thank you for your letter dated May 10 quoting rates for insurance cover of stock already in our warehouse at the address as specified above. The value of the stock held totals US50,000. Please arrange cover in this sum for all the risks mentioned in your letter and on the terms quoted.

Yours faithfully

9.4 USEFUL TERMS AND EXPRESSIONS

1.	cargo transportation insurance	货物运输保险
2.	insured	被保险人
3.	applicant	投保人
4.	insurer/underwriter	保险人
5.	insurable interest	保险利益
6.	utmost good faith	最大诚信
7.	principle of indemnity	补偿原则
8.	perils of the sea	海上风险
9.	extraneous risks	外来风险
10.	theft pilferage	偷窃
11.	non-delivery	提货不着
12.	rain damage	雨淋
13.	shortage in weight	短量
14.	leakage	渗漏
15.	clash and breakage	碰损和破碎
16.	sweating and heating	受潮受热
17.	hook damage	钩损
18.	insurance policy	保险单
19.	insurance certificate	保险凭证
20.	combined insurance certificate	联合保险凭证
21.	open policy	预约保险单
22.	cover note	暂保单
23.	endorsement	批单
24.	constructive total loss	推定全损
25.	partial loss	部分损失
26.	general average	共同海损
27.	free from particular average	平安险
28.	with average /with particular average	水渍险

9.5 COMMUNICATION LABORATORY

Application Exercises

A. **Translate the following into Chinese.**
1. We shall appreciate it if the above-mentioned goods could be insured at favorable rate.
2. We would very much like to place the insurance with PICC and are currently trying to get in touch with PICC Shanghai.
3. The prevailing rate for the proposed shipment against all risks is ... %, subject to our own Ocean Marine Cargo Clauses, copies thereof are enclosed for your reference.
4. If you find our rate acceptable, please fill in the application form enclosed and send it back, preferably by fax, so that we may issue insurance policy accordingly.
5. We are in receipt of your letter of June 10, 2007 requesting for an extension of the above policy for a period of 30 days to cover all risks whilst the goods are lying in the Custom's warehouse in Shanghai.
6. In response to your letter dated June 10, we request you to cover insurance on the vessel at 1.75‰ and on the cargo at 2.25‰ with the Eastern Star Marine Insurance Company.
7. In compliance with your orders of the June 10, I have effected the insurance with the Eastern Star Marine Insurance Company at the premiums already mentioned. Copy of Policy is enclosed.
8. To meet our clients' requirement and to facilitate handling of claim, we suggest that the business be co-insured by our two companies on 50/50 basis.

B. **Translate the following sentences into English.**
1. "海上风险"仅指海上偶发的意外事故或灾难,而不包括风浪的正常作用。(refer to)
2. 我方建议对以上的变更不再增加额外的保费,并希望此事已得到圆满解决。(in order)
3. 在此情况下,由于涉及的保险凭证早以过期,很遗憾我们不能满足贵方的要求。(comply with)
4. 此报单的被保险人名称应更换为江苏国际贸易公司,其他条款不变。(amend)
5. 我们已收到贵方 2007 年 6 月 10 日发出的关于延长保单的信函及相关附件。(acknowledge)

C. **Cloze**

Founded on April 27, 1961 as the pioneer of international shipping c_____ in China, together with the reconstruction of national transportation resources on February 16, 1993, China Ocean Shipping (Group) Company (COSCO) has grown into a $17 billion corporation by clearly f_____ on the goal of enabling commerce around the globe. It is an international giant, s_____ in shipping and modern logistics, serving as a shipping agency and providing with services in freight f_____, shipbuilding, ship repairing, terminal operation, trade, financing, real estate and IT industry as well with an aim at taking one of the leading roles in these areas. Today, followed by more than 40 years of arduous efforts, COSCO has successfully molded itself into a global company with one of the most recognized and admired brand name in the world. As far as the fleet c_____ is concerned, we now own and operate a variety of m_____ fleet of some 600 vessels with total carrying capacity of up to 35 million DWT, which help make a hit with achieving annual traffic v_____ of more than 300 million tons.

As a global company with shipping and modern logistics as the c_____ business, COSCO cherishes its abundant resources of hundreds of member units and service networks both at home and abroad. In China, our wholly-owned s_____ scattering in Guangzhou, Shanghai, Tianjin, Qingdao, Dalian, Xiamen and Hong Kong own and operate various types of ocean shipping fleets for the shipment of containership, bulk carrier, oil tanker as well as specialized carrier. Abroad, with North America, Europe, Japan, South Korea, Singapore, Australia, South Africa and West Asia as lucrative markets linked by shipping routes, we have formed a transnational operating network capable of reaching all major areas of the world. Ships and containers with the conspicuous "COSCO" l_____ are shuttling among 1,300 ports in more than 160 countries and regions around the world.

All of our efforts are designed to help our customers be more efficient and effective. All of our efforts are designed to help our customers save time and money. All of our efforts are set to help our customers be more energetic and promising and above all strive to be more competitive in the world.

Case study

Read the following Marine Cargo Transportation Insurance Policy and Cover Note to analyze possible differences between the two.

	中国人民保险公司
	THE PEOPLE'S INSURANCE COMPANY OF CHINA
	总公司设于北京　1949 年创立
发票号码	INVOICE JH-FLSINVO
保险单	INSURANCE POLICY
保险单号次	POLICY NO. JH-FLSBD 07 NO. 6

中国人民保险公司(以下简称本公司)
THIS POLICY OF INSURANCE WITNESSES THAT THE PEOPLE'S INSURANCE COMPANY OF CHINA (HEREINAFTER CALLED "THE COMPANY")
根据
AT THE REQUEST OF ORIENTAL STAR TRADING CORP.

Unit 9　Insurance

标记 MARKS & NO. S	包装及数量 QUANTITY	保险货物项目 DESCRIPTION OF GOODS	保险金额 AMOUNT INSURED
AS PER INVOICE NO. JH. FLSINV06	1,200 CARTONS	FOREVER BRAND BICYCLE	US $90,420.00

（以下简称被保险人）的要求，由被保险人向本公司缴付约
(HEREINAFTER CALLED "THE INSURED") AND IN CONSIDERATION OF THE AGREED PREMIUM PAID TO THE COMPANY BY THE
定的保险，按照本保险单承保险别和背面所载条款下列
INSURED UNDERTAKES TO INSURE THE UNDERMENTIONED GOODS IN TRANSPORTATION SUBJECT TO THE CONDITIONS OF THIS POLICY
特款承保下述货物运输保险，特立本保险单
AS PER THE CLAUSES PRINTED OVERLEAF AND OTHER SPECIAL CLAUSES ATTACHED HEREON
总保险金额：
TOTAL AMOUNT INSURED：
UNITED STATES DOLLARS NINETY THOUSAND FOUR HUNDRED AND TWENTY ONLY

保费　PREMIUM　AS ARRANGED
费率　RATE　AS ARRANGED
装载运输工具　CONVEYANCE SS. YIXIANG V307
开航日期　SLG. ON OR ABT. AS PER BILL OF LADING
自　　　　　FROM GUANGZHOU
至　　　　　TO COPENHAGEN
承保险别：
CONDITIONS
　　　　　　　ALL RISKS AND WAR RISK
　　　　　AS PER CIC OF PICC DATED 1/1/2007
　　　　　　　L/C NO. FLS. JHLC06

所保货物，如遇出险，本公司凭本保险单及其他有关证件给付赔款。
CLAIMS, IF ANY, PAYABLE ON SURRENDER OF THIS POLICY TOGETHER WITH OTHER RELEVANT DOCUMENTS
所保货物，如发生本保险单项下负责赔偿的损失或事故，
IN THE EVENT OF ACCIDENT WHEREBY LOSS OR DAMAGE MAY RESULT IN A CLAIM UNDER THIS POLICY IMMEDIATE NOTICE
应立即通知本公司下述代理人查勘。
APPLYING FOR SURVEY MUST BE GIVEN TO THE COMPANY'S AGENT AS MENTIONED HEREUNDER：
J. G. SAFE & CO. A/S63 1 MAPLE ALLE, DK-3240 VALBY
COPENHAGEN TEL：(01)4l3277　FAX：(01)4l3376

赔款偿付地点
CLAIM PAYABLE AT/IN　　DENMARK IN US DOLLARS

中国人民保险公司广州分公司
THE PEOPLE'S INSURANCE COMPANY OF CHINA GUANGZHOU BRANCH
地址:中国广州中山路56号 TEL: 87562398 Telex: 87569824 PICCS
ADDRESS:56 ZHONGSHANLU GUANGZHOU, CHINA

Cover Note

According to the request of _____ (hereinafter referred to as the "Insured"), the People's Insurance Company of China (hereinafter referred to as the "Company") agrees that before the Insured submits the application and the Company signs and issues the official policy, it will cover _____ (the type of risks) of _____ (the name of the subject matter insurance) for the Insured from _____ on the following major terms and conditions.

Insured:

Coverage:

Period of Insurance: From _____ to _____

Subject Matter Insured:

Location:

Insured Amount:

Rate:

Premium:

Clause Used:

Other Conditions: (such as territory scope of coverage, aggregate limit of indemnity nature of business, etc.)

Hereby stated that this Cover Note will expire on _____, the Insured shall submit to the Company a signed application _____ days before the termination of this Cover Note showing the detailed contents of all items of the application. The above application shall form an integral part of the official Policy to be issued by the Company within _____ days of receipt thereof.

In case of loss prior to the issuance of the official Policy, the liability of the Company is to be subject to the terms and conditions of the official Policy and any indemnity payable will be made only after signing and issuing the official Policy and upon payment of the agreed premium due by the insured.

This Cover Note shall be returned to the Company after the official Policy is signed and issued.

Date:

Place:

The People's Insurance Company of China

Unit 10 Complaints, Claims and Adjustments

10.1 GENERAL INTRODUCTION TO COMPLAINTS, CLAIMS AND ADJUSTMENTS

10.1.1 Comparison Between Complaints and Claims

Successful international business communication should avoid complaints or claims as much as possible; however, due to certain reasons, they still exist in international transactions and therefore how to handle complaints, claims and adjustments becomes increasingly important since to a certain extent they decide the possibility of future business between the seller and the buyer.

At a certain stage of international business communication, the seller and the buyer will agree on a sales contract, the terms and conditions of which should be observed by both parties, and if it is breached by one party, troubles or losses will be caused. If the trouble or loss is not very serious, the affected party can call attention of the other party to avoid such things in the future. In this case, a "complaint" is made; however, if the trouble or loss is very serious, the affected party can ask for compensation based on the provisions of the said contract and therefore a "claim" is put up instead.

Complaints or claims can be justified or unjustified. Justified complaints or claims are those genuine ones, which are caused by wrong goods, unsatisfactory quality or delivery, damage or late arrival, overcharged goods or non-complied prices, etc. On the other hand, unjustified complaints or claims are those excuses made by one party of the contract to find fault with the goods or escape contract obligations due to reasons like better business opportunities with a third party.

10.1.2 Classification of Claims

Claims can be classified into three categories, i. e., claims made on exporters/importers, claims made on carriers, and claims made on insurance companies.

Claims Made on Exporters/Importers. In international business transactions, claims are usually made by importers on exporters for faults made by the latter, such as non-delivery of goods, delay of shipment, wrong goods, insufficient quantity or insufficient quality of goods, losses due to improper packing, lack of shipment documents, etc.

However, exporters sometimes send claims to importers when losses are caused by the lateness or refusal of shipment procedures or L/C opening by the latter.

Claims Made on Carriers. Claims of this category are often caused by reasons including loss of goods, improper transportation of transit, improper piling, pilferage, damage caused by sea water, and unseaworthiness of the ship.

Claims Made on Insurance Companies. Prerequisites for claims of this category include an insurance contract and damage caused by an accident within the insurance scope of the insurance company.

10.1.3 Adjustments

There are usually three kinds of responses to a complaint or a claim, i.e., settling the claim, making adjustments and rejecting the claim.

Thus adjustment letters include both those accepting the complaint or claim and those of non-acceptance. The former is made when the complaint or claim is justified, while the latter is made usually when the complaint or claim is unjustified.

10.2 PRINCIPLES FOR MAKING COMPLAINTS, CLAIMS AND ADJUSTMENTS

10.2.1 Principles for Making Complaints and Claims

When making a complaint or a claim, you should convince the reader that the complaint or claim is legitimate and deserves a desired response. Therefore, you should follow these specific principles summed up as investigation, immediacy, clearness, dispassion and legitimacy.

Investigation. Complaints and claims should be based on careful investigation and consideration. Thus you should investigate thoroughly the matter and ask if it is worthwhile to make the complaint or claim.

Immediacy. Complaints or claims should be made as immediately as possible upon the occurrence of the problem since any delay will weaken your favorable status.

Clearness. Make the complaint or claim brief and to the point, which means you should organize your thoughts or better draw an outline before making the complaint or claim. Do not enter a long story about the problems caused.

Dispassion. Make sense and use humor if necessary. Always keep in your mind that the purpose of the complaint or claim is to make the other party give prompt response to minimize the damage and improve the quality of further transactions. Therefore, you should avoid anger or passion in your language, but state facts only in your complaint or claim. Do not assume the supplier should take the whole responsibility. You can even start with a compliment.

Legitimacy. Make the complaint or claim in accordance with the legitimate procedures as much as possible. Try to direct it to the right person and remember to include details of your contact in it to make response easy and fast. If necessary, copies of the complaint or claim should be made to avoid inconvenience in the follow-ups if your complaint or claim is not properly handled.

10.2.2 Principles for Making Adjustments

Receiving a complaint or claim is better than losing your customer without knowing the reason. When you receive a complaint or claim, it means that you can know what is wrong in your goods or services and thus you are provided with an opportunity to improve, adjust or change it.

When you have to deal with a complaint or claim, you should keep the following in mind:

- Assume the customer is right and deal with all complaints or claims seriously with thorough investigation. No matter whether the complaint or claim is justified or not, you should always thank the customer for pointing out the fault first.
- If you cannot deal with the complaint or claim immediately, you have to state that you have received the complaint or claim and proper investigation is underway.
- If the complaint or claim is ill-founded, you should point this out in a friendly and courteous way.
- If it is proved that the problem is at your fault, you should admit it readily, express your regret and promise to correct it.

Thus when you make adjustments, you should observe the following principles:

- Express your desire to build goodwill and be restrained and tactful, as worsening the situation will do no good to either party.
- Explain any favorable facts in an honest and reassuring way. State briefly the reason for the problem and be quick to admit your fault if it is proved so.
- Ask for any necessary cooperation from the customer.
- End pleasantly with a forward look. Do not repeatedly recall or apologize for the fault but state improvement and provide assurance for future development.

10.3 STRUCTURES OF COMPLAINTS, CLAIMS AND ADJUSTMENTS

10.3.1 Structure of Complaint and Claim Letters

A complaint letter is usually outlined as follows:

- The opening:
  - —Regret of the need to complain
  - —Statement of the problem
- The body:
  - —Brief introduction to the inconvenience and loss caused by the error and statement of your dissatisfaction
  - —Asking for an explanation and future improvement
  - —Suggestion of solutions
- The closing:

—Requesting better service in the future and expectation of future cooperation

A claim letter is with a similar structure but with slight differences.

- The opening:
  —Regret of the need to claim
  —Statement of the problem with as much information as possible, including the specific problem, the exact date, name of the goods, contract number, etc., for the convenience of investigation by the other party
- The body:
  —Introduction to the inconvenience and loss caused by the error
  —Suggestion of possible solutions or necessary measures
- The closing:
  —Wish of early settlement of the problem and expectation of future cooperation

10.3.2 Structure of Adjustment Letters

Adjustment letters of agreement usually follow such a pattern:

- The opening:
  —Mentioning receipt of the letter politely
  —Regret for the inconvenience or loss caused
- The body:
  —Admitting the mistake
  —Explanation of the cause of the problem
  —Agreement of the settlement of the complaint or claim
- The closing:
  —Apology or promise of improvement
  —Hope of more future business

While adjustment letter of disagreement can usually be structured as follows:

- The opening:
  —Mentioning receipt of the letter politely
  —Regret for the inconvenience or loss caused with clear statement of your position
- The body:
  —Giving reasons why the complaint or claim cannot be accepted or why your company is not at fault
  —Possible solutions
- The closing:
  —Expressing thankfulness to the party in his efforts to make things clear
  —Expectation of more future business

10.4 SAMPLE LETTERS

Sample Letter 10 (1)

Dear Mr. Ben Fisher,

<u>Re: ORDER NO.1507</u>

We would like to inform you of our dissatisfaction with the wrong color of the basketball shirts you sent us in your consignment of March 3.

If you refer to our Order No. 1507, you will find that the color of the garments we ordered is Red No. 1 but what you sent to us is Red No. 8.

We are at a loss to explain this to our clients and this does not suit your normally reliable service. We need you to arrange for the dispatch of replacement of the shirts of the color we asked for before March 30 and at the same time please note that we have shipped back at your expense the shirts of Red No. 8 to Jakarta, which is supposed to arrive on March 20.

We hope such mistakes will never happen again in our future cooperation.

Sincerely yours

Sample Letter 10 (2)

Dear Ms. Billings,

Thank you for your letter of March 5 informing us of the shipment of your Order No. 1507 for basketball shirts. Your complaint was immediately sent to our Customer Relations representative for investigation.

We have confirmed through our inventory and shipping documents that a mistake was indeed made on your February 25 order. The slip-up occurred in our new, automated inventory control system that is causing errors during the data entry stage. Your order number was unfortunately confused with another one (Order No. 1509), and the error was not caught before the shirts were sent out.

We are very sorry for this mistake and the inconvenience it has caused you and we want to do everything possible to help you satisfy your clients promptly. We offer to redeliver the correct shirts under Order No. 1511 by Express Mail upon receiving your directions. As to the non-conforming shirts, we take the carriage forward shipment you sent to us.

You are a valued customer and we sincerely regret this mistake. We assure you that every possible action will be taken by our management to prevent a repetition of the same mistake in future orders.

Sincerely yours

Sample Letter 10 (3)

Dear President Patrick Lenoir,

Re: ORDER NO.125

We thank you for your so promptly delivering the coffee we ordered on August 18 with the Order No. 125. However, the number of bags delivered by your carrier this morning was 200 whereas our order was 400.

Owing to the sudden shortage of your coffee, we have no alternatives but to cancel some orders, which has led to the loss of one of our major clients. The full consignment is urgently required to complete the rest of our orders so it is absolutely essential that you ship the additional 200 bags of coffee on the earliest possible flight from Santiago. And meanwhile, we want you to undertake the compensation of USD2,000 asked for by our clients due to the shortage of goods. We are enclosing the bill of lading and compensation bills from our clients for your investigation.

This is the third time in the last twelve months that you have short-shipped our orders. If there is any further repetition of this, we will be forced to look for an alternative supplier.

We look forward to your prompt settlement to this.

Sincerely yours

Sample Letter 10 (4)

Dear Mr. Williams,

We regret to learn from your letter of October 18 that 13 cartons of carpets shipped under your Order No. 310 were found soiled and we are required to grant you a 15% allowance on the invoice value of the order.

We took your case seriously and have looked into the matter in detail. The packing department of our company informed us that the carpets were properly packed first in waterproof paper and then in double thickness of canvas as stipulated in the contract. Furthermore, the clean B/L covering the goods indicates that they were received for shipment in apparent good condition. Therefore, we are certain that the damage must have occurred through careless handling in transit.

Such being the case, we are afraid that we cannot accept your request. We would advise that you take up the case with the shipping company and have the claim settled to your satisfaction.

Sincerely yours

10.5 USEFUL TERMS AND EXPRESSIONS

1.	complaint	投诉
2.	claim	索赔
3.	settlement of claims	理赔
4.	compensation	赔偿,补偿
5.	inventory	存货清单
6.	slip-up	疏忽
7.	inconvenience	不方便
8.	express mail	快递
9.	carriage/freight forward	运费到付
10.	freight prepaid	运费预付
11.	freight paid	运费已付
12.	clean B/L	清洁提单
13.	breach of contract	违反合同,违约
14.	dispute	纠纷
15.	fault	差错
16.	faulty goods	有毛病的货物
17.	faulty packing	包装不良
18.	non-conformity of quality	质量不符
19.	non-performance of the contract	不履行合同
20.	short shipment	短装,装卸不足
21.	short weight	短量
22.	refund	退款,偿还的钱
23.	education and sporting goods	文体类商品
24.	adhesive tape seat	胶座
25.	adhesive tape	胶带
26.	art supplies	美术用品
27.	book stand	书立
28.	boring machine	打孔机
29.	chest card	胸卡

30.	hard glue wrap	硬胶套
31.	marked price	标价器
32.	material book	资料册
33.	numbering machine	号码机
34.	name card wraps	名片包
35.	palette	画板
36.	paper cutting machine	切纸机
37.	paster	贴纸
38.	pen bag	笔袋
39.	pencil sharpener	卷笔刀
40.	pencil vase	笔筒
41.	register of alumni	题名录
42.	sealing machine	塑封机
43.	short note box	便签盒
44.	short note paper	便笺纸
45.	show shelf	展示架
46.	price tag	标价贴
47.	stapler	订书机
48.	tape cutter	胶带机
49.	double-sided adhesives	双面胶
50.	bookbinding clips	装订夹
51.	teaching models	教学模型
52.	alpenstock	登山杖
53.	badminton rackets	羽毛球拍
54.	beach umbrella	沙滩伞
55.	billiard table	台球桌
56.	camping kettle	旅行壶
57.	camping supplies	野营用品
58.	chesses	国际象棋
59.	cuffs	护腕
60.	developer devices	拉力器

Unit 10 Complaints, Claims and Adjustments

61. dryland skates	旱冰鞋
62. fishing gears	渔具
63. gate bats	门球棒
64. golf bags	高尔夫球杆包
65. extreme hand grips	握力器
66. ice skates	溜冰鞋
67. kneecaps	护膝
68. military chess	军棋
69. mountaineering bags	登山包
70. sports shoes	运动鞋
71. tennis rackets	网球拍
72. tent	帐篷
73. dispatch	发送,办理

10.6 COMMUNICATION LABORATORY

Application Exercises

A. Translate the following sentences into Chinese.

1. We are very sorry to inform you that your last shipment is not up to your usual standard.
2. However, the B/L shows that when the shipping company received the goods, they were in apparent good condition. The liability is certainly not on our side.
3. We find that the quality of your shipment is not in conformity with the agreed specification.
4. These errors on your part cause us to disappoint our important customers.
5. This is the maximum concession we can afford. Should you not agree to accept our proposal, we would like to settle by arbitration.
6. It is natural that you should be responsible for all the losses resulting from the delay in shipment.
7. There is a difference of 35 tons between the actual landed weight and the invoiced weight of this consignment.
8. Since this claim was filed two months after their arrival at your port, we regret that it cannot be accepted.
9. We propose to compensate you by 3% of the total value plus inspection fee.
10. We have received your remittance in settlement of our claim.

B. Translate the following sentences into English.

1. 贵公司要赔偿我方合同全部金额的5%。(compensate ... by)
2. 我们已经对这个索赔案件做了详细的调查研究。(investigation)
3. 我们想处理一下关于销售确认书第1254E号100吨漂白废棉的索赔问题。(settle the claim)
4. 这批货的质量低于合同规定的标准,现向你方提出索赔。(up to the standard)
5. 根据检查员报告,损坏是由于运输中操作不小心造成的。(rough handling)
6. 若数日内货物不能运到,我们就提出全额清偿索赔。(file a claim)
7. 请核实此事,并尽快通知我们处理误送货物的指示。(check up)
8. 很抱歉,损坏主要是由于没有很好加固、包装极差造成的。(poor packing)
9. 我们将在下期装运时补上短缺的重量。(deficiency)
10. 考虑到我们之间的业务关系,我们准备赔偿35吨短缺。(shortweight)

C. Cloze

Dear Mr. Lenoir,

As someone who has worked with you for over 12 years, we were very d_____ to see the work that you did on one of the houses we subcontracted to you in the Camas development.

As our oral a_____ stipulated, we expected 5 black armoire units to be installed in the master bedroom, but instead, we found that 3 w_____ particle-board desks were put in. I think you will agree that a c_____ problem exists.

We would like you to send out a crew to take out the white desks and put the black armoire units in immediately, or provide us with a r_____.

Yours faithfully

Case Study

You work at the Customer Relations Department for a cloth manufacturer and received the following letter of complaint from St. Louis Clothes Co. Ltd., Paris, one of your cloth importers one day.

Dear Sir,

We have recently received a number of complaints from customers about your linens. The linens clearly do not match the samples you left with us.

The linens complained about are part of the batch of 100 pieces supplied to our Order No. 190 of May 15. We have ourselves examined some of the linens complained about and there is little doubt that some of them are shrinkable and others not color fast.

We are therefore writing to ask you to accept return the unsold balance of the batch referred to, amounting to 35 pieces in all, and to replace them by linens of the same quality as the sample.

Sincerely yours
St. Louis Clothes Co., Ltd.

Suppose the complaint could be justified, write an adjustment letter of agreement. You can follow a structure like this:

—Indicate your regret
—Admit the possibility of mistake
—Indicate that you are arranging your local representatives to examine the materials
—Suggest replacement if the inferiority proves to be true

Then suppose the complaint is ill-founded, write another adjustment letter of disagreement with a structure as follows:

—Indicate your regret
—Indicate that you are the best manufacturer in this field and you have a very strict product examination system
—Regret for the rejection of the complaint and offer some possible solution such as a 5% discount

Unit 11 Contracts

11.1 DRAFTING CONTRACTS

A contract is an agreement between two or more parties, especially one that is written and enforceable by law. A valid contract typically requires the following four elements:

(1) A meeting of the minds between the parties, demonstrating that they both understand and agree to the essentials of the deal;

(2) Consideration, that is something of value exchanged by each of the parties, such as cash, goods, or a promise to perform a service;

(3) An agreement to enter into the contract, which is typically evidenced by both parties signing a written contract, although oral contracts can be valid in some situations;

(4) The legal competence of each party, meaning that the parties are not minors and are of sound mind.

Meeting of the Minds. The first step in creating a contract is making sure both parties are talking about the same deal, so that when they subsequently agree to enter into the contract they are both agreeing to the same thing.

Consideration. Once the parties have had a "meeting of the minds" as to the deal, they must each exchange something of value in order to create a contract. Often one party provides its goods or services in exchange for the cash of the other party. But consideration can take many other forms, as long as each party is giving up something of value to convince the other party to enter into the contract.

Agreement to Enter into the Contract. Once both parties understand the deal and understand what type of consideration will be exchanged by each party, they are ready to form an agreement. Usually the parties demonstrate that negotiations have ended and an agreement has been reached when the parties sign the contract.

Legal Competence. Be sure that the party you're working with is legally competent to enter into a contract. Otherwise your signed contract may be void and unenforceable.

According to the *Contract Law of the People's Republic of China*, a contract shall be null and void under any of the following circumstances:

- A contract is concluded through the use of fraud or coercion by one party to damage the interests of the State;
- Malicious collusion is conducted to damage the interests of the State, a collective or a third party;

- An illegitimate purpose is concealed under the guise of legitimate acts;
- Damaging the public interests;
- Violating the compulsory provisions of the laws and administrative regulations.

According to the *Contract Law of the People's Republic of China*, the contents of a contract shall be agreed upon by the parties, and shall contain the following clauses in general:

- Title or name and domicile of the parties;
- Contract object;
- Quantity;
- Quality;
- Price or remuneration;
- Time limit, place and method of performance;
- Liability for breach of contract;
- Methods to settle disputes.

A contract should be carefully drafted. It must be precise, concise and clear. The draftsman must take pains to say precisely what he means, no more and no less, so that the contract can not be construed to bind his company to more than intended or to bind the other party to less than intended. To be concise, a sentence should contain no unnecessary words. To achieve clarity, one must guard against obscurity and ambiguity.

In the 1970s, the consumer-rights movement in the United States won legislation that required plain language in contracts, insurance policies, and government regulations. In determining whether a contract meets the requirements of subsection(a), a court shall consider the following language guidelines:

- The contract should use short words, sentences and paragraphs.
- The contract should use active verbs.
- The contract should not use technical legal terms, other than commonly understood legal terms, such as "mortgage", "warranty" and "security interest".
- The contract should not use Latin and foreign words or any other word whenever its use requires reliance upon an obsolete meaning.
- If the contract defines words, the words should be defined by using commonly understood meanings.
- When the contract refers to the parties to the contract, the reference should use personal pronouns, the actual or shortened names of the parties, the terms "seller" and "buyer" or the terms "lender" and "borrower".
- The contract should not use sentences that contain more than one condition.
- The contract should not use cross references, except cross references that briefly and clearly describe the substances of the item to which reference is made.
- The contract should not use sentences with double negatives or exceptions to exceptions.

11.2 SAMPLE CONTRACTS

11.2.1 Sample Agency Agreement

Commercial Agency Agreement

THIS AGREEMENT is made the day (…) of (…)

BETWEEN:

(a) (Principal's name) ("Principal"); and

(b) (Agent's name), whose principal place of business is at (address) ("Agent")

1. Appointment

Principal appoints Agent as its exclusive agent for the Products in the Territory listed on the Schedule and undertakes that, for the duration of this Agreement, Principal will neither sell nor market the Products in the Territory other than through Agent and shall not appoint any other agent for the Territory.

2. Best efforts: competitive lines and other business

2.1 Agent shall devote its best efforts to marketing the Products and servicing accounts which carry the Products in the Territory.

2.2 Agent shall neither market nor sell in the Territory any products which compete with the Products.

2.3 Agent shall be given samples of the products and marketing literature by Principal.

2.4 Agent shall pass all orders for the Products to Principal who shall deal with such orders promptly and ensure goods supplied are of satisfactory quality.

3. Commission

3.1 Principal shall pay Agent a commission of the percentage set out on the Schedule on all sales of the Products in the Territory, whether such sale is generated by the Agent or not. Such commission shall be on the invoiced (FOB/FCA) value, charged by Principal to customers.

3.2 Commission shall be paid each month by the first week of the month on sales invoiced by Principal in the preceding month. Whether a customer subsequently defaults in payment of any invoice, where Principal is not to blame for such default, then Principal may deduct commission already paid for such sale from the next commission due to Agent.

3.3 With each such monthly commission payment Principal shall send Agent a full commission statement showing all sales of the Products made to the Territory in the preceding month, sufficient to enable Agent to check the commission due.

4. Term and termination

4.1 This Agreement is for an initial minimum period of two years and shall continue after unless and until terminated by at least one year's written notice by one party to the other to expire on the third or any subsequent anniversary of the date of this Agreement.

4.2 On termination of this Agreement commission shall be paid to Agent on all orders received up to the date of termination.

5. General

5.1 This Agreement is subject to Australian law and the parties agree to submit to the jurisdiction of the Australian courts in respect of any dispute.

5.2 This Agreement replaces any earlier agreement or arrangement between the parties, verbal or written, and is the entire agreement between them. It may only be modified by written agreement of both parties.

5.3 Nothing in this Agreement shall prevent Agent from sub-contracting its obligations under this Agreement nor from using a sub-agent. Either party may assign all its rights under this Agreement to a third party, but only with the prior written consent of the other party.

SCHEDULE

The Products are:
(insert details)

The Exclusive Territory is:
(specify)

The Commission Rate is:
(specify)

SIGNATURES

Signed
by ....
For and on behalf of ....
(Principal)

In the presence of:
Witness'
Signature ....
Name ....

Address ···
Occupation ···
Signed
by ···

In the presence of:
Witness'
Signature ··
Name ··
Address ···
Occupation ··
Signed
by ···

11.2.2 Sample Sales Contract

Sales Contract

No. :
Date:

This contract is made by and between the Sellers and the Buyers, whereby the Sellers agree to sell and the Buyers agree to buy the under-mentioned goods according to the terms and conditions stipulated below and overleaf:

(1) Names of Commodity(ies) and Specification(s):

(2) Quantity:

(3) Unit Price:

(4) Amount:

(5) Packing:

(6) Port of Loading:

(7) Port of Destination:

(8) Shipping Marks:

(9) Time of Shipment: within _____ days after receipt of L/C, allowing transshipment and partial shipments.

(10) Terms of Payment: 100% by confirmed, irrevocable sight Letter of Credit to remain valid for negotiation in China until the 15th day after shipment.

(11) Insurance: To be effected by the Buyers for 110% of the invoice value against all risks and war risk as per the China Insurance Clauses of PICC Property and Casualty Company Limited.

(12) The Buyers shall establish the covering Letter of Credit before _____ ; failing

which, the Seller reserves the right to rescind this Sales Contract without further notice, or to accept whole or any part of this Sales Contract, or to lodge claim for direct losses sustained, if any.

(13) Documents: The Sellers shall present to the negotiating bank, Clean On Board Bill of Lading, Invoice, Certificate on Quality/Quantity/Weight issued by the General Administration of Quality Supervision, Inspection and Quarantine of the People's Republic of China, and Transferable Insurance Policy or Certificate when this contract is made on CIF basis.

(14) If the Buyers ask to increase the insurance premium or scope of risks, they should get the permission of the Sellers before time of loading, and all the charges thus incurred should be borne by the Buyers.

(15) Quality/Quantity Discrepancy: In case of quality discrepancy, claim should be filed by the Buyers within 30 days after the arrival of the goods at port of destination; while for quantity discrepancy, claim should be filed by the Buyers within 15 days after the arrival of the goods at port of destination. It is understood that the Sellers shall not be liable for any discrepancy of the goods shipped due to causes for which the Insurance Company, Shipping Company, other transportation organizations and/or Post Office are liable.

(16) The Sellers shall not be held liable for failure or delay in delivery of the entire lot or a portion of the goods under this Sales Contract in consequence of any Force Majeure incidents.

(17) Arbitration: All disputes in connection with this contract or the execution thereof shall be settled friendly through negotiations. In case no settlement can be reached, the case may then be submitted for arbitration to China International Economic and Trade Arbitration Commission in accordance with the Arbitration Rules promulgated by the said Arbitration Commission. The arbitration shall take place in Beijing and the award of the Arbitration Commission shall be final and binding upon both parties; neither party shall seek recourse to a law court or other authorities to appeal for revision of the decision. Arbitration fee shall be borne by the losing party. Or arbitration may be settled in the third country mutually agreed upon by both parties.

(18) The Buyers are requested always to quote THE NUMBER OF THE SALES CONTRACT in the Letter of Credit to be opened in favour of the Sellers.

Seller: Buyer:

11.2.3 Sample Joint Venture Contract

Contract for Sino-Foreign Joint Venture

Chapter 1 General Provisions

In accordance with the *Law of the People's Republic of China on Joint Ventures Using Chinese and Foreign Investment* and other relevant Chinese laws and regulations,

_____ Company and _____ Company, in accordance with the principle of equality and mutual benefit and through friendly consultations, agree to jointly set up a joint venture in _____ the People's Republic of China.

Chapter 2 Parties to the Joint Venture

Article 1

Parties to this contract are as follows:

_____ Company (hereinafter referred to as Party A) , registered with _____ in China, and its legal address is at _____ (street) _____ (district) _____ (city) _____ China.

Legal representative:

Name:

Position:

Nationality:

_____ Company (hereinafter referred to as Party B) , registered with _____ and its legal address is at _____.

Legal representative:

Name:

Position:

Nationality:

Chapter 3 Establishment of the Joint Venture Company

Article 2

In accordance with the Joint Venture Law and other relevant Chinese laws and regulations, both parties of the cooperative venture agree to set up _____ Joint Venture Limited Liability Company(hereinafter referred to as the Joint Venture Company).

Article 3

The name of the Joint Venture Company shall be _____ in Chinese and shall be known as _____ in English.

The legal address of the Joint Venture Company shall be at _____ street _____ (city) _____ province.

Article 4

All activities of the Joint Venture Company shall be governed by the laws, decrees and pertinent rules and regulations of the People's Republic of China.

Article 5

The organization form of the Joint Venture Company is a limited liability company. The profits, risks and losses of the joint venture company shall be shared by the parties according to the relevant provisions thereafter.

Chapter 4 Purpose, Scope and Scale of Production and Business

Article 6

The goals of the parties to the joint venture are to enhance economic cooperation and technical exchanges, improve the product quality, develop new products, and gain a competitive position in the world marketing quality and price by adopting advanced and appropriate technology and scientific management methods, so as to raise economic results and ensure satisfactory economic benefits for both parties.

Article 7

The production and business scope of the Joint Venture Company is to produce _____ products, provide maintenance service after the sale of the products and develop new products.

Article 8

The production scale of the Joint Venture Company is as follows:
1. The production capacity after the joint venture is put into operation is _____.
2. The production scale may be increased up to _____ with the development of the production and operation. The product varieties may be developed into _____.

Chapter 5 Total Amount of Investment and Registered Capital

Article 9

The total amount of investment of the Joint Venture Company is RMB _____ (or a foreign currency agreed upon by both parties).

Article 10

The registered capital of the Joint Venture Company is RMB _____ (exclusive of the right to the use of the site or the right to the exploitation of the natural resources and premises contributed by Party A).

Article 11

Party A and Party B shall contribute the following to the Joint Venture Company:

Party A: premises _____ m²
    The right to the use of the site _____ m²

Party B: cash _____ Yuan
    Machines and equipment _____ Yuan
    Industrial property right _____ Yuan
    Others _____ Yuan in all.

Article 12

The right to the use of site contributed by Party A shall be for the use of the Joint Venture Company within _____ days after the approval of the contract.

The cash contributed by Party B shall be paid in _____ installment(s). Each installment shall be as follows:

Article 13

The machines and equipment contributed by Party B as investment shall meet the needs of the Joint Venture Company, and shall be carried to the Chinese port _____ days before the completion of the premises construction.

Chapter 6 Responsibilities of Each Party to the Joint Venture

Article 14

Party A and Party B shall be respectively responsible for the following matters:

Responsibilities of Party A:
- Applications for approval, registration, business license and other matters concerning the establishment of the Joint Venture Company from competent departments in China;
- Application for the right to the use of a site to the authority in charge of the land;
- Organizing the design and construction of the premises and other engineering facilities of the Joint Venture Company;
- Assisting Party B with import customs declaration for the machinery and equipment contributed by Party B as investment and arranging the transportation within the Chinese territory;
- Assisting the Joint Venture Company in purchasing or leasing equipment, materials, raw materials, articles for office use, means of transportation and communication facilities, etc. ;
- Assisting the Joint Venture Company in settling infrastructure such as water, electricity, transportation;
- Assisting the Joint Venture Company in recruiting Chinese management personnel, technical personnel, workers and other personnel needed;
- Assisting foreign staff and workers in applying for entry visas, work permits and providing convenience for their traveling on business in China;
- Responsible for handling other matters entrusted by the Joint Venture Company.

Responsibilities of Party B:
- Providing cash, machinery and equipment, industrial property in accordance with the provisions of Articles 11, 12 and 13, and responsible for arranging for shipment of the capital goods such as machinery and equipment contributed as investment to a Chinese port;
- Handling the matters entrusted by the Joint Venture Company, such as purchasing machinery and equipment outside China, etc. ;
- Providing necessary technical personnel for installing, testing and trial production of the equipment as well as the technical personnel for production and inspecting;
- Training the technical personnel and workers of the Joint Venture Company;

- In case Party B is the licensor, it shall be responsible for the stable production of qualified products of the Joint Venture Company in the light of design capacity within the specified period;
- Responsible for other matters entrusted by the Joint Venture Company.

Chapter 7 Distribution of Profits and Repayment for Party B's Investment

Article 15

The Joint Venture Company shall distribute its profits in accordance with the following procedure after paying the income tax:

_____% as allocations for reserve funds, expansion funds, welfare funds and bonuses for staff and workers of the Joint Venture Company;

_____% as repayment for Party B's investment and

_____% of the remaining to be distributed to Party A and _____% to Party B.

Chapter 8 Sale of Products

Article 16

The products of the Joint Venture Company shall be sold both on the Chinese and the overseas markets; the export portion accounts for _____%, whereas the other _____% is for the domestic market.

Article 17

Products may be sold on overseas markets through the following channels:

The Joint Venture Company may directly sell its products on the overseas markets, accounting for _____%.

The Joint Venture Company may sign sales contracts with Chinese foreign trade companies, entrusting them to be sales agents or exclusive sales agents, accounting for _____%.

The Joint Venture Company may entrust Party B to sell its products, accounting for _____%.

Article 18

The Joint Venture Company's products may be sold in China by the Joint Venture Company directly or by means of sales agents.

Article 19

In order to provide maintenance service to the products sold both in China and abroad, the Joint Venture Company may set up sales branches for maintenance service both in China and abroad subject to the approval of the relevant Chinese department.

Chapter 9 Board of Directors

Article 20

The date of registration of the Joint Venture Company shall be the date of the establishment of the board of directors of the Joint Venture Company.

Article 21

The board of directors is composed of _____ directors, of which _____ shall be appointed by Party A, _____ by Party B. The chairman of the board shall be appointed by Party A, and its vice-chairman by Party B. The term of office for the directors, chairman and vice-chairmen is four years. Their terms of office may be renewed if continuously appointed by the relevant party.

Article 22

The highest authority of the Joint Venture Company shall be its board of directors. It shall decide all major issues concerning the Joint Venture Company. Unanimous approval shall be required for any decisions concerning major issues. As for other matters, approval by majority or a simple majority shall be required.

Article 23

The chairman of the board is the legal representative of the Joint Venture Company. Should the chairman be unable to exercise his responsibilities for any reason, he shall authorize the vice-chairman or any other directors to represent the Joint Venture Company temporarily.

Article 24

The board of directors shall convene at least one meeting every year. The meeting shall be summoned and presided over by the chairman of the board. The chairman may convene an interim meeting based on a proposal made by more than one third of the total directors. Minutes of the meetings shall be placed on file.

Article 25

The meeting shall be valid only when more than two thirds of the directors attend. In case of absence, the director shall entrust another person to attend and vote for him with a trust deed.

Chapter 10 Business Management Office

Article 26

The Joint Venture Company shall establish a management office which shall be responsible for its daily management. The management office shall have a general manager, appointed by Party _____, _____ deputy general managers, _____ by Party _____; _____ by Party _____. The general manager and deputy general managers whose term of office is _____ years shall be appointed by the board of directors.

Article 27

The responsibility of the general manager is to carry out the decisions of the board and organize and conduct the daily management of the Joint Venture Company. The deputy general managers shall assist the general manager with his work.

Article 28

The general manager shall report to the board of directors the operation conditions of the Joint Venture Company every three months, and make a financial report every six months.

Article 29

In case of graft or serious dereliction of duty on the part of the general manager and deputy general managers, the board of directors shall have the power to dismiss them at any time.

Chapter 11 Labor Management

Article 30

Labor contracts covering the recruitment, employment, dismissal and resignation, wages, labor insurance, welfare, awards and punishments and other matters concerning the staff and workers of the Joint Venture Company shall be drawn up and signed between the Joint Venture Company and the Trade Union of the Joint Venture Company as a whole, or between the Joint Venture Company and its staff and workers on an individual basis in accordance with the *Law of the People's Republic of China on Joint Ventures Using Chinese and Foreign Investment.*

The labor contracts shall, after being signed, be filed with the local labor management department.

Article 31

The appointment of high-ranking administrative personnel recommended by both parties, their salaries, social insurance, welfare, the standard of traveling expenses, etc. shall be decided by the meeting of the board of directors.

Chapter 12 Taxes, Finance and Audit

Article 32

The Joint Venture Company shall pay taxes in accordance with the provisions of Chinese laws and other relative regulations.

Article 33

Staff members and workers of the Joint Venture Company shall pay individual income tax according to the *Individual Income Tax Law of the People's Republic of China.*

Article 34

The fiscal year of the Joint Venture Company shall be from January 1 to December 31. All vouchers, receipts, statistic statements and reports shall be written in Chinese. A foreign language can be used concurrently with mutual consent.

Article 35

Financial checking and examination of the Joint Venture Company shall be conducted by an auditor registered in China and reports shall be submitted to the board of directors and the general manager.

In case Party B considers it necessary to employ a foreign auditor registered in another country to undertake annual financial checking and examination, Party A shall give its consent. All the expenses thereof shall be borne by Party B.

Article 36

In the first three months of each fiscal year, the general manager shall prepare the previous year's balance sheet, profit and loss statement and proposal regarding the disposal of profits, and submit them to the board of directors for examination and approval.

Chapter 13 Duration of the Joint Venture

Article 37

The duration of the Joint Venture Company is _____ years. The establishment date of the Joint Venture Company shall be the date on which the business license of the Joint Venture Company is issued.

An application for the extension of the duration, proposed by one party and unanimously approved by the board of directors, shall be submitted to the Ministry of Commerce (or the examination and approval authority entrusted by it) six months prior to the expiry date of the Joint Venture Company.

Chapter 14 Disposal of Assets after the Expiration of the Duration

Article 38

Upon the expiration of the duration, the assets shall belong to Party A.

Chapter 15 Insurance

Article 39

Insurance of the Joint Venture Company against various risks shall be effected with the People's Insurance Company of China. Types, value and duration of insurance shall be decided by the board of directors in accordance with the provisions of the People's Insurance Company of China.

Chapter 16 Amendment, Alteration and Termination of the Contract

Article 40

The amendment to the contract or other appendices shall come into force only after a written agreement has been signed by and between Party A and Party B and approved by the original examination and approval authority.

Article 41

In case of inability to fulfill the contract or to continue operation due to heavy losses in successive years as a result of force majeure, the duration of the joint venture and the contract shall be terminated before the time of expiration after being unanimously agreed upon by the board of directors and approved by the original examination and approval authority.

Chapter 17 Liability for Breach of Contract

Article 42

Should the Joint Venture Company be unable to continue its operation or achieve its business purpose due to the fact that one of the contracting parties fails to fulfill the obligations prescribed by the contract and articles of association, or seriously violates the provisions of the contract and articles of association, that party shall be deemed to have unilaterally terminated the contract. The other party shall have the right to terminate the contract in accordance with the provisions of the contract after approval by the original examination and approval authority, and to claim damages. In case Party A and Party B of the Joint Venture Company agree to continue the operation, the party who fails to fulfill its obligations shall be liable for the financial losses caused thereby to the Joint Venture Company.

Article 43

Should either Party A or Party B fail to provide on schedule the contributions in accordance with the provisions defined in Chapter 5 of this contract, the party in breach shall pay to the other party _____ Yuan, or _____% of the contribution starting from the first month after exceeding the time limit. Should the party in breach fail to provide after _____ months, _____ Yuan, or _____% of the contribution shall be paid to the other party, who shall have the right to terminate the contract and to claim damages from the party in breach in accordance with the provisions of Article 42 of the contract.

Article 44

Should all or part of the contract and its appendices be unable to be fulfilled owing to the fault of one party, the party in breach shall bear liability therefore. Should it be the fault of both parties, they shall bear their respective liabilities according to the actual situation.

Article 45

In order to guarantee the performance of the contract and its appendices, both Party A and Party B shall provide each other with bank guarantees for performance of the contract within _____ days after the contract comes into force.

Chapter 18 Force Majeure

Article 46

Should either of the parties to the contract be prevented from executing the contract by force majeure, such as earthquake, typhoon, flood, fire, war or other unforeseen events, and their occurrence and consequences are unpreventable and unavoidable, the prevented party shall notify the other party by fax without any delay, and within fifteen (15) days thereafter provide detailed information of the events and a valid document for evidence issued by the relevant public notary organization explaining the reason for its inability to execute or delay the execution of all or part of the contract. Both parties shall, through consultations, decide whether to terminate the contract or to exempt part of the obligations for implementation of the contract or whether to delay the execution of the contract according to the effects of the events on the performance of the contract.

Chapter 19 Applicable Law

Article 47

The formation, validity, interpretation, execution and settlement of disputes in respect of this contract shall be governed by the relevant laws of the People's Republic of China.

Chapter 20 Settlement of Disputes

Article 48

Any dispute arising from the execution of, or in connection with, the contract shall be settled through friendly consultations between both parties. In case no settlement can be reached through consultations, the disputes shall be submitted to the China International Economic and Trade Arbitration Commission in accordance with the Arbitration Rules promulgated by the said Arbitration Commission. The arbitral award is final and binding upon both parties.

Article 49

During the arbitration, the contract shall be observed and enforced by both parties except for the matters in dispute.

Chapter 21 Language

Article 50

The contract shall be written in Chinese and in English. Both language versions are equally authentic. In the event of any discrepancy between the two aforementioned versions, the Chinese version shall prevail.

Chapter 22 Effectiveness of the Contract and Miscellaneous

Article 51

The appendices drawn up in accordance with the principles of this contract are integral parts of this contract, including the project agreement, the technology transfer agreement, the sales agreement, etc.

Article 52

The contract and its appendices shall come into force commencing from the date of approval of the Ministry of Commerce of the People's Republic of China (or its entrusted examination and approval authority).

Article 53

Should notices in connection with any party's rights and obligations be sent by either Party A or Party B by telex or fax, the written letter notices shall also be required afterwards. The legal addresses of Party A and Party B listed in this contract shall be the post addresses.

Article 54

The contract is signed in _____, China by the authorized representatives of both parties on _____, 20 _____.

For Party A   For Party B
(Signature)   (Signature)

11.3 USEFUL TERMS AND EXPRESSIONS

1.	consideration	对价
2.	breach of contract	违约
3.	agency agreement	代理协议
4.	exclusive agent	独家代理
5.	sole agent	独家代理
6.	principal	委托人
7.	commission	佣金
8.	defaults in payment	未按期付款
9.	termination	终止
10.	sub-contract	转包
11.	sales contract	售货合同

12.	purchasing contract	购货合同
13.	General Administration of Quality Supervision, Inspection and Quarantine	国家质量监督检验检疫总局
14.	quality/quantity discrepancy	质量/数量差异
15.	Force Majeure incidents	不可抗力事件
16.	arbitration	仲裁
17.	China International Economic and Trade Arbitration Commission	中国国际经济贸易仲裁委员会
18.	award	裁决
19.	joint venture	合资经营
20.	parties to the contract	合约当事人
21.	Party A	甲方
22.	Party B	乙方
23.	legal representative	法定代表人
24.	scale of production and business	生产经营规模
25.	economic cooperation and technical exchanges	经济合作与技术交流
26.	maintenance service after sale	售后维修服务
27.	production capacity	生产能力
28.	registered capital	注册资本
29.	premises	厂房
30.	right to the use of the site	土地使用权
31.	industrial property right	工业产权
32.	business license	营业执照
33.	competent department	主管部门
34.	customs declaration	报关
35.	leasing equipment	设备租赁
36.	infrastructure	基础设施
37.	entry visas	入境签证
38.	work permits	工作许可证

39.	capital goods	资本货物；实物
40.	distribution of profits	利润分配
41.	reserve funds	储备基金
42.	expansion funds	发展基金
43.	welfare funds and bonuses	奖励及福利基金
44.	director	董事
45.	board of directors	董事会
46.	chairman of the board	董事长
47.	vice-chairman	副董事长
48.	the highest authority	最高权力机构
49.	simple majority	简单多数
50.	absolute majority	绝对多数
51.	exercise one's responsibilities	履行职责
52.	convene a meeting	召集会议
53.	minutes of the meeting	会议纪要
54.	business management office	经营管理机构
55.	daily management	日常管理
56.	general manager and deputy general manager	总经理和副总经理
57.	financial report	财务报告
58.	graft or serious dereliction of duty	营私舞弊或严重失职
59.	labor management	劳动管理
60.	labor contract	劳动合同
61.	recruitment, employment, dismissal	招聘、雇用、解雇
62.	awards and punishments	奖惩
63.	Trade Union	工会
64.	high-ranking administrative personnel	高级行政管理人员
65.	individual income tax	个人所得税
66.	fiscal year	会计年度

67.	vouchers	记账凭证
68.	statistic statements and reports	统计报表
69.	financial checking and examination	财务稽核
70.	auditor	审计师
71.	certified public accountant (CPA)	注册会计师
72.	balance sheet	资产负债表
73.	profit and loss statement	损益表
74.	examination and approval	审批
75.	duration of the joint venture	合资经营期限
76.	Ministry of Commerce	商务部
77.	losses in successive years	连年亏损
78.	liquidation	清理
79.	amendment to and alteration of the contract	合同修改和变更
80.	financial losses	经济损失
81.	notary public / public notary	公证人
82.	applicable law	适用法律
83.	formation of contract	合同订立
84.	validity, interpretation, execution of the contract	合同的效力、解释和履行
85.	settlement of disputes	争议的解决
86.	technology transfer agreement	技术转让协议
87.	project agreement	项目协议
88.	articles of association	章程
89.	trust deed	委托书

11.4 COMMUNICATION LABORATORY

Application Exercises

A. Translate the following into Chinese.

1. We have noted your request to act as our agent in your district, but before going further into the matter, we would like to know your plan for promoting sales and

minimum annual turnover you may realize in your market.

2. All disputes in connection with this contract or the execution thereof shall be settled friendly through negotiations. In case no settlement can be reached, the case may then be submitted for arbitration to China International Economic and Trade Arbitration Commission in accordance with the Arbitration Rules promulgated by the said Arbitration Commission.

3. Agent shall pass all orders for the Products to Principal who shall deal with such orders promptly and ensure goods supplied are of satisfactory quality.

4. The chairman may convene an interim meeting based on a proposal made by more than one third of the total directors.

5. The general manager shall report to the board of directors the operation conditions of the Joint Venture Company every three months, and make a financial report every six months.

6. Should the Joint Venture Company be unable to continue its operation or achieve its business purpose due to the fact that one of the contracting parties fails to fulfill the obligations prescribed by the contract and articles of association, or seriously violates the provisions of the contract and articles of association, that party shall be deemed to have unilaterally terminated the contract.

7. Should either of the parties to the contract be prevented from executing the contract by force majeure, such as earthquake, typhoon, flood, fire, war or other unforeseen events, and their occurrence and consequences are unpreventable and unavoidable, the prevented party shall notify the other party by fax without any delay, and within fifteen (15) days thereafter provide detailed information of the events and a valid document for evidence issued by the relevant public notary organization explaining the reason for its inability to execute or delay the execution of all or part of the contract.

8. Both language versions are equally authentic. In the event of any discrepancy between the two aforementioned versions, the Chinese version shall prevail.

B. **Translate the following into English.**
   1. 中国政府依法保护外国合营者按照经中国政府批准的协议、合同、章程在合资企业的合法权益。(protect by the legislation in force)
   2. 合营企业设董事会,其人数组成由合营各方协商。(size and composition)
   3. 合营企业各方可以现金、实物、工业产权等进行投资。(contribute ... as investment)
   4. 经研究你方的提议以及了解你们的业务情况,我们决定委任你方为我们在你地区的代理。(appoint)
   5. 本法自公布之日起施行。(promulgation)

C. **Cloze**

This is to inform you that we are acting as agents on a sole agency basis. We s_____ in the trade of household and decorative wares, such as porcelain wares, lacquer wares and crystals.

We have been working with the Ceramics Department of your Shenzhen Office and our relations have proved m_____ satisfactory. You may r_____ to them for any information concerning our firm.

We are much interested in entering into an e_____ arrangement with you for the p_____ of sales of your products in Rome.

We a_____ your news with keen interest.

Case Study

Prepare a contract with information gathered from the following correspondences.

1 (Outgoing Letter)

Dear Sirs,

Thank you for your enquiry of October 29 for Women's Nylon Garments. In compliance with your request, we have enclosed a pricelist and an illustrated brochure. Although we still have certain amount of stock, we feel it necessary to inform you that we can hardly keep them for a long time because of the heavy demand.

We are looking forward to your early reply.

Yours faithfully
Yangtze Garments Import and Export Corp.

2 (Incoming Letter)

Dear Sirs,

Many thanks for your quotation of November 1 and the samples of Women's Nylon Garments. We are satisfied with the quality and pleased to enclose our Order No. 789 for sizes mentioned in your latest catalogue.

We note that you can supply these items form stock and hope you will dispatch them before December 31, 2019. Our company will reserve the right to cancel this order or reject the goods for any late arrival.

For your reference, we wish to effect payment by D/P at 60 days sight. Please kindly let us have your confirmation.

Yours faithfully
Evan Brown & Sons

ORDER NO. 789

Yangtze Garments Import and Export Corp.
Beijing, China

Please supply the following items:

Quantity(Doz.)	Item	Size	Unit Price CIF London
20	Women's Nylon Garments	small	US$105.00 per doz.
30	ditto	medium	US$130.00 per doz.
15	ditto	large	US$160.00 per doz.

Unit 12　Documentation in International Trade

12.1　INTRODUCTION

The main objectives of this unit are to learn about different types of documents used in international trade, which documents are usually required by customs, the requirements for various documents and how to fill in these documents correctly.

When trading internationally the right paperwork is crucial. Missing or inaccurate documents can increase risks, lead to delays and extra costs, or even prevent a deal from being complete, all of which may affect future business relations between the two trading partners.

This part explains the key documentations you should be aware of. It outlines what paperwork you need for customs, transport and payment, etc. Whether you are importing or exporting, you need to understand what paperwork is required. Even if you use a freight forwarder or an agent, it is still up to you to make sure the right documentation is available.

Most international trade transactions require certain transport documents, administrative documents, commercial documents and insurance documents. There are a great variety of documents that may need to be produced to complete export/import transactions; some estimates indicate over 200 different documents are used in international trade. Different documents are required for different transactions, depending on the nature of the deal, the terms of delivery, the type of commodity, stipulations of credit, regulations and practices in different countries, etc. And documents fulfill the following functions:

Proof of Contract. Documents such as transport documents (bill of lading), insurance documents, etc. evidence the existence of contracts of sale and conditions stipulated there.

Title to the Goods. Certain transport documents represent title to the goods, that is, they give the right to collect the goods from the carrier (just as a bank draft gives you the right to collect funds against the drawer).

Information. Certain documents provide information on the price for the goods (invoice), the contents of package units (packing list), etc.

Customs. The customs of the country of destination require documents that evidence the origin of the goods, etc. in order to establish whether the goods are importable to the country and in order to charge appropriate taxes and duties.

Proof of Compliance. Certain documents serve as proof that the conditions stipulated in the contract of sale are complied with, such as date of shipment (transport documents), the origin of the goods (certificate of origin), etc.

12.2 COMMERCIAL DOCUMENTS

Commercial documents are generally issued by the importer, exporter or some business organizations.

12.2.1 Commercial Invoice

The export invoice should show normal invoice details plus a full description of the goods including item price, net weight and the country of origin. Customs authorities use the commercial invoice to verify the details of the consignment; it is therefore a good practice that the invoice has a signed and dated declaration that the facts are true and correct.

For some countries there are specific requirements on the layout, form or content of the invoice. You can find out more about these special invoices from SITPRO, or your freight forwarder or specialist trade publications. You could also ask your customer if there is any special wording or clauses that you should include on the invoice.

The commercial invoice issued by the imported and called "Invoice" for short, is not the documents of the title but one of the most important documents in international trade. It constitutes the basis on which other documents are to be presented. A commercial invoice normally should include the following: invoice number and the date; name and address of the seller and the buyer; L/C number and contract number; means of transportation and routine; shipping marks; description of goods; total amount and seal or signature of the exporter.

Sample 12(1)

Issuer NANJING JAVASOFT CO., LTD. 7/F, HUAXIN BLDING, XINJIEKOU, NANJING, CHINA		南京杰华科技有限公司 江苏省南京市新街口华新大厦7楼 商业发票 COMMERCIAL INVOICE	
To ABC ABC		No. 20002MXD001	Date January 01, 2000
Transport Details FROM HK TO KANDAHA BY VESSEL		S/C No. JA12-97	L/C No. 2000XYZ001
			Terms of Payment L/C AT SIGHT	
Marks and Numbers	Mumber and Kind of Packages; Description of Goods	Quantity	Unit Price	Amount

MADE IN CHINA
  YWMC001 YSPGG001
  MAN SHIRT
  100% COTTON
		100DZ
		700DZ
			USD20.00/DZ
			USD45.00/DZ
				CIF KANDAHA
				USD2,000.00
				USD31,500.00

			CIF LESS COMMISION PLUS SAMPLE FEE	USD33,500.00 USD2,030.00 USD100.00
			TOTAL	USD31,570.00

TOTAL QUANTITY: 800DZ IN 80CTNS

TOTAL AMOUNT: SAY U.S. DOLLARS THIRTY-ONE THOUSANO FIVE HUNDRED AND SEVENTY ONLY.

L/C No.
1234567890

Sample 12 (2)

INVOICE

Invoice No.: __45675__   Date: __July 20, 2006__

Seller: __HANGZHOU WULIN TRANDING CO., LTD.__
       __SOUTH YAN'AN ROAD, HANGZHOU, CHINA__

Buyer: __DAIWAN ART AND FRAFTS CO., LTD.__
      __NO. 5002 SEOCHO-DONG SECCHO-GU__
      __SEOUL, KOREA__

L/C No.: __TF003MO56789__   Contract No.: __RS304/009__

Shipped by __EASTWIND V. 009E__ from __SHANGHAI, CHINA__ to __BUSAN PORT, KOREA__

Shipping Mark	Description of Goods			Total Amount
N/M	GLASSWARE AS PER SALES CONFIRMATION NO. RS304/009 DATED 7. 15. 2006 QTY: 294 CARTONS G.W. 4557KGS N.W. 3960KGS			USD1,959 CIF BUSHAN PORT, KOREA
	ART. NO.	QTY(PCS)	UNIT PRICE	AMOUNT (USD)
	03-21/22	100	6.53	653
	03-11/20	100	6.53	653
	03-27/30	100	6.53	653

HANGZHOU WULIN TRADING CO., LTD.

_____

(Signature)

12.2.2 Customs Invoice

Customs invoice is required by the importing country to clear the customs, to verify the country of origin for import duty and tax purpose, to compare export and domestic price to fix anti-dumping duty, etc. The fundamental points in it are similar to that in common commercial invoice. Currently, this kind of invoice is required for exporting for

US, Canada, New Zealand, Australia, Jamaica, countries sharing Caribbean Common Market and some African countries.

12.2.3 Proforma Invoice

It is issued by the exporter as a structure response to an inquiry under the circumstance that the importer's country requires that an import license be issued for each import and must approve the proforma invoice before making foreign exchange available for payment by the importer.

A proforma invoice has no legal status. It clearly states that it is proforma and if it is accepted the details are normally transferred to a commercial invoice against which payment will be made, although in some cases payment will be made against a proforma invoice. It is only a means to facilitate the buyer to accomplish the above-mentioned tasks. It is often used in some developing countries to control import and disbursement of foreign exchange.

12.2.4 Packing Documents

Packing documents completed by the shipper, provide a list of the contents of a consignment and are often attached to the bill of lading, airway bill, or consignment. The purpose is to give an inventory of the shipped goods. There are a variety of packing documents. The common ones we are familiar with include:

- Packing List / Packing Slip;
- Packing Specification;
- Detail Packing List;
- Packing Summary;
- Weight List / Weight Note;
- Weight Certificate / Certificate of Weight;
- Weight Memo;
- Measurement List;
- Assortment List.

Usually, the packing document offered by the exporter varies with different goods and L/C as required. A packing list is very useful for the consignments which are composite. It is usually required by the customs for clearance purpose. The specification list is similar to the packing list but emphasizes the description of the specifications of the goods. The weight list, weight note, or weight memo put emphasis on the weight of the goods and are generally used for goods which are based on the weight for price calculation. The weight certificate is usually required by the importer to confirm that the weight of the goods is in accordance with the sales contract at the time of shipment.

Sample 12 (3)

装箱单
PACKING LIST

客户：
To Messres：_____
船名：
Shipped by：_____ From   to

日期
Date：_____
发票编号：
Invoice No.：_____
合约号：
Contract No.：_____
付款条件：
Terms of Payment：_____

箱号 Ctn. No.	货物名称及规格 Description	总箱数 Ctns	总数量 Quantity	总毛重 G. W.	总净重 N. W.
合计： Total					

12.3 TRANSPORTATION DOCUMENTS

Transport documentation is needed to provide instructions to the carrier on what should be done with the goods. They can be used to pass responsibility for, and sometimes ownership of, the goods during their journey. They are also an essential part of some payment procedures. A single transportation involves a lot of different transportation documents to ensure the goods to reach the final consignee. Some of the transportation documents are: shipping note, shipping order, mates receipt, bill of lading, combined transportation documents, and airway bill.

12.3.1 Shipping Note

A shipping note offers information about a particular export consignment for shipment and serves the shipping company as a delivery or receipt for the consignment. It is normally completed by the exporter but others e. g. freight forwarders or agents may also do so. It is the receiving document for ports and container bases and advises them of the necessary information to process and handle the goods.

12.3.2 Bill of Lading

The bill of lading, shortened as B/L, is the most important document required to establish legal ownership and facilitate financial transactions. The B/L has been used for hundreds of years as a document related to the sale of goods in international trade. It provides evidence of the contract between the exporter and carrier, receipt that the goods have been received into the custody of the carrier and is a document of title—allowing the ownership of the goods to be transferred while the goods are at sea. The B/L is usually completed by the agent or carrier.

The major contents of the bill of lading include the following:
- The B/L No.;
- The shipper or consignor, which is normally the exporter;
- The consignee, which is generally either the importer or made out "to order or to order of the shipper";
- The notify party. It is often the agent of the consignee or the consignee himself;
- Ocean vessel, voyage number;
- The port of loading;
- The port of discharge;
- The final destination;
- Number of original Bs/L;
- Shipping marks & numbers;
- A general description of the goods including the name, number and kind of packages, gross weight (kgs) and measurement (cubic meter);
- Freight clause. For FOB and FAS it should be "Freight collect", or "Freight to collect", or "freight payable at destination"; for CIF and CFR, it should be "freight prepaid", or "Freight paid";
- Total packages (in words);
- Freight and charges;
- The place and the date of issue;
- The carrier and signed for the carrier;

The B/L can be classified into the following types.

On Board or Shipped B/L and Received for Shipment B/L or Alongside Bills

On Board B/L is issued by the shipping company after the goods are actually shipped on board the designated vessel.

Received for Shipment B/L arises where the word "shipped" does not appear on the bill of lading. It merely confirms that the goods have been handed over to the ship-owner. The buyer under a CIF contract will not accept such a B/L because he is not able to anticipate the arrival of the consignment in the absence of the date of shipment.

Since shipped B/L provides better guarantee for the consignee to receive the cargo at the destination, the importer usually requires the exporter to produce shipped B/L and most bill of lading forms are preprinted as "shipped bill".

Clean B/L and Unclean B/L

A clean B/L states that the goods have been "shipped in apparent good order and condition" when the goods do not show any defects on their exteriors at the time of loading at the port of shipment. While defects are found on the exteriors of the goods, or the shipping company does not agree to any of the statements in the bill of lading, the bill will be marked as "unclean", "foul" or "packages in damaged condition". This includes: inadequate packaging, second-hand cases, damaged crates, etc. Unclean bill of lading is unacceptable to the buyer and banks.

If certain defects of the goods are unavoidable, for instance, timber often has "split ends", or chemicals cause discoloration on packing, the exporter must get the agreement of the importer to certain clauses on the B/L. These clauses must be agreed on before the export contract is established and the importer should tell their bank about the agreed clauses.

Straight, Blank or Open and Order B/L

Straight B/L has a designated consignee. As it is not transferable, it is not commonly used in international trade. Blank B/L also called Open B/L or Bearer B/L refers to the bill in which there is no definite consignee of the goods. There usually appear in the box of consignee words like "to bearer". Anyone who holds the bill is entitled to the goods the bill represents. No endorsement is needed for the transfer of the blank bill. Owing to the high risk involved, this bill is rarely used.

Order B/L means that the goods are consigned or destined to the order of a named person. In the box of consignee, words like "To order", "To order of the shipper", or "To order of the consignee" are marked. It can be transferred only after endorsement is made. If the B/L is made out "To order of the shipper", the shipper will endorse the bill. If it is made out "To the order of the consignee", the consignee will endorse the bill to transfer it. It is widely used in international trade.

Direct and Transshipment B/L

There is direct service between the shipment port and the destination port when the direct bill of lading is issued. A transshipment B/L means the goods need to be transshipped at the intermediate port as there is not direct service between the shipment port and the destination port.

Stale B/L

It is important that the bill of lading is available at the port of destination before the goods arrival. Bills, presented to the consignee or buyer or his bank after the goods are due at the port of destination, are described as "Stale B/L". As a cargo cannot be collected by the buyer without the bill of lading, the late arrival of this important document may have undesirable consequences and therefore should be avoided. Sometimes in the case of short sea voyages, it is necessary to add a clause of "Stale B/L is acceptable".

Container B/L

Such kind of B/L is becoming more common in use with the development of containerization. There are, generally, two styles of such bills with words "Containerized" or "Combined Transport B/L" in it. Normally, it is essential to add a clause of "Combined Transport B/L Acceptable" in the L/C.

On Deck B/L

On Deck B/L is issued when the cargo has to be loaded on the ship's deck. It applies to goods like livestock, plants, dangerous cargo, or awkwardly-shaped goods that can not fit into the ship's holds. As the goods are exposed to greater risks, specific insurance must be taken out against additional risks, in this case.

Through B/L

In many cases, it is necessary to employ two or more carriers to get the goods to their final destination. Usually, the first carrier will sign and issue a through bill of lading. The on-carriage may be by different form of transport.

In terms of negotiability and non-negotiability, bill of lading can also be categorized into negotiable bill of lading and non-negotiable bill of lading. Basically, negotiable B/L is a negotiable document, which allows the goods to be transferred by endorsement. In a non-negotiable B/L, the consignee cannot transfer the property or goods by transfer of the bills. This particular type will normally apply when goods are shipped on a non-commercial basis.

Sample 12 (4)

SHIPPER/EXPORTER	Bill of Lading Nr	SPHA025
JSC SYKTYVKAR FOREST ENTERPRISE 2, PR.BUMAZHNIKOV 167026 SYKTYVKAR, KOMI REPUBLIC, RUSSIA	Reference Nr	84/0366. EXPRESS RELEASE

ESF EUROSERVICES N.V.
St. Pietersvliet 7 B-2000 Antwerpen

CONSIGNEE (NOT NEGOTIABLE UNLESS CONSIGNED TO ORDER)
WWW SHIPMENTS MR. JORG WOERDEMANN HAMBURG

EUROSERVICES

MANAGERS: EURO SHIPPING & FORWARDING
5, Merhnevoy Canal,
198035, St.Petersburg
PHONE (812) 327 41 41
FAX (812) 327 41 44
TELEX 622825 ESF RU

NOTIFY PARTY
THE SAME AS CONSIGNEE

COPY NOT NEGOTIABLE

PRE-CARRIAGE (BY/BY)	PLACE OF INITIAL RECEIPT
VESSEL / VOYAGE	PORT OF LOADING
JOHANNA / 02041	ST. PETERSBURG
PORT OF DISCHARGE	PLACE OF DELIVERY
HAMBURG	

PARTICULARS FURNISHED BY THE MERCHANT

MARKS & NOS./CONTAINER NOS.	NO. OF PKGS.	KIND OF PACKAGES; DESCRIPTION OF GOODS	GROSS WEIGHT	MEASUREMENT
		2 X 40' CONTAINERS STC: COPY PAPER	TARE NETTO	GROSS
RWNU 9045191 L.C:hc SEAL:0167357		24 CASES	3970 26184	30154KGS
NOCU 6044074 L.C:hc SEAL:1336064		17 CASES	4550 18796	23346KGS
		41 CASES	8520 44980	53500KGS

SHIPPER'S LOAD, COUNT, STOWAGE AND SEAL   FREIGHT COLLECT

VALUE DECLARED $ .... IF NO VALUE IS DECLARED THE LIABILITY OF THE CARRIER ANDOR THE VESSEL SHALL NOT EXCEED US $ 500.00 PER PACKAGE OR CUSTOMARY FREIGHT UNIT. THE MERCHANT ACKNOWLEDGES THAT HE HAS BEEN GIVEN THE OPPORTUNITY TO CLAIM HIGHER COMPENSATION IF THE VALUE OF THE GOODS IS DECLARED HERE AND EXTRA FREIGHT IF REQUIRED IS PAID. SEE CLAUSE 7.3, 41.3)	FREIGHT PAYABLE AT	
	NUMBER OF ORIGINAL B(S)/L	ZERO

RECEIVED BY THE CARRIER FROM THE MERCHANT IN APPARENT GOOD ORDER AND CONDITION, UNLESS OTHERWISE INDICATED HEREIN, THE GOODS OR THE CONTAINER OR OTHER PACKAGES OR UNITS SAID BY THE MERCHANT TO CONTAIN THE CARGO HEREIN MENTIONED, TO BE CARRIED SUBJECT TO ALL THE TERMS AND CONDITIONS PROVIDED FOR ON THE FACE AND THE BACK OF THIS BILL OF LADING AND BY CARRIER'S TARIFF RULES AND REGULATIONS, BY THE VESSEL NAMED HEREIN OR ANY SUBSTITUTE AT THE CARRIER'S OPTION INCLUDING THE USE OF FEEDER SHIPS, BARGES, AIRPLANES, TRACTOR CARRIERS OR RAILCARS, FROM THE PLACE OF RECEIPT OR THE LOADING PORT TO THE PORT OF DISCHARGE OR PLACE OF DELIVERY SHOWN HEREIN. WHEN THIS PLACE OF RECEIPT IS AN INLAND POINT ANY NOTATION ON THIS BILL OF LADING OF "ON BOARD", "LOADING ON BOARD", "SHIPPED ON BOARD" OR WORDS TO LIKE EFFECT, SHALL BE DEEMED TO MEAN ON BOARD THE TRUCK, RAILCAR, AIRCRAFT, BARGE OR OTHER INLAND CONVEYANCE (AS THE CASE MAY BE). FOR ON-BOARD CARRIAGE FROM THE PLACE OF RECEIPT TO THE PORT OF LOADING. IN WITNESS WHEREOF THE NUMBER OF ORIGINAL BILLS OF LADING STATED ABOVE HAVE BEEN SIGNED ALL OF THE SAME TENOR AND DATE, ONE OF WHICH BEING ACCOMPLISHED, THE OTHER(S) TO STAND VOID.

IN ACCEPTING THIS BILL OF LADING THE MERCHANT EXPRESSLY ACCEPTS AND AGREES TO ITS STIPULATIONS ON BOTH PAGES, WHETHER WRITTEN, PRINTED, STAMPED OR OTHERWISE INCORPORATED, AS FULLY AS IF THEY WERE ALL SIGNED BY THE MERCHANT.

PLACE AND DATE OF ISSUE St.Petersburg

SIGNED FOR THE CARRIER
11 JUN 2002

ESF EUROSERVICES
St. P........
B-2000 A......

Sample 12 (5)

[Bill of Lading document]

SHANDONG PROVINCE YANTAI INTERNATIONAL MARINE SHIPPING CO.

Port-to-Port or Combine Transport BILL OF LADING

BILL OF LADING NO.: SYSHKBZJ6168560

SHIPPER: WUHAN KONJAC TECHNOLOGY CO.,LTD.
202 HANQIANG STREET, WEDZ, WUHAN, CHINA

CONSIGNEE: TO THE ORDER OF KOOKMIN BANK

NOTIFY PARTY: DONG YANG FOOD COMPANY
339-3 JANGRIM-2DONG, SAHA-KU,
PUSAN KOREA

VESSEL/VOY: KMTU XXX V.0614E
PORT OF LOADING: WUHAN, CHINA
PORT OF DISCHARGE: BUSAN PORT, KOREA
PLACE OF DELIVERY: BUSAN PORT, KOREA
No. of Original Bills of Lading: THREE

CONTAINER NO./SEAL NO. MARKS & NUMBERS: N/M
1X20'GP FCL CY-CY
U□□U2364308/D50594

DESCRIPTION OF GOODS (SAID TO CONTAIN):
SHIPPER'S LOAD & COUNT & SEAL
1787 CTNS
KONNYAKU PRODUCTS
L/C NO.M10T0603NS20032
TT-16B
TT-16BC
YT-16B

SAY ONE THOUSAND SEVEN HUNDRED AND EIGHTY SEVEN CARTONS ONLY

ON BOARD: APR.08,2006

GROSS WEIGHT (KILOS): 15162.565KGS
MEASUREMENT (CU METRES): 28.661 CBM

ON BOARD(1)

AGENT: CENTRANS KOREA
5TH FL., KYUNGNAM BLDG., 56-4, 4-GA,
CHUNGANG-DONG, CHUNG-GU, BUSAN, KOREA
TEL:0082-51-441-9951 FAX:0082-51-441-9740

FREIGHT PREPAID

WUHAN AMT SHIPPING AGENCY LTD.

PLACE OF ISSUE: WUHAN
DATE OF ISSUE: APR.08,2006

SIGNED BY AS AGENT FOR THE CARRIER
SHANDONG PROVINCE YANTAI INTERNATIONAL MARINE SHIPPING CO.

12.3.3 Combined Transport Documents

Combined transport document evidences the contract of carriage of goods by at least two modes of transport, issued by a combined transport operator under a combined transport contract. It is similar to "through B/L" and "combined transport B/L", but broader than them. Through B/L and combined transport B/L are always connected with sea, used for any transport combined with sea, while combined transport document can be applied to any kind of combined transport. Several carriers are involved in through B/L, while combined transport document is issued by only one carrier, that is, combined transport operator. Combined transport document can be made out either negotiable or non-negotiable.

12.3.4 Airway Bill

The airway bill is basically a receipt of the goods for dispatch and evidence of the contract of carriage between the carrier and the consignor. It is the consignment note used for the carriage of goods by air. This document is approximately the equivalent to the sea freight bill of lading, but the airway bill is not a negotiable title to goods in the same way as is an ocean bill of lading although it is widely used as a valuable receipt and evidence of dispatch and can be utilized within the framework of letters of credit, etc. Airway bills are made out in three originals. Normally the exporter would retain No. 1 original, No. 3 would be retained by the airline and No. 2 would automatically go forward with the consignment to the consignee at the destination point. Copies are used as circumstances demand.

Efficient service depends on the accuracy and completeness of the airway bill. Shippers themselves must give clear and complete forwarding instructions to the airline or agent.

12.4 FINANCE DOCUMENTS

In the course of international trade, payment is indispensable and there are quite a few finance documents used to ensure that the exporter receives full and timely payment for the shipment. If payment is not ensured, then, all will be meaningless. Basically, there are three modes of payment in international trade: Remittance, Collection and Letter of Credit. The most generally used method of payment in international trade is Letter of Credit (L/C), which has been discussed in Unit 6.

12.4.1 Bill of Exchange/Draft

A bill of exchange is also called a draft, which is an unconditional order in writing, usually drawn and signed by the exporter (also called the drawer), requiring the paying bank (or the drawee) to pay on demand, or at a fixed future time, a certain sum of money to the person specified. It is either a sight or a term bill. The former is one that is payable on presentation to the drawee. The other type is payable at a fixed time in the future, or a number of months or days after the bill has been sighted. In foreign trade the bill of exchange is mostly a documentary bill, that is, the bill of exchange is accompanied by the documents relating to the goods for which payment is to be settled. Documentary collections and documentary credits are payment methods often used in international trade.

With a documentary collection, the exporter prepares a bill of exchange stating how much is to be paid and when. Once the customer accepts this bill of exchange, the customer is legally liable for payment. Only then does the exporter, usually through the bank in the overseas country, allow the customer to have the transport documents needed to take possession of the goods. A documentary collection falls into two categories:

(1) Documents against Payment (D/P)

The exporter makes shipment and sends the shipping documents to the exporter's bank for collection. The bank then sends the shipping documents along with a bill of exchange to the importer's bank, which then sends the bill of exchange to the importer, who has to make payment immediately upon receiving the bill of exchange.

(2) Documents against Acceptance (D/A)

The importer does not have to pay immediately when the documents are presented under the term of D/A. The importer has to accept the bill of exchange to signify his formal commitment to pay on the due date. Thus, the accepted bill of exchange is paid by the importer on the day, which may be 30, 60 or 90 days later, as originally agreed upon with the seller.

With a documentary credit, the customer arranges a letter of credit from their bank. The bank agrees to pay the exporter once all the right documentation—such as transport documents showing the right goods have been dispatched—is received. The exporter must provide the required paperwork within the agreed time limit and with no discrepancies. Regardless of what payment method you agree, it's important to understand what documentation is required and ensure it is accurate.

Compared with a letter of credit, the collection method is of the low cost. But, this is offset by the risk that the importer might reject the documents for some reason or other. The collection arrangement involves a high level of trust between the exporter and the importer. Since the cargo would have already been loaded, the exporter has little recourse against the importer in cases of non-payment.

In the collection method of payment for goods, the exporter always uses the banking system to send the importer a bill of exchange to get paid. That is to say, the exporter uses a draft to draw on an overseas buyer for the sum agreed in the export contract. By using a draft with other shipping documents through the banking system, an exporter can ensure greater control of the goods, because until the draft is accepted by the buyer the goods cannot be released.

In general, the following items are included in the draft:
- No. ;
- Place and Date of Issue;
- Amount in Figures of Draft;
- Amount in Words of Draft;
- Drawn Clause;

Unit 12 Documentation in International Trade

- Tenor;
- Payee;
- Drawee;
- Signature of the Drawer.

Sample 12 (6)

ORIGINAL

No.: RX6080800   Dalian China, 1 AUG., 2021

Exchange for USD3,857.28

At   * * * * *   sight of this FIRST of Exchange (second of the same tenor and date unpaid) pay to the order of   BANK OF CHINA   the sum of US DOLLARS THREE THOUSAND EIGHT HUNDRED AND FIFTY-SEVEN AND CENTS TWENTY-EIGHT ONLY

Drawn under   INDUSTRIAL BANK OF KOREA, SEOUL L/C NO. MO389701NU30057 DATED 030514

To   INDUSTRIAL BANK OF KOREA (HEAD OFFICE SEOUL) SEOUL 50, ULCHIRO 2-GA, CHUNG-GU SEOUL, KOREA, REPUBLIC OF

DALIAN E. T. D. Z.
YUXI TRADING CO., LTD

DUPLICATE

No.: RX6080800   Dalian China, 1 AUG., 2021

Exchange for USD3,857.28

At   * * * * *   sight of this SECOND of Exchange (first of the same tenor and date unpaid) pay to the order of   BANK OF CHINA   the sum of US DOLLARS THREE THOUSAND EIGHT HUNDRED AND FIFTY-SEVEN AND CENTS TWENTY-EIGHT ONLY

Drawn under   INDUSTRIAL BANK OF KOREA, SEOUL L/C NO. MO389701NU30057 DATED 060614

To   INDUSTRIAL BANK OF KOREA (HEAD OFFICE SEOUL) SEOUL 50, ULCHIRO 2-GA, CHUNG-GU SEOUL, KOREA, REPUCLIC OF

DALIAN E. T. D. Z.
YUXI TRADING CO., LTD

Sample 12 (7)

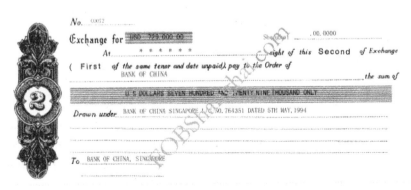

12.4.2 Remittance

Remittance happens when a payer asks his bank to send a sum of money to a beneficiary abroad by one of the transfer methods at his option. The beneficiary can be paid at the designated bank, which is either the remitting bank's overseas branch or its correspondent. This method is basically carried out in three ways, namely,

- Mail Transfer (M/T);
- Telegraphic Transfer (T/T);
- Demand Draft (D/D).

Remittance by airmail transfers funds by means of a payment order, a mail advice, or sometimes an advice issued by a remitting bank at the request of the remitter. It is generally known as mail transfer or M/T.

Remittance by cable/telex is often referred to as cable transfer or telegraphic transfer, namely T/T. It is exactly the same as a mail transfer, except that instructions from the remitting bank to the paying bank are transmitted by cable instead of by airmail.

Remittance by banker's demand draft is often referred to as demand draft, namely, D/D. A bank's draft is a negotiable instrument drawn by a bank on its overseas branch or its correspondent abroad ordering the latter to pay on demand the stated amount to the holder of the draft.

This method is fast and of low cost, but is least safe since the payer does not have any guarantee whatsoever for receiving the goods after payment. Generally speaking, airmail remittance is less used than T/T or D/D, except for small amount remittance. T/T is quicker, yet, more expensive. It is often used when the remittance amount is large and the transfer of funds is subject to a time limit.

12.5 OTHER DOCUMENTS

International trade involves complex flows of goods and services between many countries. A set of documents is used to monitor and control these flows by countries. Besides the documents mentioned above, these also include:

- Insurance Policy;
- Inspection Certificate;
- Certificate of Origin;
- Import License;
- Export License;
- Foreign Authorization.

12.5.1 Insurance Policy

In order to protect the goods against possible losses, the buyer or seller usually applies to an insurance company for insurance covering the goods in transit before the transportation of goods. In insurance, the contract made between the insurer and the insured is an insurance policy or certificate.

Sample 12 (8)

AIU INSURANCE COMPANY GUANGZHOU BRANCH

13/F., GuangFa Finance Centre, 83 NongLin Xia Road, Guangzhou, P.R. China 510080
Telephone: (8620)87311888 Fax: (8620)87310166

INSURANCE CERTIFICATE

ORIGINAL

NO: 0000001323

THE ASSURER:	AIU INSURANCE COMPANY GUANGZHOU BRANCH	
THE ASSURED: 万通实业（国际）有限公司 &/OR ONAN SEA-AIR LOGISTICS (CHINA) LTD.		AMOUNT INSURED: HKD 50,000.00
VESSEL/CONVEYANCE: 桃园 V.9809		SAILING ON /ABOUT: MAR. 25, 1998
AT AND FROM: HUANGPU, GUANGZHOU, CHINA	TO: SHANGHAI, CHINA	TRANSHIPMENT AT:
SUBJECT-MATTER INSURED: FIBER GLASS VASES PACKING: IN CARTON		MARKS & NUMBERS:
	SO VALUED	
SETTLING AGENT: AIU Insurance Company Guangzhou Branch 13/F., GuangFa Finance Centre, 83, NongLin Xia Road Guangzhou, P.R.China, Post Code: 510080 Tel: (86 20) 87011888 Fax: (86 20) 87310166		CLAIM REPRESENTATIVE: AIU Insurance Company Guangzhou Branch 13/F., GuangFa Finance Centre, 83, NongLin Xia Road Guangzhou, P.R.China, Post Code: 510080 Tel: (86 20) 87011888 Fax: (86 20) 87310166
CLAIM, IF ANY, PAYABLE AT : DESTINATION		Nos. of ORIGINAL: 1

INSURANCE CONDITIONS

INSTITUTE CARGO CLAUSES (A) -1/1/82
INSTITUTE WAR CLAUSES (CARGO)-1/1/82
INSTITUTE STRIKES CLAUSES (CARGO)-1/1/82
INSTITUTE CLASSIFICATION CLAUSE-13/4/92
INSTITUTE THEFT, PILFERAGE & NON-DELIVERY CLAUSES-1/12/82

Subject to the conditions of Marine Open Policy No. 80062 of AIU Insurance Company Guangzhou Branch.

Loss if any payable to the ASSURED or order upon surrender of this Certificate.

It is understood and agreed that this Certificate represents and takes the place of the policy and conveys all the rights of the original policy holder (for the purpose of collecting any loss or claims), as fully as if the property were covered by a special policy direct through the holder of this Certificate, and free from any liability for unpaid premium.

It is agreed that, upon the payment of any loss or damage, the Insurers are to be subrogated to the extent of such payments, to all the rights of Assured under their bills of lading or other contracts of carriage.

It is hereby understood and agreed that in case of claim for loss under this Certificate the same shall be reported as soon as the goods are landed or the loss known, to the Agent of the Company as endorsed hereon to whom proofs of loss must in all cases be submitted for verification.

Claims to be adjusted according to the usage of Lloyds in Great Britain or of the ports of settlement elsewhere, but subject to the conditions of the policy and contract of insurance.

ISSUED AT: GUANGZHOU, CHINA   Date: MARCH 25, 1998

This Certificate is not valid unless countersigned by:

ORIGINAL

For and on behalf of
AIU INSURANCE COMPANY
GUANGZHOU BRANCH

Authorised Representative

12.5.2 Inspection Certificate

An inspection certificate is a statement issued and signed by the appropriate authority, either a government entity or a private inspection company, providing evidence that the goods were inspected and detailing the results of such inspection. For certain commodities or for certain countries, such an inspection certificate must be issued by a government entity.

The inspection certificate contains details of the shipment to which it relates, states the results of the inspection, and bears the signature, the stamp or the seal of the inspection entity. According to its different functions, the inspection certificate can be generally classified into quality certificate, quantity certificate, weight certificate, phytosanitary certificate, veterinary certificate, sanitary/heath certificate, disinfection certificate, etc.

12.5.3 Certificate of Origin

A certificate of origin is a document stating the country of origin of the goods. It is usually required by countries which do not use customs invoice or consular invoice to set the appropriate duties for the imports. It mainly contains the nature, quantity, value of the goods shipped and their place of manufacture. No particular format exists internationally. It enables the buyer not only to process the importation of the goods, but also permits preferential import duties where appropriate. In China, this certificate is generally issued by the Import and Export Commodity Inspection Bureau or China Council for Promotion of International Trade.

Sample 12 (9)

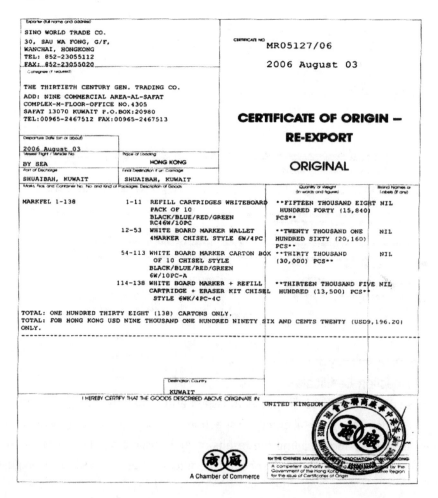

12.5.4 Import or Export License and Foreign Authorization

If your business is considering importing or exporting goods, sometimes you need a license. There are controls on exports of military or paramilitary goods, technology, artworks, plants and animals, medicines and chemicals. License requirements may depend on the potential use of the item—if it has a military application (usually referred to as dual use goods)—and where you are exporting to. There are also controls on imports including firearms, plants and animals, foods, medicines, textiles and chemicals. Some countries also use import license and foreign authorization system to restrict imports. If the planned importation or exportation is legal and meets current requirement, the license will be issued. Exporting or importing controlled goods without the right license is a criminal offence, so it's important to get the license before the goods are shipped.

Sample 12 (10)

中华人民共和国敏感物项和技术出口许可证
EXPORT LICENCE FOR SENSITIVE ITEMS AND TECHNOLOGIES OF PRC
No. 4000000

1. 出口商: Exporter	2. 出口许可证号: Export licence No.
3. 出口经营登记证号: Registration number	4. 许可证有效日期至: Export licence expiry date
5. 贸易方式: Terms of trade	6. 付款方式: Payment
7. 进口国（地区）: Country/Region of purchase	8. 最终目的国(地区): Destination
9. 合同号: Contract No.	10. 合同签订日期: Date of contract signed
11. 收货人: Consignee	12. 最终用户: End-user
13. 报关口岸: Place of clearance	14. 运输方式: Mode of transport
15. 商品名称: Description of goods	商品编码: Code of goods

16. 规格、等级 Specification	17. 单位 Unit	18. 数量 Quantity	19. 单价（ ） Unit price	20. 总值（ ） Amount	21. 总值折美元 Amount in USD
总 计 Total					

22. 备 注 Supplementary details	23. 发证机关签章 Issuing authority's stamp & signature
	24. 发证日期 Licence date

12.6 USEFUL TERMS AND EXPRESSIONS

1.	documentation	制单
2.	customs invoice	海关发票
3.	consular invoice	领事发票
4.	bill of lading (B/L)	提货单
5.	packing list	装箱单
6.	shipping note	托运单
7.	clean B/L, unclean B/L	清洁/不清洁提单
8.	on board or shipped B/L	已装船提单
9.	Straight, Blank or Open and Order B/L	记名、不记名以及指示提单
10.	direct and transshipment B/L	直船、转船提单
11.	stable B/L	过期提单
12.	container B/L	集装箱提单
13.	on deck B/L	舱面提单
14.	through B/L	联运提单
15.	airway bill	航空提单
16.	finance documents	金融单据
17.	shipping mark	运输标志
18.	inspection certificate	检验证书
19.	certificate of origin	原产地证
20.	import/export license	进口/出口许可证
21.	quality license	品质检验证书
22.	quantity certificate	数量检验证书
23.	weight certificate	重量检验证书
24.	phytosanitary certificate	植物检疫证书
25.	veterinary certificate	兽医检验证书
26.	sanitary/heath certificate	卫生/健康检验证书
27.	disinfection certificate	消毒检验证书

12.7 COMMUNICATION LABORATORY

Prepare a bill of exchange, commercial invoice and packing list with details given below.

出口商：SHANGHAI SUNDING CO., LTD.
　　　　60 ZHONGSHAN ROAD, SHANGHAI, CHINA
进口商：NYCS AMERICA, INC.
　　　　32 MOUNT VERNON, NEW YORK, NY, USA
开证银行：CITIBANK, NEWYORK, NY, USA
信用证号码：901L/C251991
开证日期：2019 年 4 月 20 日
发票日期：2019 年 5 月 12 日
发票号码：SDCH128
合同号码：SDCH1806
装运港：SHANGHAI, CHINA
目的港：NEW YORK, USA
运输标志：　　　　　NYCS
　　　　　　　　　SDCH128
　　　　　NEW YORK C/No.1 –1000
货名：CONNECTER
数量：20000 PCS
包装：纸箱装，每箱 20PCS
毛重：6800KGS
净重：6600KGS
体积：57CBM
单价：USD 13.00/PC CIF NEW YORK
付款期限：见票后 60 天支付
授权签署人：孙达

(1) BILL OF EXCHANGE

BILL OF EXCHANGE

凭 Drawn Under （1）＿＿＿＿＿＿＿＿＿＿　　不可撤销信用证 Irrevocable　L/C No. （2）＿＿＿＿＿＿＿

日期 DATED （3）＿＿＿＿＿＿＿　　支取 Payable With interest @ ___ % 按 息 付款

号码 No. （4）＿＿＿＿　　汇票金额 Exchange for （5）＿＿＿＿＿　　中国上海 Shanghai, China

见票 At （6）＿＿＿＿＿ sight of this FIRST of Exchange (Second of Exchange 日后（本汇票之副本未付）付交

Being unpaid) Pay to the order of （7）＿＿＿＿＿＿＿＿

金额 the sum of （8）＿＿＿＿＿＿＿＿＿＿＿＿＿＿＿＿

此致 To
　　（9）＿＿＿＿＿＿＿

　　　　　　　　　　　（10）＿＿＿＿＿＿＿＿

(2) COMMERCIAL INVOICE

SHANGHAI SUNDING CO., LTD.

60 ZHONGSHAN ROAD, SHANGHAI, CHINA

COMMERCIAL INVOICE

TO:

INVOICE NO.: _____

DATE: _____

S/C NO.: _____

L/C NO.: _____

FROM _____ TO _____ BY _____

MARKS & NUMBERS	DESCRIPTION OF GOODS	QUANTITY	UNIT PRICE	AMOUNT
TOTAL AMOUNT				

(3) PACKING LIST

SHANGHAI SUNDING CO., LTD.

60 ZHONGSHAN ROAD, SHANGHAI, CHINA

PACKING LIST

TO:

INVOICE NO.: _____

DATE: _____

S/C NO.: _____

L/C NO.: _____

FROM _____ TO _____ BY _____

MARKS & NUMBERS	DESCRIPTION OF GOODS	QUANTITY	NOS. & KINDS OF PKGS.	G.W. (KG)	N.W. (KG)	MEAS. (CBM)
TOTAL PACKAGES (IN WORDS)						

Appendix 1 — Foreign Trade Law of The People's Republic of China

Passed on May 12, 1994 during the 7th meeting of the Standing Committee of the Eighth National People's Congress and amended during the 8th meeting of the Standing Committee of the Tenth National People's Congress on April 6, 2004.

Index

Chapter One	General Provisions
Chapter Two	Foreign Trade Operator
Chapter Three	Import and Export of Goods and Technologies
Chapter Four	International Service Trade
Chapter Five	Trade-related Intellectual Property Protection
Chapter Six	Foreign Trade Order
Chapter Seven	Foreign Trade Investigation
Chapter Eight	Foreign Trade Relief
Chapter Nine	Foreign Trade Promotion
Chapter Ten	Legal Liabilities
Chapter Eleven	Supplementary Provisions

Chapter One   General Provisions

Article 1   This Law is promulgated with a view to enhancing the opening-up to the outside world, developing foreign trade, maintaining order in foreign trade activities and promoting a healthy development of socialist market economy.

Article 2   This Law shall be applicable to foreign trade and trade-related intellectual property protection.

The term foreign trade in this Law shall refer to the import and export of goods and technologies and international service trade.

Article 3   The department in charge of foreign trade under the State Council shall take charge of all foreign trade work in the whole country in accordance with this Law.

Article 4   The State shall adopt a unified foreign trade system, encourage foreign trade development and safeguard a fair and free foreign trade order.

Article 5   The People's Republic of China shall promote and develop trading relations with all other countries and regions, establish or participate in agreements of tariff unions, free trade agreements and other regional economic and trade agreements and participate in regional economic organizations in the principle of equality and mutual benefit.

Article 6 In foreign trade, the People's Republic of China shall, in accordance with the international treaties or agreements that she has signed or entered into, grant the contractual parties and participants the most favor nation or national treatment of China, or grant the most favor nation or national treatment of China to the counterparts in accordance with the principle of equality and mutual benefit.

Article 7 The People's Republic of China shall have the right to adopt, in accordance with the actual circumstances, corresponding measures against any country or region to counter their discriminatory measures on the banning, restriction or other similar acts in trading with the People's Republic of China.

Chapter Two   Foreign Trade Operator

Article 8 The term foreign trade operator in this Law shall refer to a legal person or other organization or individual engaged in foreign trade activities that have gone through the industry and commerce registration or other business formalities in compliance with the provisions of this Law and other laws and administrative rules.

Article 9 A foreign trade operator engaged in import and export of goods or technologies shall make registration for record with the department in charge of foreign trade under the State Council or institutions entrusted by it; but those that are exempted from registration for record by laws, administrative rules and rules of the department in charge of foreign trade under the State Council shall be excluded. The detailed rules on the registration for record shall be stipulated by the department in charge of foreign trade under the State Council. Customs shall not handle the declaration and clearance procedure for goods imported or exported by a foreign trade operator who fails to go through the registration for record in accordance with the rules.

Article 10 The operation of international service trade shall abide by the provisions of this Law and other relevant laws and administrative rules. Organizations engaged in the undertaking of overseas projects or overseas labor collaboration shall possess the corresponding capability or qualifications. The detailed rules shall be promulgated by the State Council.

Article 11 The State may place the import and export of certain goods under the administration of state-trading regime. Import and export of goods subject to state-trading regime may only be handled by the authorized enterprises; but, the certain volume of goods subject to state-trading regime that is permitted by the State to be imported or exported by non-authorized enterprises shall be excluded from the administration of state-trading regime. Catalogues for the goods subject to state-trading regime and list of the authorized enterprises shall be drawn up, adjusted and published by the department in charge of foreign trade under the State Council in consultation with other relevant departments under the State Council. Goods subject to state-trading regime imported or exported without permission and in violation of this Article shall not be cleared by the Customs.

Article 12 A foreign trade operator may accept entrustment from others to conduct foreign trade within its business scope by acting as an agent.

Article 13 A foreign trade operator shall provide documents and materials related to its foreign trade activities to the relevant departments in accordance with the rules that are stipulated by the department in charge of foreign trade under the State Council or other relevant departments under the State Council according to laws. The relevant departments shall undertake to protect the commercial secrets of the foreign trade operator.

Chapter Three Import and Export of Goods and Technologies

Article 14 The State shall allow the free import and export of goods and technologies, except otherwise provided for by other laws and administrative rules.

Article 15 The department in charge of foreign trade under the State Council may place certain goods of free import and export under the administration of automatic licensing regime and publish the catalogues in view of the need to monitor the import and export situation. For importing and exporting of goods subject to automatic licensing regime, if consigners or consignees file applications for automatic licensing before the customs declaration, the department in charge of foreign trade under the State Council or institutions entrusted by it shall approve the applications; the Customs shall not clear the goods without going through the formality of automatic licensing. Contracts of importing or exporting technologies subject to automatic import and export shall be registered for record with the department in charge of foreign trade under the State Council or the institutions entrusted by it.

Article 16 The State may restrict or ban the import or export of goods or technologies due to the following reasons: Being necessary to restrict or ban the import or export because of national security, public interests or public ethics; Being necessary to restrict or ban the import or export in view of protecting the health or safety of the people, life or health of animals and plants and the ecological environment; Being necessary to restrict or ban the import or export in view of implementing the measures on import and export of gold or silver; Being necessary to restrict or ban the export because of shortage of supplies at home or as important natural resources that are in danger of depletion; Being necessary to restrict the export as the limited market in the importing countries or regions; Being necessary to restrict the export due to the severe disruption in the export order; Being necessary to restrict the import by the State to establish or accelerate to establish certain industries at home; Agricultural, animal husbandry and fishery products in any form that are necessary to be restricted of importing by the State; Being necessary to restrict the import by the State in view of maintaining the financial position of the country in the world or ensuring a balance of international payments; Being necessary to restrict or ban the import or export due to other reasons in accordance with laws and administrative rules; and subject to restriction or ban of import and export by international treaties or agreements to which the People's Republic of China is a signatory or has entered.

Article 17 The State may take any necessary measures on the import and export of goods and technologies related to fissile and fusion matters or matters that may derive these matters and import and export of weapons and ammunitions and other materials for military use to protect the security of the State. At wartime or to maintain world peace and security, the State may take any necessary measures concerning the import and export of goods and technologies.

Article 18 The department in charge of foreign trade under the State Council shall, in consultation with other relevant departments under the State Council, draw up, revise and publish the catalogues of goods and technologies whose import or export are restricted or banned in accordance with the provisions of Article 16 and 17 of this Law. The department in charge of foreign trade under the State Council may, independently or in consultation with other relevant departments under the State Council, make decisions to provisionally restrict or ban the import or export of special goods or technologies that are not listed in the aforementioned catalogues within the provisions of Article 16 and 17 of this Law.

Article 19 The State implements quota or licence administration on goods whose import or export is restricted and licence administration on technologies whose import or export is restricted. Goods and technologies subject to quota or licence administration can be imported or exported only when it has been approved by the department in charge of foreign trade under the State Council independently or in consultation with other relevant departments under the State Council in accordance with the provisions promulgated by the State Council. The State may implement tariff quota administration on the import of certain goods.

Article 20 The import and export quotas shall be allocated by the departments in charge of foreign trade under the State Council or by other relevant departments under the State Council within their terms of reference in line with the principle of being open, fair, just and efficient. The detailed measures of quota allocation shall be worked out by the State Council.

Article 21 The State implements a unified appraisal system on the quality of goods by conducting accreditation, inspection and quarantine on imported and exported goods in accordance with the provisions of the relevant laws and administrative rules.

Article 22 The State implements the country of origin administration on the imported and exported goods. The detailed rules shall be worked out by the State Council.

Article 23 For cultural relics, wild animals and plants and their products whose import and export are banned or restricted according to other laws and administrative rules, the provisions of other laws and administrative regulations shall apply.

Chapter Four International Service Trade

Article 24　In the context of international service trade, the People's Republic of China shall grant other signatories and participants market access and national treatment in accordance with the commitments made in the international treaties and agreements to which China is a signatory or a participant.

Article 25　The department in charge of foreign trade under the State Council and other relevant departments under the State Council shall exercise administration on international service trade in accordance with this Law and other relevant laws and administrative rules.

Article 26　Restrictions or bans may be imposed on the international service trade by the State in view of the following reasons: Being necessary to restrict or ban because of national security, public interests or public morals; Being necessary to restrict or ban to protect the health or safety of the people, life or health of animals and plants and the ecological environment; Being necessary to restrict to establish or accelerate to establish certain domestic service industries; Being necessary to restrict by the State to maintain the balance of foreign exchange payment; Being necessary to restrict or ban due to other reasons in accordance with laws and administrative rules; and other restrictions or ban provided for by the international treaties or agreements to which the People's Republic of China is a signatory or has entered.

Article 27　The State may take any necessary measures on the international service trade related to military purposes and international service trade related to fissile and fusion matters or matters that may derive these matters to safeguard the State security. At wartime or to maintain world peace and security, the State may take any necessary measures concerning the international service trade.

Article 28　The department in charge of foreign trade under the State Council shall, in consultation with other relevant departments under the State Council, draw up, revise and publish the catalogues of market access for international service trade in accordance with the provisions of Article 26 and 27 of this law and other relevant laws and administrative rules.

Chapter Five Trade-related Intellectual Property Protection

Article 29　The State shall protect trade-related intellectual property in accordance with laws and administrative rules on intellectual property. For imported goods that infringe upon intellectual property and disrupt foreign trade order, the department in charge of foreign trade under the State Council may take measures as ban of import of the relevant goods produced or sold by those who infringe upon the intellectual property within a certain period.

Article 30 Should the person who holds the intellectual property have any one of acts as forbidding the concessionaire from questioning on the effectiveness of the intellectual property in the concession contract, imposing package concession or inserting terms of exclusive re-granting in the concession contract and the act disrupt the fair competition order in foreign trade, the department in charge of foreign trade may take necessary measures to eliminate the disruption.

Article 31 Should other countries or regions fail to grant the legal persons, other organizations or individuals from the People's Republic of China national treatment, or not be able to provide effective intellectual property protection to the goods, technologies or services originating from the People's Republic of China, the department in charge of foreign trade under the State Council may take necessary measures on the trade with the countries or regions in accordance with this Law and other relevant laws and administrative regulations and in line with the international treaties and agreements that People's Republic of China has signed or entered into.

Chapter Six   Foreign Trade Order

Article 32 In the operation of foreign trade, monopolistic activities in violation of anti-trust laws and administrative rules shall not be conducted. Monopolistic activities in the operation of foreign trade that disrupt the fair market competition shall be punished in accordance with the laws and administrative rules on anti-trust. For the aforementioned activities violating laws and disrupting the foreign trade order, the department in charge of foreign trade under the State Council shall take necessary measures to eliminate the disruption.

Article 33 In the operation of foreign trade, illegitimate business operations such as selling products at unreasonably low prices, colluded bidding, disseminating advertisements containing false contents and offering bribe in commercial activities shall not be conducted. The illegitimate business operations in foreign trade shall be punished in accordance with the laws and administrative rules on anti-illegitimate competition. For the aforementioned activities violating laws and disrupting the foreign trade order, the department in charge of foreign trade under the State Council may ban the import and export of the relevant goods and technologies conducted by the operators to eliminate the impairment.

Article 34 In the operation of foreign trade, the following activities shall be prohibited:Falsifying, modifying certificates of country of origin, falsifying, modifying or trading in certificates of country of origin and import and export licences, import and export quota certificates or other import and export documents; Obtaining export rebate by deception; Smuggling or trafficking; Evading accreditation, inspection and quarantine required by laws and administrative rules; and Committing acts that violate the provisions of other laws and administrative rules.

Article 35 In the operation of foreign trade, regulations on foreign exchange promulgated by the State shall be abided by.

Article 36 The department in charge of foreign trade under the State Council may publish notifications to the public on activities that violate this Law and disrupt foreign trade order.

Chapter Seven Foreign Trade Investigation

Article 37 Tomaintain the foreign trade order, the department in charge of foreign trade under the State Council may, independently or in consultation with other relevant departments under the State Council, conduct investigations on the following matters: Import and export of goods, import and export of technologies and international service trade's impact on domestic industries and their competitiveness; Relevant countries and regions' trade barriers; Matters that are necessary to be investigated to decide whether or not to adopt such foreign trade relief measures as anti-dumping, anti-subsidy and safeguards in accordance with laws; Acts that circumvent foreign trade relief measures; Issues concerning state safety and interests in foreign trade; Matters that are necessary to be investigated to implement Article 7, ii of Article 29, Article 30, 31, iii of Article 32 and iii of Article 33; and Other matters that disrupt foreign trade order and are necessary to be investigated.

Article 38 The department in charge of foreign trade under the State Council shall issue notifications to initiate foreign trade investigations. The investigation may be conducted in the form of written questionnaire, hearing, on-the-spot investigation and entrusted investigation. The department in charge of foreign trade under the State Council shall present investigation report or render rulings and publish notifications according to the outcome of the investigations.

Article 39 The relevant workplaces and individuals shall cooperate and assist the foreign trade investigation. The department in charge of foreign trade under the State Council and other relevant departments under the State Council and their staff shall undertake to protect the state and commercial secrets that they are aware of or familiar with.

Chapter Eight Foreign Trade Relief

Article 40 The State may take corresponding foreign trade relief measures according to the outcome of foreign trade investigation.

Article 41 Should products originating from other countries or regions enter the Chinese market at price below-the-normal-value or dumping, which causes material injury or threat of such material injury to an established domestic industry or causes material barrier to the establishment of a domestic industry, the State may take anti-dumping measures to eliminate or mitigate such injury or the threat of injury or barrier.

Article 42 Should products originating from other countries or regions be exported to the market of the third country at price below-the-normal-value, which causes material injury or threat of such material injury to an established domestic industry or causes material barrier to the establishment of a domestic industry, upon the petition filed by a domestic industry, the department in charge of foreign trade under the State Council may conduct consultation with the government of the third country and request it to take corresponding measures.

Article 43 Should the imported products directly or indirectly accept the exclusive subsidy in any form offered by the exporting countries or regions, which causes material injury or threat of such material injury to an established domestic industry or causes material barrier to the establishment of a domestic industry, the State may take anti-subsidy measures to eliminate or mitigate such injury or the threat of injury or barrier.

Article 44 Should the substantially increasing import cause material injury or threat of material injury to the domestic industry that produces like-products or directly competing products, the State may take necessary safeguard measures to eliminate or mitigate such injury or the threat of injury and provide necessary support to the industry.

Article 45 Should the increasing service provided by service providers from other countries or regions cause material injury or threat of such material injury to a domestic industry that provide the same service or directly competing service, the State may take relief measures to eliminate or mitigate such injury or the threat of injury.

Article 46 Should the import of a certain product increase substantially due to the restriction of import exercised by the third country, which causes material injury or threat of such material injury to an established domestic industry or causes material barrier to the establishment of a domestic industry, the State may take necessary relief measures to limit the import of the product.

Article 47 Should a country or region that has signed with the People's Republic of China or jointly entered into economic and trade treaties and agreements violate the provisions of the treaties or agreements and thus lead to losses or impairment of the interests that are enjoyed by the People's Republic of China in accordance with the treaties and agreements, or hamper the realization of the purposes set forth in the treaties or agreements, the People's Republic of China has the right to request the governments of the relevant countries or regions to take corresponding remedial measures and suspend or terminate fulfillment of relevant responsibilities in accordance with the relevant treaties or agreements.

Article 48 The department in charge of foreign trade under the State Council shall conduct the bilateral or multilateral consultations, negotiations and dispute settlement in accordance with this Law and other relevant laws.

Article 49 The department in charge of foreign trade under the State Council and other relevant departments under the State Council shall establish a pre-warning and response mechanism on the import and export of goods, import and export of technologies and international service trade to counter the unexpected and unusual situations and safeguard state economic safety.

Article 50   The State may take necessary anti-circumvention measures to the acts that circumvent the foreign trade relief measures provided for by this Law.

Chapter Nine   Promotion of Foreign Trade

Article 51   The State shall draw up the foreign trade development strategy, establish and perfect the foreign trade promotion mechanism.

Article 52   The State shall, in accordance with the need of foreign trade development, make efforts to set up and improve special financial institutions that are to serve foreign trade as well as establish development and risk funds for the trade.

Article 53   The State shall adopt various promotion measures to develop foreign trade including issuing of import and export credits, export credit insurance and setting up of export rebates.

Article 54   The State shall establish foreign trade public information service system to provide information to foreign trade operators and other social mass of people.

Article 55   The State shall take measures to encourage foreign trade operators to explore the international market, take such measures as overseas investment, undertaking of overseas projects and overseas labor collaboration to develop foreign trade.

Article 56   Foreign trade operators may establish or enter into associations and chambers of commerce in accordance with laws. The relevant associations and chambers of commerce shall abide by laws and administrative rules, provide the members with services related to production, marketing, information and training in accordance with the articles of association, perform the function of coordination and self-discipline, file petitions for foreign trade relief measures in accordance with laws, safeguard the interests of their members and industry, convey to the relevant government departments proposals on promoting foreign trade and carry out foreign trade promotion activities.

Article 57   Chinese organizations for the promotion of international trade shall according to their articles of association, develop contacts with overseas businesses, hold exhibitions, provide information and consultancy services and engage in other foreign trade promotion activities.

Article 58   The State shall support and promote small and medium-sized enterprises to develop foreign trade.

Article 59   The State shall make special efforts to promote foreign trade in ethnic autonomous regions and economically less developed areas.

Chapter Ten Legal Liabilities

Article 60 For import and export of goods subject to state-trading regime without permission in violation of Article 11 of this Law, the department in charge of foreign trade under the State Council or other relevant departments under the State Council may impose a fine of 50,000 Yuan or less; for a serious case, the application for import and export of goods subject to state-trading regime filed by the law-breaker shall not be accepted within three years as of the date when the administrative punishment enters into effect or his right to conduct the import and export of other goods subject to state-trading regime shall be revoked.

Article 61 Import and export of goods that are banned from import or export or import and export of goods that are restricted for import and export without permission shall be handled and punished by the Customs in accordance with the provisions of laws and administrative rules; if crime is constituted, the criminal liabilities shall be ascertained. Import and export of technologies that are banned from import or export or import and export of technologies that are restricted for import and export without permission shall be handled and punished in accordance with the provisions of laws and administrative rules; if the act is not provided for by laws and regulations, the department in charge of foreign trade under the State Council shall order the act to be rectified, confiscate the illegal gains and impose a fine of more than one time but no more than five times of the amount of the illegal gains, if there is no illegal gains achieved or the illegal gains is less than 10,000 Yuan, the fine shall be between 10,000 and 50,000 Yuan; if crime is constituted, the criminal liabilities shall be ascertained. The department in charge of foreign trade under the State Council or other relevant departments under the State Council may refuse to accept the application filed by the law-breaker for import and export quota or licence within three years as of date when the administrative punishment provided for by the above two paragraphs enters into force or when the criminal punishments enter into force, or forbid the law-breaker from operation of import and export of goods and technologies for more than one year but less than three years.

Article 62 Undertaking of banned international service trade, or undertaking of restricted international service trade without permission shall be punished in accordance with the relevant laws and administrative rules, the department in charge of foreign trade under the State Council shall order the act to be rectified, the illegal gains shall be confiscated and a fine of more than one time but no more than five times of the amount of the illegal gains shall be imposed, if there is no illegal gains achieved or the illegal gains is less than 10,000 Yuan, the fine shall be between 10,000 and 50,000 Yuan; if crime is constituted, the criminal liabilities shall be ascertained. The department in charge of foreign trade under the State Council may forbid the law-breaker from operation of the relevant international service trade for more than one year but less than three years as of the date when the administrative punishment provided for by the above paragraph enters into force or when the criminal punishment enters into force.

Article 63 Acts in violation of Article 34 of this Law shall be punished in accordance with the relevant laws and administrative rules; if crime is constituted, the criminal liabilities shall be ascertained. The department in charge of foreign trade under the State Council may forbid the law-breaker from operation of the relevant foreign trade for more than one year but less than three years as of the date when the administrative punishment provided for by the above paragraph enters into force or when the criminal punishment enters into force.

Article 64 In accordance with Article 61 to 63 of this law, the Customs shall not handle the declaration and clearance procedure for the goods imported or exported by foreign trade operators who are forbidden from operation of foreign trade in accordance with the forbidding decision made by the department in charge of foreign trade under the State Council, foreign exchange administrations or banks designated to deal with foreign exchange shall not handle the relevant foreign exchange settlement and purchase for them.

Article 65 If staff with the departments in charge of foreign trade is found committing dereliction of duty, resorting to deception for personal gains or abusing their powers, if crime is constituted, the criminal liability shall be ascertained; otherwise, administrative punishments shall be meted out. If staff with the departments in charge of foreign trade is found taking advantage of his/her position to extort belongings from others or seek interests for others after accepting benefits, if crime is constituted, the criminal liability shall be ascertained; otherwise, administrative punishments shall be meted out.

Article 66 Foreign trade operators who hold dissents to the administrative decisions conducted by the departments in charge of foreign trade in accordance with this Law may apply for administrative review or file administrative litigation to the People's Court in accordance with laws.

Chapter Eleven Supplementary Provisions

Article 67 If laws and administrative rules have other provisions on the foreign trade administration on goods for military use, fissile and fusion matters or matters that may derive these matters and import and export administration on cultural products, these provisions shall apply.

Article 68 The State shall adopt flexible measures and grant preferential treatment and facilities to promote trade between towns of China and neighboring countries and trading among border residents at fairs within each other's territories. The detailed procedures shall be formulated by the State Council.

Article 69 This Law shall not apply to exclusive tariff areas of the People's Republic of China.

Article 70 This Law shall enter into force as of July 1, 2004.

Appendix 2: Uniform Customs and Practice For Documentary Credits, UCP 600

(ICC Publication No. 600)

Article 1 Application of UCP

The Uniform Customs and Practice for Documentary Credits, 2007 Revision, ICC Publication No. 600 ("UCP") are rules that apply to any documentary credit ("credit") (including, to the extent to which they may be applicable, any standby letter of credit) when the text of the credit expressly indicates that it is subject to these rules. They are binding on all parties thereto unless expressly modified or excluded by the credit.

Article 2 Definitions

For the purpose of these rules:

Advising bank means the bank that advises the credit at the request of the issuing bank.

Applicant means the party on whose request the credit is issued.

Banking day means a day on which a bank is regularly open at the place at which an act subject to these rules is to be performed.

Beneficiary means the party in whose favour a credit is issued.

Complying presentation means a presentation that is in accordance with the terms and conditions of the credit, the applicable provisions of these rules and international standard banking practice.

Confirmation means a definite undertaking of the confirming bank, in addition to that of the issuing bank, to honour or negotiate a complying presentation.

Confirming bank means the bank that adds its confirmation to a credit upon the issuing bank's authorization or request.

Credit means any arrangement, however named or described, that is irrevocable and thereby constitutes a definite undertaking of the issuing bank to honour a complying presentation.

Honour means:

a. to pay at sight if the credit is available by sight payment.

b. to incur a deferred payment undertaking and pay at maturity if the credit is available by deferred payment.

Appendix 2　Uniform Customs and Practice For Documentary Credits, UCP 600

c. to accept a bill of exchange ("draft") drawn by the beneficiary and pay at maturity if the credit is available by acceptance.

Issuing bank means the bank that issues a credit at the request of an applicant or on its own behalf.

Negotiation means the purchase by the nominated bank of drafts (drawn on a bank other than the nominated bank) and/or documents under a complying presentation, by advancing or agreeing to advance funds to the beneficiary on or before the banking day on which reimbursement is due to (to be paid the nominated bank).

Nominated bank means the bank with which the credit is available or any bank in the case of a credit available with any bank.

Presentation means either the delivery of documents under a credit to the issuing bank or nominated bank or the documents so delivered.

Presenter means a beneficiary, bank or other party that makes a presentation.

Article 3　Interpretations

For the purpose of these rules:

Where applicable, words in the singular include the plural and in the plural include the singular.

A credit is irrevocable even if there is no indication to that effect.

A document may be signed by handwriting, facsimile signature, perforated signature, stamp, symbol or any other mechanical or electronic method of authentication.

A requirement for a document to be legalized, visaed, certified or similar will be satisfied by any signature, mark, stamp or label on the document which appears to satisfy that requirement.

Branches of a bank in different countries are considered to be separate banks.

Terms such as "first class", "well known", "qualified", "independent", "official", "competent" or "local" used to describe the issuer of a document allow any issuer except the beneficiary to issue that document.

Unless required to be used in a document, words such as "prompt", "immediately" or "as soon as possible" will be disregarded.

The expression "on or about" or similar will be interpreted as a stipulation that an event is to occur during a period of five calendar days before until five calendar days after the specified date, both start and end dates included.

The words "to", "until", "till", "from" and "between" when used to determine a period of shipment include the date or dates mentioned, and the words "before" and "after" exclude the date mentioned.

The words "from" and "after" when used to determine a maturity date exclude the date mentioned.

The terms "first half" and "second half" of a month shall be construed respectively as the 1st to the 15th and the 16th to the last day of the month, all dates inclusive.

The terms "beginning", "middle" and "end" of a month shall be construed respectively as the 1st to the 10th, the 11th to the 20th and the 21st to the last day of the month, all dates inclusive.

Article 4 Credits v. Contracts

a. A credit by its nature is a separate transaction from the sale or other contract on which it may be based. Banks are in no way concerned with or bound by such contract, even if any reference whatsoever to it is included in the credit. Consequently, the undertaking of a bank to honor, to negotiate or to fulfill any other obligation under the credit is not subject to claims or defences by the applicant resulting from its relationships with the issuing bank or the beneficiary.

A beneficiary can in no case avail itself of the contractual relationships existing between banks or between the applicant and the issuing bank.

b. An issuing bank should discourage any attempt by the applicant to include, as an integral part of the credit, copies of the underlying contract, proforma invoice and the like.

Article 5 Documents v. Goods, Services or Performance

Banks deal with documents and not with goods, services or performance to which the documents may relate.

Article 6 Availability, Expiry Date and Place for Presentation

a. A credit must state the bank with which it is available or whether it is available with any bank. A credit available with a nominated bank is also available with the issuing bank.

b. A credit must state whether it is available by sight payment, deferred payment, acceptance or negotiation.

c. A credit must not be issued available by a draft drawn on the applicant.

d. i. A credit must state an expiry date for presentation. An expiry date stated for honour or negotiation will be deemed to be an expiry date for presentation.

ii. The place of the bank with which the credit is available is the place for presentation. The place for presentation under a credit available with any bank is that of any bank. A place for presentation other than that of the issuing bank is in addition to the place of the issuing bank.

e. Except as provided in sub-article 29 (a), a presentation by or on behalf of the beneficiary must be made on or before the expiry date.

Article 7 Issuing Bank Undertaking

a. Provided that the stipulated documents are presented to the nominated bank or to the issuing bank and that they constitute a complying presentation, the issuing bank must honour if the credit is available by:

i. sight payment, deferred payment or acceptance with the issuing bank;

ii. sight payment with a nominated bank and that nominated bank does not pay;

iii. deferred payment with a nominated bank and that nominated bank does not incur its deferred payment undertaking or, having incurred its deferred payment undertaking, does not pay at maturity;
iv. acceptance with a nominated bank and that nominated bank does not accept a draft drawn on it or, having accepted a draft drawn on it, does not pay at maturity;
v. negotiation with a nominated bank and that nominated bank does not negotiate.

b. An issuing bank is irrevocably bound to honour as of the time it issues the credit.

c. An issuing bank undertakes to reimburse a nominated bank that has honoured or negotiated a complying presentation and forwarded the documents to the issuing bank. Reimbursement for the amount of a complying presentation under a credit available by acceptance or deferred payment is due at maturity, whether or not the nominated bank prepaid or purchased before maturity. An issuing bank's undertaking to reimburse a nominated bank is independent of the issuing bank's undertaking to the beneficiary.

Article 8 Confirming Bank Undertaking

a. Provided that the stipulated documents are presented to the confirming bank or to any other nominated bank and that they constitute a complying presentation, the confirming bank must:

i. honour, if the credit is available by:
a. sight payment, deferred payment or acceptance with the confirming bank;
b. sight payment with another nominated bank and that nominated bank does not pay;
c. deferred payment with another nominated bank and that nominated bank does not incur its deferred payment undertaking or, having incurred its deferred payment undertaking, does not pay at maturity;
d. acceptance with another nominated bank and that nominated bank does not accept a draft drawn on it or, having accepted a draft drawn on it, does not pay at maturity;
e. negotiation with another nominated bank and that nominated bank does not negotiate.
ii. negotiate, without recourse, if the credit is available by negotiation with the confirming bank.

b. A confirming bank is irrevocably bound to honour or negotiate as of the time it adds its confirmation to the credit.

c. A confirming bank undertakes to reimburse another nominated bank that has honoured or negotiated a complying presentation and forwarded the documents to the confirming bank. Reimbursement for the amount of a complying presentation under a credit available by acceptance or deferred payment is due at maturity, whether or not another nominated bank prepaid or purchased before maturity. A confirming bank's undertaking to reimburse another nominated bank is independent of the confirming bank's undertaking to the beneficiary.

d. If a bank is authorized or requested by the issuing bank to confirm a credit but is not prepared to do so, it must inform the issuing bank without delay and may advise the credit without confirmation.

Article 9   Advising of Credits and Amendments

a. A credit and any amendment may be advised to a beneficiary through an advising bank. An advising bank that is not a confirming bank advises the credit and any amendment without any undertaking to honour or negotiate.

b. By advising the credit or amendment, the advising bank signifies that it has satisfied itself as to the apparent authenticity of the credit or amendment and that the advice accurately reflects the terms and conditions of the credit or amendment received.

c. An advising bank may utilize the services of another bank ("second advising bank") to advise the credit and any amendment to the beneficiary. By advising the credit or amendment, the second advising bank signifies that it has satisfied itself as to the apparent authenticity of the advice it has received and that the advice accurately reflects the terms and conditions of the credit or amendment received.

d. A bank utilizing the services of an advising bank or second advising bank to advise a credit must use the same bank to advise any amendment thereto.

e. If a bank is requested to advise a credit or amendment but elects not to do so, it must so inform, without delay, the bank from which the credit, amendment or advice has been received.

f. If a bank is requested to advise a credit or amendment but cannot satisfy itself as to the apparent authenticity of the credit, the amendment or the advice, it must so inform, without delay, the bank from which the instructions appear to have been received. If the advising bank or second advising bank elects nonetheless to advise the credit or amendment, it must inform the beneficiary or second advising bank that it has not been able to satisfy itself as to the apparent authenticity of the credit, the amendment or the advice.

Article 10   Amendments

a. Except as otherwise provided by article 38, a credit can neither be amended nor cancelled without the agreement of the issuing bank, the confirming bank, if any, and the beneficiary.

b. An issuing bank is irrevocably bound by an amendment as of the time it issues the amendment. A confirming bank may extend its confirmation to an amendment and will be irrevocably bound as of the time it advises the amendment. A confirming bank may, however, choose to advise an amendment without extending its confirmation and, if so, it must inform the issuing bank without delay and inform the beneficiary in its advice.

c. The terms and conditions of the original credit (or a credit incorporating previously accepted amendments) will remain in force for the beneficiary until the beneficiary communicates its acceptance of the amendment to the bank that advised such amendment. The beneficiary should give notification of acceptance or rejection of an amendment. If the beneficiary fails to give such notification, a presentation that complies with the credit and to any not yet accepted amendment will be deemed to be notification of acceptance by the beneficiary of such amendment. As of that moment the credit will be amended.

d. A bank that advises an amendment should inform the bank from which it received the amendment of any notification of acceptance or rejection.

e. Partial acceptance of an amendment is not allowed and will be deemed to be notification of rejection of the amendment.

f. A provision in an amendment to the effect that the amendment shall enter into force unless rejected by the beneficiary within a certain time shall be disregarded.

Article 11 Teletransmitted and Pre-Advised Credits and Amendments

a. An authenticated teletransmission of a credit or amendment will be deemed to be the operative credit or amendment, and any subsequent mail confirmation shall be disregarded.

If a teletransmission states "full details to follow" (or words of similar effect), or states that the mail confirmation is to be the operative credit or amendment, then the teletransmission will not be deemed to be the operative credit or amendment. The issuing bank must then issue the operative credit or amendment without delay in terms not inconsistent with the teletransmission.

b. A preliminary advice of the issuance of a credit or amendment ("pre-advice") shall only be sent if the issuing bank is prepared to issue the operative credit or amendment. An issuing bank that sends a pre-advice is irrevocably committed to issue the operative credit or amendment, without delay, in terms not inconsistent with the pre-advice.

Article 12 Nomination

a. Unless a nominated bank is the confirming bank, an authorization to honour or negotiate does not impose any obligation on that nominated bank to honour or negotiate, except when expressly agreed to by that nominated bank and so communicated to the beneficiary.

b. By nominating a bank to accept a draft or incur a deferred payment undertaking, an issuing bank authorizes that nominated bank to prepay or purchase a draft accepted or a deferred payment undertaking incurred by that nominated bank.

c. Receipt or examination and forwarding of documents by a nominated bank that is not a confirming bank does not make that nominated bank liable to honour or negotiate, nor does it constitute honour or negotiation.

Article 13 Bank-to-Bank Reimbursement Arrangements

a. If a credit states that reimbursement is to be obtained by a nominated bank ("claiming bank") claiming on another party ("reimbursing bank"), the credit must state if the reimbursement is subject to the ICC rules for bank-to-bank reimbursements in effect on the date of issuance of the credit.

b. If a credit does not state that reimbursement is subject to the ICC rules for bank-to-bank reimbursements, the following apply:

i. An issuing bank must provide a reimbursing bank with a reimbursement authorization that conforms to the availability stated in the credit. The reimbursement authorization should not be subject to an expiry date.

ii. A claiming bank shall not be required to supply a reimbursing bank with a certificate of compliance with the terms and conditions of the credit.

iii. An issuing bank will be responsible for any loss of interest, together with any expenses incurred, if reimbursement is not provided on first demand by a reimbursing bank in accordance with the terms and conditions of the credit.

iv. A reimbursing bank's charges are for the account of the issuing bank. However, if the charges are for the account of the beneficiary, it is the responsibility of an issuing bank to so indicate in the credit and in the reimbursement authorization. If a reimbursing bank's charges are for the account of the beneficiary, they shall be deducted from the amount due to a claiming bank when reimbursement is made. If no reimbursement is made, the reimbursing bank's charges remain the obligation of the issuing bank.

c. An issuing bank is not relieved of any of its obligations to provide reimbursement if reimbursement is not made by a reimbursing bank on first demand.

Article 14   Standard for Examination of Documents

a. A nominated bank acting on its nomination, a confirming bank, if any, and the issuing bank must examine a presentation to determine, on the basis of the documents alone, whether or not the documents appear on their face to constitute a complying presentation.

b. A nominated bank acting on its nomination, a confirming bank, if any, and the issuing bank shall each have a maximum of five banking days following the day of presentation to determine if a presentation is complying. This period is not curtailed or otherwise affected by the occurrence on or after the date of presentation of any expiry date or last day for presentation.

c. A presentation including one or more original transport documents subject to articles 19, 20, 21, 22, 23, 24 or 25 must be made by or on behalf of the beneficiary not later than 21 calendar days after the date of shipment as described in these rules, but in any event not later than the expiry date of the credit.

d. Data in a document, when read in context with the credit, the document itself and international standard banking practice, need not be identical to, but must not conflict with, data in that document, any other stipulated document or the credit.

e. In documents other than the commercial invoice, the description of the goods, services or performance, if stated, may be in general terms not conflicting with their description in the credit.

f. If a credit requires presentation of a document other than a transport document, insurance document or commercial invoice, without stipulating by whom the document is to be issued or its data content, banks will accept the document as presented if its content appears to fulfil the function of the required document and otherwise complies with sub-article 14 (d).

g. A document presented but not required by the credit will be disregarded and may be returned to the presenter.

h. If a credit contains a condition without stipulating the document to indicate compliance with the condition, banks will deem such condition as not stated and will disregard it.

i. A document may be dated prior to the issuance date of the credit, but must not be dated later than its date of presentation.

j. When the addresses of the beneficiary and the applicant appear in any stipulated document, they need not be the same as those stated in the credit or in any other stipulated document, but must be within the same country as the respective addresses mentioned in the credit. Contact details (telefax, telephone, e-mail and the like) stated as part of the beneficiary's and the applicant's address will be disregarded. However, when the address and contact details of the applicant appear as part of the consignee or notify party details on a transport document subject to articles 19, 20, 21, 22, 23, 24 or 25, they must be as stated in the credit.

k. The shipper or consignor of the goods indicated on any document need not be the beneficiary of the credit.

l. A transport document may be issued by any party other than a carrier, owner, master or charterer provided that the transport document meets the requirements of articles 19, 20, 21, 22, 23 or 24 of these rules.

Article 15 Complying Presentation

a. When an issuing bank determines that a presentation is complying, it must honour.

b. When a confirming bank determines that a presentation is complying, it must honour or negotiate and forward the documents to the issuing bank.

c. When a nominated bank determines that a presentation is complying and honours or negotiates, it must forward the documents to the confirming bank or issuing bank.

Article 16 Discrepant Documents, Waiver and Notice

a. When a nominated bank acting on its nomination, a confirming bank, if any, or the issuing bank determines that a presentation does not comply, it may refuse to honour or negotiate.

b. When an issuing bank determines that a presentation does not comply, it may in its sole judgment approach the applicant for a waiver of the discrepancies. This does not, however, extend the period mentioned in sub-article 14 (b).

c. When a nominated bank acting on its nomination, a confirming bank, if any, or the issuing bank decides to refuse to honour or negotiate, it must give a single notice to that effect to the presenter.

The notice must state:

i. that the bank is refusing to honour or negotiate; and

ii. each discrepancy in respect of which the bank refuses to honour or negotiate; and

iii. a) that the bank is holding the documents pending further instructions from the presenter; or

b) that the issuing bank is holding the documents until it receives a waiver from the applicant and agrees to accept it, or receives further instructions from the presenter prior to agreeing to accept a waiver; or

c) that the bank is returning the documents; or

d) that the bank is acting in accordance with instructions previously received from the presenter.

d. The notice required in sub-article 16 (c) must be given by telecommunication or, if that is not possible, by other expeditious means no later than the close of the fifth banking day following the day of presentation.

e. A nominated bank acting on its nomination, a confirming bank, if any, or the issuing bank may, after providing notice required by sub-article 16 (c) (iii) (a) or (b), return the documents to the presenter at any time.

f. If an issuing bank or a confirming bank fails to act in accordance with the provisions of this article, it shall be precluded from claiming that the documents do not constitute a complying presentation.

g. When an issuing bank refuses to honour or a confirming bank refuses to honour or negotiate and has given notice to that effect in accordance with this article, it shall then be entitled to claim a refund, with interest, of any reimbursement made.

Article 17　Original Documents and Copies

a. At least one original of each document stipulated in the credit must be presented.

b. A bank shall treat as an original any document bearing an apparently original signature, mark, stamp, or label of the issuer of the document, unless the document itself indicates that it is not an original.

c. Unless a document indicates otherwise, a bank will also accept a document as original if it:

i. appears to be written, typed, perforated or stamped by the document issuer's hand; or

ii. appears to be on the document issuer's original stationery; or

iii. states that it is original, unless the statement appears not to apply to the document presented.

d. If a credit requires presentation of copies of documents, presentation of either originals or copies is permitted.

e. If a credit requires presentation of multiple documents by using terms such as "in duplicate", "in two fold" or "in two copies", this will be satisfied by the presentation of at least one original and the remaining number in copies, except when the document itself indicates otherwise.

Article 18   Commercial Invoice

a. A commercial invoice:

i. must appear to have been issued by the beneficiary, except as provided in article 38;

ii. must be made out in the name of the applicant, except as provided in sub-article 38 (g);

iii. must be made out in the same currency as the credit; and need not be signed.

b. A nominated bank acting on its nomination, a confirming bank, if any, or the issuing bank may accept a commercial invoice issued for an amount in excess of the amount permitted by the credit, and its decision will be binding upon all parties, provided the bank in question has not honoured or negotiated for an amount in excess of that permitted by the credit.

c. The description of the goods, services or performance in a commercial invoice must correspond with that appearing in the credit.

Article 19   Transport Document Covering at Least Two Different Modes of Transport

a. A transport document covering at least two different modes of transport (multimodal or combined transport document), however named, must appear to:

i. bear and be signed by:

a) the carrier or a named agent for or on behalf of the carrier, or

b) the master or a named agent for or on behalf of the master.

Any signature by the carrier, master or agent must be identified as that of the carrier, master or agent.

Any signature by an agent must indicate whether the agent has signed for or on behalf of the carrier or for or on behalf of the master.

ii. indicate that the goods have been dispatched, taken in charge or shipped on board at the place stated in the credit, by:

a) pre-printed wording, or

b) a stamp or notation indicating the date on which the goods have been dispatched, taken in charge or shipped on board.

The date of issuance of the transport document will be deemed to be the date of dispatch, taking in charge or shipped on board, and the date of shipment. However, if the transport document indicates, by stamp or notation, a date of dispatch, taking in charge or shipped on board, this date will be deemed to be the date of shipment.

    iii. indicate the place of dispatch, taking in charge or shipment and the place of final destination stated in the credit, even if:
        a) the transport document states, in addition, a different place of dispatch, taking in charge or shipment or place of final destination, or
        b) the transport document contains the indication "intended" or similar qualification in relation to the vessel, port of loading or port of discharge.
    iv. sole original transport document or, if issued in more than one original, be the full set as indicated on the transport document.
    v. contain terms and conditions of carriage or make reference to another source containing the terms and conditions of carriage (short form or blank back transport document). Contents of terms and conditions of carriage will not be examined.
    vi. contain no indication that it is subject to a charter party.

b. For the purpose of this article, transhipment means unloading from one means of conveyance and reloading to another means of conveyance (whether or not in different modes of transport) during the carriage from the place of dispatch, taking in charge or shipment to the place of final destination stated in the credit.

    c. i. A transport document may indicate that the goods will or may be transhipped provided that the entire carriage is covered by one and the same transport document.
       ii. A transport document indicating that transhipment will or may take place is acceptable, even if the credit prohibits transhipment.

Article 20   Bill of Lading

    a. A bill of lading, however named, must appear to:
       i. indicate the name of the carrier and be signed by:
         —the carrier or a named agent for or on behalf of the carrier, or
         —the master or a named agent for or on behalf of the master.

Any signature by the carrier, master or agent must be identified as that of the carrier, master or agent.

Any signature by an agent must indicate whether the agent has signed for or on behalf of the carrier or for or on behalf of the master.

       ii. indicate that the goods have been shipped on board a named vessel at the port of loading stated in the credit by:
         a) pre-printed wording, or
         b) an on board notation indicating the date on which the goods have been shipped on board.

The date of issuance of the bill of lading will be deemed to be the date of shipment unless the bill of lading contains an on board notation indicating the date of shipment, in which case the date stated in the on board notation will be deemed to be the date of shipment.

If the bill of lading contains the indication "intended vessel" or similar qualification in relation to the name of the vessel, an on board notation indicating the date of shipment and the name of the actual vessel is required.

    iii. indicate shipment from the port of loading to the port of discharge stated in the credit.

If the bill of lading does not indicate the port of loading stated in the credit as the port of loading, or if it contains the indication "intended" or similar qualification in relation to the port of loading, an on board notation indicating the port of loading as stated in the credit, the date of shipment and the name of the vessel is required. This provision applies even when loading on board or shipment on a named vessel is indicated by pre-printed wording on the bill of lading.

    iv. be the sole original bill of lading or, if issued in more than one original, be the full set as indicated on the bill of lading.

    v. contain terms and conditions of carriage or make reference to another source containing the terms and conditions of carriage (short form or blank back bill of lading). Contents of terms and conditions of carriage will not be examined.

    vi. contain no indication that it is subject to a charter party.

b. For the purpose of this article, transhipment means unloading from one vessel and reloading to another vessel during the carriage from the port of loading to the port of discharge stated in the credit.

    c. i. A bill of lading may indicate that the goods will or may be transhipped provided that the entire carriage is covered by one and the same bill of lading.

    ii. A bill of lading indicating that transhipment will or may take place is acceptable, even if the credit prohibits transhipment, if the goods have been shipped in a container, trailer or LASH barge as evidenced by the bill of lading.

d. Clauses in a bill of lading stating that the carrier reserves the right to tranship will be disregarded.

Article 21 Non-Negotiable Sea Waybill

a. A non-negotiable sea waybill, however named, must appear to:

i. indicate the name of the carrier and be signed by:

    a) the carrier or a named agent for or on behalf of the carrier, or

    b) the master or a named agent for or on behalf of the master.

Any signature by the carrier, master or agent must be identified as that of the carrier, master or agent.

Any signature by an agent must indicate whether the agent has signed for or on behalf of the carrier or for or on behalf of the master.

ii. indicate that the goods have been shipped on board a named vessel at the port of loading stated in the credit by:
   a) pre-printed wording, or
   b) an on board notation indicating the date on which the goods have been shipped on board.

The date of issuance of the non-negotiable sea waybill will be deemed to be the date of shipment unless the non-negotiable sea waybill contains an on board notation indicating the date of shipment, in which case the date stated in the on board notation will be deemed to be the date of shipment.

If the non-negotiable sea waybill contains the indication "intended vessel" or similar qualification in relation to the name of the vessel, an on board notation indicating the date of shipment and the name of the actual vessel is required.

   iii. indicate shipment from the port of loading to the port of discharge stated in the credit.

If the non-negotiable sea waybill does not indicate the port of loading stated in the credit as the port of loading, or if it contains the indication "intended" or similar qualification in relation to the port of loading, an on board notation indicating the port of loading as stated in the credit, the date of shipment and the name of the vessel is required. This provision applies even when loading on board or shipment on a named vessel is indicated by pre-printed wording on the non-negotiable sea waybill.

   iv. be the sole original non-negotiable sea waybill or, if issued in more than one original, be the full set as indicated on the non-negotiable sea waybill.
   v. contain terms and conditions of carriage or make reference to another source containing the terms and conditions of carriage (short form or blank back non-negotiable sea waybill). Contents of terms and conditions of carriage will not be examined.
   vi. contain no indication that it is subject to a charter party.

b. For the purpose of this article, transhipment means unloading from one vessel and reloading to another vessel during the carriage from the port of loading to the port of discharge stated in the credit.

   c. i. A non-negotiable sea waybill may indicate that the goods will or may be transhipped provided that the entire carriage is covered by one and the same non-negotiable sea waybill.
   ii. A non-negotiable sea waybill indicating that transhipment will or may take place is acceptable, even if the credit prohibits transhipment, if the goods have been shipped in a container, trailer or LASH barge as evidenced by the non-negotiable sea waybill.

d. Clauses in a non-negotiable sea waybill stating that the carrier reserves the right to tranship will be disregarded.

Article 22 Charter Party Bill of Lading

a. A bill of lading, however named, containing an indication that it is subject to a charter party (charter party bill of lading), must appear to:

   i. be signed by:

   a) the master or a named agent for or on behalf of the master, or

   b) the owner or a named agent for or on behalf of the owner, or

   c) the charterer or a named agent for or on behalf of the charterer.

Any signature by the master, owner, charterer or agent must be identified as that of the master, owner, charterer or agent.

Any signature by an agent must indicate whether the agent has signed for or on behalf of the master, owner or charterer.

An agent signing for or on behalf of the owner or charterer must indicate the name of the owner or charterer.

   ii. indicate that the goods have been shipped on board a named vessel at the port of loading stated in the credit by:

   a) pre-printed wording, or

   b) an on board notation indicating the date on which the goods have been shipped on board.

The date of issuance of the charter party bill of lading will be deemed to be the date of shipment unless the charter party bill of lading contains an on board notation indicating the date of shipment, in which case the date stated in the on board notation will be deemed to be the date of shipment.

   iii. indicate shipment from the port of loading to the port of discharge stated in the credit. The port of discharge may also be shown as a range of ports or a geographical area, as stated in the credit.

   iv. be the sole original charter party bill of lading or, if issued in more than one original, be the full set as indicated on the charter party bill of lading.

b. A bank will not examine charter party contracts, even if they are required to be presented by the terms of the credit.

Article 23 Air Transport Document

a. An air transport document, however named, must appear to:

   i. indicate the name of the carrier and be signed by:

   —the carrier, or

   —a named agent for or on behalf of the carrier.

Any signature by the carrier or agent must be identified as that of the carrier or agent.

Any signature by an agent must indicate that the agent has signed for or on behalf of the carrier.

   ii. indicate that the goods have been accepted for carriage.

   iii. indicate the date of issuance. This date will be deemed to be the date of shipment unless the air transport document contains a specific notation of the actual date of shipment, in which case the date stated in the notation will be deemed to be the date of shipment.

Any other information appearing on the air transport document relative to the flight number and date will not be considered in determining the date of shipment.

 iv. indicate the airport of departure and the airport of destination stated in the credit.

 v. be the original for consignor or shipper, even if the credit stipulates a full set of originals.

 vi. contain terms and conditions of carriage or make reference to another source containing the terms and conditions of carriage. Contents of terms and conditions of carriage will not be examined.

b. For the purpose of this article, transhipment means unloading from one aircraft and reloading to another aircraft during the carriage from the airport of departure to the airport of destination stated in the credit.

 c. i. An air transport document may indicate that the goods will or may be transhipped, provided that the entire carriage is covered by one and the same air transport document.

 ii. An air transport document indicating that transhipment will or may take place is acceptable, even if the credit prohibits transhipment.

Article 24 Road, Rail or Inland Waterway Transport Documents

a. A road, rail or inland waterway transport document, however named, must appear to:

 i. indicate the name of the carrier and:

  —be signed by the carrier or a named agent for or on behalf of the carrier, or

  —indicate receipt of the goods by signature, stamp or notation by the carrier or a named agent for or on behalf of the carrier.

Any signature, stamp or notation of receipt of the goods by the carrier or agent must be identified as that of the carrier or agent.

Any signature, stamp or notation of receipt of the goods by the agent must indicate that the agent has signed or acted for or on behalf of the carrier.

If a rail transport document does not identify the carrier, any signature or stamp of the railway company will be accepted as evidence of the document being signed by the carrier.

 ii. indicate the date of shipment or the date the goods have been received for shipment, dispatch or carriage at the place stated in the credit. Unless the transport document contains a dated reception, stamp, an indication of the date of receipt or a date of shipment, the date of issuance of the transport document will be deemed to be the date of shipment.

iii. indicate the place of shipment and the place of destination stated in the credit.

b. i. Road transport document must appear to be the original for consignor or shipper or bear no marking indicating for whom the document has been prepared.

ii. A rail transport document marked "duplicate" will be accepted as an original.

iii. A rail or inland waterway transport document will be accepted as an original whether marked as an original or not.

c. In the absence of an indication on the transport document as to the number of originals issued, the number presented will be deemed to constitute a full set.

d. For the purpose of this article, transhipment means unloading from one means of conveyance and reloading to another means of conveyance, within the same mode of transport, during the carriage from the place of shipment, dispatch or carriage to the place of destination stated in the credit.

e. i. A road, rail or inland waterway transport document may indicate that the goods will or may be transhipped provided that the entire carriage is covered by one and the same transport document.

ii. A road, rail or inland waterway transport document indicating that transhipment will or may take place is acceptable, even if the credit prohibits transhipment.

Article 25 Courier Receipt, Post Receipt or Certificate of Posting

a. A courier receipt, however named, evidencing receipt of goods for transport, must appear to:

i. indicate the name of the courier service and be stamped or signed by the named courier service at the place from which the credit states the goods are to be shipped; and

ii. indicate a date of pick-up or of receipt or wording to this effect. This date will be deemed to be the date of shipment.

b. A requirement that courier charges are to be paid or prepaid may be satisfied by a transport document issued by a courier service evidencing that courier charges are for the account of a party other than the consignee.

c. A post receipt or certificate of posting, however named, evidencing receipt of goods for transport, must appear to be stamped or signed and dated at the place from which the credit states the goods are to be shipped. This date will be deemed to be the date of shipment.

Article 26 "On Deck", "Shipper's Load and Count", "Said by Shipper to Contain" and Charges Additional to Freight

a. A transport document must not indicate that the goods are or will be loaded on deck. A clause on a transport document stating that the goods may be loaded on deck is acceptable.

b. A transport document bearing a clause such as "shipper's load and count" and "said by shipper to contain" is acceptable.

c. A transport document may bear a reference, by stamp or otherwise, to charges additional to the freight.

Article 27　Clean Transport Document

A bank will only accept a clean transport document. A clean transport document is one bearing no clause or notation expressly declaring a defective condition of the goods or their packaging. The word "clean" need not appear on a transport document, even if a credit has a requirement for that transport document to be "clean on board".

Article 28　Insurance Document and Coverage

a. An insurance document, such as an insurance policy, an insurance certificate or a declaration under an open cover, must appear to be issued and signed by an insurance company, an underwriter or their agents or their proxies.

Any signature by an agent or proxy must indicate whether the agent or proxy has signed for or on behalf of the insurance company or underwriter.

b. When the insurance document indicates that it has been issued in more than one original, all originals must be presented.

c. Cover notes will not be accepted.

d. An insurance policy is acceptable in lieu of an insurance certificate or a declaration under an open cover.

e. The date of the insurance document must be no later than the date of shipment, unless it appears from the insurance document that the cover is effective from a date not later than the date of shipment.

f. i. The insurance document must indicate the amount of insurance coverage and be in the same currency as the credit.

ii. A requirement in the credit for insurance coverage to be for a percentage of the value of the goods, of the invoice value or similar is deemed to be the minimum amount of coverage required.

If there is no indication in the credit of the insurance coverage required, the amount of insurance coverage must be at least 110% of the CIF or CIP value of the goods.

When the CIF or CIP value cannot be determined from the documents, the amount of insurance coverage must be calculated on the basis of the amount for which honour or negotiation is requested or the gross value of the goods as shown on the invoice, whichever is greater.

iii. The insurance document must indicate that risks are covered at least between the place of taking in charge or shipment and the place of discharge or final destination as stated in the credit.

g. A credit should state the type of insurance required and, if any, the additional risks to be covered. An insurance document will be accepted without regard to any risks that are not covered if the credit uses imprecise terms such as "usual risks" or "customary risks".

h. When a credit requires insurance against "all risks" and an insurance document is presented containing any "all risks" notation or clause, whether or not bearing the heading "all risks", the insurance document will be accepted without regard to any risks stated to be excluded.

i. An insurance document may contain reference to any exclusion clause.

j. An insurance document may indicate that the cover is subject to a franchise or excess (deductible).

Article 29 Extension of Expiry Date or Last Day for Presentation

a. If the expiry date of a credit or the last day for presentation falls on a day when the bank to which presentation is to be made is closed for reasons other than those referred to in article 36, the expiry date or the last day for presentation, as the case may be, will be extended to the first following banking day.

b. If presentation is made on the first following banking day, a nominated bank must provide the issuing bank or confirming bank with a statement on its covering schedule that the presentation was made within the time limits extended in accordance with sub-article 29 (a).

c. The latest date for shipment will not be extended as a result of sub-article 29 (a).

Article 30 Tolerance in Credit Amount, Quantity and Unit Prices

a. The words "about" or "approximately" used in connection with the amount of the credit or the quantity or the unit price stated in the credit are to be construed as allowing a tolerance not to exceed 10% more or 10% less than the amount, the quantity or the unit price to which they refer.

b. A tolerance not to exceed 5% more or 5% less than the quantity of the goods is allowed, provided the credit does not state the quantity in terms of a stipulated number of packing units or individual items and the total amount of the drawings does not exceed the amount of the credit.

c. Even when partial shipments are not allowed, a tolerance not to exceed 5% less than the amount of the credit is allowed, provided that the quantity of the goods, if stated in the credit, is shipped in full and a unit price, if stated in the credit, is not reduced or that sub-article 30 (b) is not applicable. This tolerance does not apply when the credit stipulates a specific tolerance or uses the expressions referred to in sub-article 30 (a).

Article 31 Partial Drawings or Shipments

a. Partial drawings or shipments are allowed.

b. A presentation consisting of more than one set of transport documents evidencing shipment commencing on the same means of conveyance and for the same journey, provided they indicate the same destination, will not be regarded as covering a partial shipment, even if they indicate different dates of shipment or different ports of loading, places of taking in charge or dispatch. If the presentation consists of more than one set of transport documents, the latest date of shipment as evidenced on any of the sets of transport documents will be regarded as the date of shipment.

A presentation consisting of one or more sets of transport documents evidencing shipment on more than one means of conveyance within the same mode of transport will be regarded as covering a partial shipment, even if the means of conveyance leave on the same day for the same destination.

c. A presentation consisting of more than one courier receipt, post receipt or certificate of posting will not be regarded as a partial shipment if the courier receipts, post receipts or certificates of posting appear to have been stamped or signed by the same courier or postal service at the same place and date and for the same destination.

Article 32 Instalment Drawings or Shipments

If a drawing or shipment by instalments within given periods is stipulated in the credit and any instalment is not drawn or shipped within the period allowed for that instalment, the credit ceases to be available for that and any subsequent instalment.

Article 33 Hours of Presentation

A bank has no obligation to accept a presentation outside of its banking hours.

Article 34 Disclaimer on Effectiveness of Documents

A bank assumes no liability or responsibility for the form, sufficiency, accuracy, genuineness, falsification or legal effect of any document, or for the general or particular conditions stipulated in a document or superimposed thereon; nor does it assume any liability or responsibility for the description, quantity, weight, quality, condition, packing, delivery, value or existence of the goods, services or other performance represented by any document, or for the good faith or acts or omissions, solvency, performance or standing of the consignor, the carrier, the forwarder, the consignee or the insurer of the goods or any other person.

Article 35 Disclaimer on Transmission and Translation

A bank assumes no liability or responsibility for the consequences arising out of delay, loss in transit, mutilation or other errors arising in the transmission of any messages or delivery of letters or documents, when such messages, letters or documents are transmitted or sent according to the requirements stated in the credit, or when the bank may have taken the initiative in the choice of the delivery service in the absence of such instructions in the credit.

If a nominated bank determines that a presentation is complying and forwards the documents to the issuing bank or confirming bank, whether or not the nominated bank has honoured or negotiated, an issuing bank or confirming bank must honour or negotiate, or reimburse that nominated bank, even when the documents have been lost in transit between the nominated bank and the issuing bank or confirming bank, or between the confirming bank and the issuing bank.

A bank assumes no liability or responsibility for errors in translation or interpretation of technical terms and may transmit credit terms without translating them.

Article 36 Force Majeure

A bank assumes no liability or responsibility for the consequences arising out of the interruption of its business by Acts of God, riots, civil commotions, insurrections, wars, acts of terrorism, or by any strikes or lockouts or any other causes beyond its control.

A bank will not, upon resumption of its business, honour or negotiate under a credit that expired during such interruption of its business.

Article 37 Disclaimer for Acts of an Instructed Party

a. A bank utilizing the services of another bank for the purpose of giving effect to the instructions of the applicant does so for the account and at the risk of the applicant.

b. An issuing bank or advising bank assumes no liability or responsibility should the instructions it transmits to another bank not be carried out, even if it has taken the initiative in the choice of that other bank.

c. A bank instructing another bank to perform services is liable for any commissions, fees, costs or expenses ("charges") incurred by that bank in connection with its instructions.

If a credit states that charges are for the account of the beneficiary and charges cannot be collected or deducted from proceeds, the issuing bank remains liable for payment of charges.

A credit or amendment should not stipulate that the advising to a beneficiary is conditional upon the receipt by the advising bank or second advising bank of its charges.

d. The applicant shall be bound by and liable to indemnify a bank against all obligations and responsibilities imposed by foreign laws and usages.

Article 38 Transferable Credits

a. A bank is under no obligation to transfer a credit except to the extent and in the manner expressly consented to by that bank.

b. For the purpose of this article:

Transferable credit means a credit that specifically states it is "transferable". A transferable credit may be made available in whole or in part to another beneficiary ("second beneficiary") at the request of the beneficiary ("first beneficiary").

Transferring bank means a nominated bank that transfers the credit or, in a credit available with any bank, a bank that is specifically authorized by the issuing bank to transfer and that transfers the credit. An issuing bank may be a transferring bank.

Transferred credit means a credit that has been made available by the transferring bank to a second beneficiary.

c. Unless otherwise agreed at the time of transfer, all charges (such as commissions, fees, costs or expenses) incurred in respect of a transfer must be paid by the first beneficiary.

d. A credit may be transferred in part to more than one second beneficiary provided partial drawings or shipments are allowed.

A transferred credit cannot be transferred at the request of a second beneficiary to any subsequent beneficiary. The first beneficiary is not considered to be a subsequent beneficiary.

e. Any request for transfer must indicate if and under what conditions amendments may be advised to the second beneficiary. The transferred credit must clearly indicate those conditions.

f. If a credit is transferred to more than one second beneficiary, rejection of an amendment by one or more second beneficiary does not invalidate the acceptance by any other second beneficiary, with respect to which the transferred credit will be amended accordingly. For any second beneficiary that rejected the amendment, the transferred credit will remain unamended.

g. The transferred credit must accurately reflect the terms and conditions of the credit, including confirmation, if any, with the exception of:
—the amount of the credit,
—any unit price stated therein,
—the expiry date,
—the period for presentation, or
—the latest shipment date or given period for shipment, any or all of which may be reduced or curtailed.

The percentage for which insurance cover must be effected may be increased to provide the amount of cover stipulated in the credit or these articles.

The name of the first beneficiary may be substituted for that of the applicant in the credit.

If the name of the applicant is specifically required by the credit to appear in any document other than the invoice, such requirement must be reflected in the transferred credit.

h. The first beneficiary has the right to substitute its own invoice and draft, if any, for those of a second beneficiary for an amount not in excess of that stipulated in the credit, and upon such substitution the first beneficiary can draw under the credit for the difference, if any, between its invoice and the invoice of a second beneficiary.

i. If the first beneficiary is to present its own invoice and draft, if any, but fails to do so on first demand, or if the invoices presented by the first beneficiary create discrepancies that did not exist in the presentation made by the second beneficiary and the first beneficiary fails to correct them on first demand, the transferring bank has the right to present the documents as received from the second beneficiary to the issuing bank, without further responsibility to the first beneficiary.

j. The first beneficiary may, in its request for transfer, indicate that honour or negotiation is to be effected to a second beneficiary at the place to which the credit has been transferred, up to and including the expiry date of the credit. This is without prejudice to the right of the first beneficiary in accordance with sub-article 38 (h).

k. Presentation of documents by or on behalf of a second beneficiary must be made to the transferring bank.

Article 39　Assignment of Proceeds

The fact that a credit is not stated to be transferable shall not affect the right of the beneficiary to assign any proceeds to which it may be or may become entitled under the credit, in accordance with the provisions of applicable law. This article relates only to the assignment of proceeds and not to the assignment of the right to perform under the credit.

Appendix 3 — UN Convention of Contracts for the International Sale of Goods

The States Parties to this Convention,

Bearing in mind the broad objectives in the resolutions adopted by the sixth special session of the General Assembly of the United Nations on the establishment of a New International Economic Order,

Considering that the development of international trade on the basis of equality and mutual benefit is an important element in promoting friendly relations among States,

Being of the Opinion that the adoption of uniform rules which govern contracts for the international sale of goods and take into account the different social, economic and legal systems would contribute to the removal of legal barriers in international trade and promote the development of international trade,

Have agreed as follows:

Part I Sphere of Application and General Provisions

CHAPTER I SPHERE OF APPLICATION

Article 1

(1) This Convention applies to contracts of sale of goods between parties whose places of business are in different States:

(a) when the States are Contracting States; or

(b) when the rules of private international law lead to the application of the law of a Contracting State.

(2) The fact that the parties have their places of business in different States is to be disregarded whenever this fact does not appear either from the contract or from any dealings between, or from information disclosed by, the parties at any time before or at the conclusion of the contract.

(3) Neither the nationality of the parties nor the civil or commercial character of the parties or of the contract is to be taken into consideration in determining the application of this Convention.

Article 2 This Convention does not apply to sales:

(a) of goods bought for personal, family or household use, unless the seller, at any time before or at the conclusion of the contract, neither knew nor ought to have known that the goods were bought for any such use;

(b) by auction;

(c) on execution or otherwise by authority of law;

(d) of stocks, shares, investment securities, negotiable instruments or money;

(e) of ships, vessels, hovercraft or aircraft;

(f) of electricity.

Article 3

(1) Contracts for the supply of goods to be manufactured or produced are to be considered sales unless the party who orders the goods undertakes to supply a substantial part of the materials necessary for such manufacture or production.

(2) This Convention does not apply to contracts in which the preponderant part of the obligations of the party who furnishes the goods consists in the supply of labour or other services.

Article 4 This Convention governs only the formation of the contract of sale and the rights and obligations of the seller and the buyer arising from such a contract. In particular, except as otherwise expressly provided in this Convention, it is not concerned with:

(a) the validity of the contract or of any of its provisions or of any usage;

(b) the effect which the contract may have on the property in the goods sold.

Article 5 This Convention does not apply to the liability of the seller for death or personal injury caused by the goods to any person.

Article 6 The parties may exclude the application of this Convention or, subject to article 12, derogate from or vary the effect of any of its provisions.

CHAPTER II GENERAL PROVISIONS

Article 7

(1) In the interpretation of this Convention, regard is to be had to its international character and to the need to promote uniformity in its application and the observance of good faith in international trade.

(2) Questions concerning matters governed by this Convention which are not expressly settled in it are to be settled in conformity with the general principles on which it is based or, in the absence of such principles, in conformity with the law applicable by virtue of the rules of private international law.

Article 8

(1) For the purposes of this Convention statements made by and other conduct of a party are to be interpreted according to his intent where the other party knew or could not have been unaware what that intent was.

(2) If the preceding paragraph is not applicable, statements made by and other conduct of a party are to be interpreted according to the understanding that a reasonable person of the same kind as the other party would have had in the same circumstances.

(3) In determining the intent of a party or the understanding a reasonable person would have had, due consideration is to be given to all relevant circumstances of the case including the negotiations, any practices which the parties have established between themselves, usages and any subsequent conduct of the parties.

Article 9

(1) The parties are bound by any usage to which they have agreed and by any practices which they have established between themselves.

(2) The parties are considered, unless otherwise agreed, to have impliedly made applicable to their contract or its formation a usage of which the parties knew or ought to have known and which in international trade is widely known to, and regularly observed by, parties to contracts of the type involved in the particular trade concerned.

Article 10 For the purposes of this Convention:

(a) if a party has more than one place of business, the place of business is that which has the closest relationship to the contract and its performance, having regard to the circumstances known to or contemplated by the parties at any time before or at the conclusion of the contract;

(b) if a party does not have a place of business, reference is to be made to his habitual residence.

Article 11 A contract of sale need not be concluded in or evidenced by writing and is not subject to any other requirement as to form. It may be proved by any means, including witnesses.

Article 12 Any provision of article 11, article 29 or Part II of this Convention that allows a contract of sale or its modification or termination by agreement or any offer, acceptance or other indication of intention to be made in any form other than in writing does not apply where any party has his place of business in a Contracting State which has made a declaration under article 96 of this Convention. The parties may not derogate from or vary the effect of this article.

Article 13 For the purposes of this Convention "writing" includes telegram and telex.

Part II Formation of the Contract

Article 14

(1) A proposal for concluding a contract addressed to one or more specific persons constitutes an offer if it is sufficiently definite and indicates the intention of the offeror to be bound in case of acceptance. A proposal is sufficiently definite if it indicates the goods and expressly or implicitly fixes or makes provision for determining the quantity and the price.

(2) A proposal other than one addressed to one or more specific persons is to be considered merely as an invitation to make offers, unless the contrary is clearly indicated by the person making the proposal.

Article 15

(1) An offer becomes effective when it reaches the offeree.

(2) An offer, even if it is irrevocable, may be withdrawn if the withdrawal reaches the offeree before or at the same time as the offer.

Article 16

(1) Until a contract is concluded an offer may be revoked if the revocation reaches the offeree before he has dispatched an acceptance.

(2) However, an offer cannot be revoked:

(a) if it indicates, whether by stating a fixed time for acceptance or otherwise, that it is irrevocable; or

(b) if it was reasonable for the offeree to rely on the offer as being irrevocable and the offeree has acted in reliance on the offer.

Article 17 An offer, even if it is irrevocable, is terminated when a rejection reaches the offeror.

Article 18

(1) A statement made by or other conduct of the offeree indicating assent to an offer is an acceptance. Silence or inactivity does not in itself amount to acceptance.

(2) An acceptance of an offer becomes effective at the moment the indication of assent reaches the offeror. An acceptance is not effective if the indication of assent does not reach the offeror within the time he has fixed or, if no time is fixed, within a reasonable time, due account being taken of the circumstances of the transaction, including the rapidity of the means of communication employed by the offeror. An oral offer must be accepted immediately unless the circumstances indicate otherwise.

(3) However, if, by virtue of the offer or as a result of practices which the parties have established between themselves or of usage, the offeree may indicate assent by performing an act, such as one relating to the dispatch of the goods or payment of the price, without notice to the offeror, the acceptance is effective at the moment the act is performed, provided that the act is performed within the period of time laid down in the preceding paragraph.

Article 19

(1) A reply to an offer which purports to be an acceptance but contains additions, limitations or other modifications is a rejection of the offer and constitutes a counteroffer.

(2) However, a reply to an offer which purports to be an acceptance but contains additional or different terms which do not materially alter the terms of the offer constitutes an acceptance, unless the offeror, without undue delay, objects orally to the discrepancy or dispatches a notice to that effect. If he does not so object, the terms of the contract are the terms of the offer with the modifications contained in the acceptance.

(3) Additional or different terms relating, among other things, to the price, payment, quality and quantity of the goods, place and time of delivery, extent of one party's liability

to the other or the settlement of disputes are considered to alter the terms of the offer materially.

Article 20

(1) A period of time for acceptance fixed by the offeror in a telegram or a letter begins to run from the moment the telegram is handed in for dispatch or from the date shown on the letter or, if no such date is shown, from the date shown on the envelope. A period of time for acceptance fixed by the offeror by telephone, telex or other means of instantaneous communication, begins to run from the moment that the offer reaches the offeree.

(2) Official holidays or non-business days occurring during the period for acceptance are included in calculating the period. However, if a notice of acceptance cannot be delivered at the address of the offeror on the last day of the period because that day falls on an official holiday or a non-business day at the place of business of the offeror, the period is extended until the first business day which follows.

Article 21

(1) A late acceptance is nevertheless effective as an acceptance if without delay the offeror orally so informs the offeree or dispatches a notice to that effect.

(2) If a letter or other writing containing a late acceptance shows that it has been sent in such circumstances that if its transmission had been normal it would have reached the offeror in due time, the late acceptance is effective as an acceptance unless, without delay, the offeror orally informs the offeree that he considers his offer as having lapsed or dispatches a notice to that effect.

Article 22 An acceptance may be withdrawn if the withdrawal reaches the offeror before or at the same time as the acceptance would have become effective.

Article 23 A contract is concluded at the moment when an acceptance of an offer becomes effective in accordance with the provisions of this Convention.

Article 24 For the purposes of this Part of the Convention, an offer, declaration of acceptance or any other indication of intention "reaches" the addressee when it is made orally to him or delivered by any other means to him personally, to his place of business or mailing address or, if he does not have a place of business or mailing address, to his habitual residence.

Part III Sale of Goods

CHAPTER I GENERAL PROVISIONS

Article 25 A breach of contract committed by one of the parties is fundamental if it results in such detriment to the other party as substantially to deprive him of what he is entitled to expect under the contract, unless the party in breach did not foresee and a reasonable person of the same kind in the same circumstances would not have foreseen such a result.

Article 26 A declaration of avoidance of the contract is effective only if made by notice to the other party.

Article 27 Unless otherwise expressly provided in this Part of the Convention, if any notice, request or other communication is given or made by a party in accordance with this Part and by means appropriate in the circumstances, a delay or error in the transmission of the communication or its failure to arrive does not deprive that party of the right to rely on the communication.

Article 28 If, in accordance with the provisions of this Convention, one party is entitled to require performance of any obligation by the other party, a court is not bound to enter a judgment for specific performance unless the court would do so under its own law in respect of similar contracts of sale not governed by this Convention.

Article 29

(1) A contract may be modified or terminated by the mere agreement of the parties.

(2) A contract in writing which contains a provision requiring any modification or termination by agreement to be in writing may not be otherwise modified or terminated by agreement. However, a party may be precluded by his conduct from asserting such a provision to the extent that the other party has relied on that conduct.

CHAPTER II OBLIGATIONS OF THE SELLER

Article 30 The seller must deliver the goods, hand over any documents relating to them and transfer the property in the goods, as required by the contract and this Convention.

Section I Delivery of the Goods and Handing Over of Documents

Article 31 If the seller is not bound to deliver the goods at any other particular place, his obligation to deliver consists:

(a) if the contract of sale involves carriage of the goods, in handing the goods over to the first carrier for transmission to the buyer;

(b) if, in cases not within the preceding sub-paragraph, the contract relates to specific goods, or unidentified goods to be drawn from a specific stock or to be manufactured or produced, and at the time of the conclusion of the contract the parties knew that the goods were at, or were to be manufactured or produced at, a particular place—in placing the goods at the buyer's disposal at that place;

(c) in other cases—in placing the goods at the buyer's disposal at the place where the seller had his place of business at the time of the conclusion of the contract.

Article 32

(1) If the seller, in accordance with the contract or this Convention, hands the goods

over to a carrier and if the goods are not clearly identified to the contract by markings on the goods, by shipping documents or otherwise, the seller must give the buyer notice of the consignment specifying the goods.

(2) If the seller is bound to arrange for carriage of the goods, he must make such contracts as are necessary for carriage to the place fixed by means of transportation appropriate in the circumstances and according to the usual terms for such transportation.

(3) If the seller is not bound to effect insurance in respect of the carriage of the goods, he must, at the buyer's request, provide him with all available information necessary to enable him to effect such insurance.

Article 33 The seller must deliver the goods:

(a) if a date is fixed by or determinable from the contract, on that date;

(b) if a period of time is fixed by or determinable from the contract, at any time within that period unless circumstances indicate that the buyer is to choose a date, or

(c) in any other case, within a reasonable time after the conclusion of the contract.

Article 34

If the seller is bound to hand over documents relating to the goods, he must hand them over at the time and place and in the form required by the contract. If the seller has handed over documents before that time, he may, up to that time, cure any lack of conformity in the documents, if the exercise of this right does not cause the buyer unreasonable inconvenience or unreasonable expense. However, the buyer retains any right to claim damages as provided for in this Convention.

Section II Conformity of the Goods and Third Party Claims

Article 35

(1) The seller must deliver goods which are of the quantity, quality and description required by the contract and which are contained or packaged in the manner required by the contract.

(2) Except where the parties have agreed otherwise, the goods do not conform with the contract unless they:

(a) are fit for the purposes for which goods of the same description would ordinarily be used;

(b) are fit for any particular purpose expressly or impliedly made known to the seller at the time of the conclusion of the contract, except where the circumstances show that the buyer did not rely, or that it was unreasonable for him to rely, on the seller's skill and judgment;

(c) possess the qualities of goods which the seller has held out to the buyer as a sample or model;

(d) are contained or packaged in the manner usual for such goods or, where there is no such manner, in a manner adequate to preserve and protect the goods.

(3) The seller is not liable under subparagraphs (a) to (d) of the preceding paragraph for any lack of conformity of the goods if at the time of the conclusion of the contract the buyer knew or could not have been unaware of such lack of conformity.

Article 36

(1) The seller is liable in accordance with the contract and this Convention for any lack of conformity which exists at the time when the risk passes to the buyer, even though the lack of conformity becomes apparent only after that time.

(2) The seller is also liable for any lack of conformity which occurs after the time indicated in the preceding paragraph and which is due to a breach of any of his obligations, including a breach of any guarantee that for a period of time the goods will remain fit for their ordinary purpose or for some particular purpose or will retain specified qualities or characteristics.

Article 37 If the seller has delivered goods before the date for delivery, he may, up to that date, deliver any missing part or make up any deficiency in the quantity of the goods delivered, or deliver goods in replacement of any non-conforming goods delivered or remedy any lack of conformity in the goods delivered, provided that the exercise of this right does not cause the buyer unreasonable inconvenience or unreasonable expense. However, the buyer retains any right to claim damages as provided for in this Convention.

Article 38

(1) The buyer must examine the goods, or cause them to be examined, within as short a period as is practicable in the circumstances.

(2) If the contract involves carriage of the goods, examination may be deferred until after the goods have arrived at their destination.

(3) If the goods are redirected in transit or redispatched by the buyer without a reasonable opportunity for examination by him and at the time of the conclusion of the contract the seller knew or ought to have known of the possibility of such redirection or redispatch, examination may be deferred until after the goods have arrived at the new destination.

Article 39

(1) The buyer loses the right to rely on a lack of conformity of the goods if he does not give notice to the seller specifying the nature of the lack of conformity within a reasonable time after he has discovered it or ought to have discovered it.

(2) In any event, the buyer loses the right to rely on a lack of conformity of the goods if he does not give the seller notice thereof at the latest within a period of two years from the date on which the goods were actually handed over to the buyer, unless this time-limit is inconsistent with a contractual period of guarantee.

Article 40 The seller is not entitled to rely on the provisions of articles 38 and 39 if the lack of conformity relates to facts of which he knew or could not have been unaware and which he did not disclose to the buyer.

Article 41 The seller must deliver goods which are free from any right or claim of a third party, unless the buyer agreed to take the goods subject to that right or claim. However, if such right or claim is based on industrial property or other intellectual property, the seller's obligation is governed by article 42.

Article 42

(1) The seller must deliver goods which are free from any right or claim of a third party based on industrial property or other intellectual property, of which at the time of the conclusion of the contract the seller knew or could not have been unaware, provided that the right or claim is based on industrial property or other intellectual property:

(a) under the law of the State where the goods will be resold or otherwise used, if it was contemplated by the parties at the time of the conclusion of the contract that the goods would be resold or otherwise used in that State; or

(b) in any other case, under the law of the State where the buyer has his place of business.

(2) The obligation of the seller under the preceding paragraph does not extend to cases where:

(a) at the time of the conclusion of the contract the buyer knew or could not have been unaware of the right or claim; or

(b) the right or claim results from the seller's compliance with technical drawings, designs, formulas or other such specifications furnished by the buyer.

Article 43

(1) The buyer loses the right to rely on the provisions of article 41 or article 42 if he does not give notice to the seller specifying the nature of the right or claim of the third party within a reasonable time after he has become aware or ought to have become aware of the right or claim.

(2) The seller is not entitled to rely on the provisions of the preceding paragraph if he knew of the right or claim of the third party and the nature of it.

Article 44

Notwithstanding the provisions of paragraph (1) of article 39 and paragraph (1) of article 43, the buyer may reduce the price in accordance with article 50 or claim damages, except for loss of profit, if he has reasonable excuse for his failure to give the required notice.

Section Ⅲ Remedies for Breach of Contract by the Seller

Article 45

(1) If the seller fails to perform any of his obligations under the contract or this Convention, the buyer may:

(a) exercise the rights provided in articles 46 to 52;

(b) claim damages as provided in articles 74 to 77.

(2) The buyer is not deprived of any right he may have to claim damages by exercising his right to other remedies.

(3) No period of grace may be granted to the seller by a court or arbitral tribunal when the buyer resorts to a remedy for breach of contract.

Article 46

(1) The buyer may require performance by the seller of his obligations unless the buyer has resorted to a remedy which is inconsistent with this requirement.

(2) If the goods do not conform with the contract, the buyer may require delivery of substitute goods only if the lack of conformity constitutes a fundamental breach of contract and a request for substitute goods is made either in conjunction with notice given under article 39 or within a reasonable time thereafter.

(3) If the goods do not conform with the contract, the buyer may require the seller to remedy the lack of conformity by repair, unless this is unreasonable having regard to all the circumstances. A request for repair must be made either in conjunction with notice given under article 39 or within a reasonable time thereafter.

Article 47

(1) The buyer may fix an additional period of time of reasonable length for performance by the seller of his obligations.

(2) Unless the buyer has received notice from the seller that he will not perform within the period so fixed, the buyer may not, during that period, resort to any remedy for breach of contract. However, the buyer is not deprived thereby of any right he may have to claim damages for delay in performance.

Article 48

(1) Subject to article 49, the seller may, even after the date for delivery, remedy at his own expense any failure to perform his obligations, if he can do so without unreasonable delay and without causing the buyer unreasonable inconvenience or uncertainty of reimbursement by the seller of expenses advanced by the buyer. However, the buyer retains any right to claim damages as provided for in this Convention.

(2) If the seller requests the buyer to make known whether he will accept performance and the buyer does not comply with the request within a reasonable time, the seller may perform within the time indicated in his request. The buyer may not, during that period of time, resort to any remedy which is inconsistent with performance by the seller.

(3) A notice by the seller that he will perform within a specified period of time is assumed to include a request, under the preceding paragraph, that the buyer make known his decision.

(4) A request or notice by the seller under paragraph (2) or (3) of this article is not effective unless received by the buyer.

Article 49

(1) The buyer may declare the contract avoided:

(a) if the failure by the seller to perform any of his obligations under the contract or this Convention amounts to a fundamental breach of contract; or

(b) in case of non-delivery, if the seller does not deliver the goods within the additional period of time fixed by the buyer in accordance with paragraph (1) of article 47 or declares that he will not deliver within the period so fixed.

(2) However, in cases where the seller has delivered the goods, the buyer loses the right to declare the contract avoided unless he does so:

(a) in respect of late delivery, within a reasonable time after he has become aware that delivery has been made;

(b) in respect of any breach other than late delivery, within reasonable time:

(i) after he knew or ought to have known of the breach;

(ii) after the expiration of any additional period of time fixed by the buyer in accordance with paragraph (1) of article 47, or after the seller has declared that he will not perform his obligations within such an additional period; or

(iii) after the expiration of any additional period of time indicated by the seller in accordance with paragraph (2) of article 48, or after the buyer has declared that he will not accept performance.

Article 50

If the goods do not conform with the contract and whether or not the price has already been paid, the buyer may reduce the price in the same proportion as the value that the goods actually delivered had at the time of the delivery bears to the value that conforming goods would have had at that time. However, if the seller remedies any failure to perform his obligations in accordance with article 37 or article 48 or if the buyer refuses to accept performance by the seller in accordance with those articles, the buyer may not reduce the price.

Article 51

(1) If the seller delivers only a part of the goods or if only a part of the goods delivered is in conformity with the contract, articles 46 to 50 apply in respect of the part which is missing or which does not conform.

(2) The buyer may declare the contract avoided in its entirety only if the failure to make delivery completely or in conformity with the contract amounts to a fundamental breach of the contract.

Article 52

(1) If the seller delivers the goods before the date fixed, the buyer may take delivery or refuse to take delivery.

(2) If the seller delivers a quantity of goods greater than that provided for in the contract, the buyer may take delivery or refuse to take delivery of the excess quantity. If the buyer takes delivery of all or part of the excess quantity, he must pay for it at the contract rate.

CHAPTER III OBLIGATIONS OF THE BUYER

Article 53   The buyer must pay the price for the goods and take delivery of them as required by the contract and this Convention.

Section I Payment of the Price

Article 54   The buyer's obligation to pay the price includes taking such steps and complying with such formalities as may be required under the contract or any laws and regulations to enable payment to be made.

Article 55   Where a contract has been validly concluded but does not expressly or implicitly fix or make provision for determining the price, the parties are considered, in the absence of any indication to the contrary, to have impliedly made reference to the price generally charged at the time of the conclusion of the contract for such goods sold under comparable circumstances in the trade concerned.

Article 56   If the price is fixed according to the weight of the goods, in case of doubt it is to be determined by the net weight.

Article 57

(1) If the buyer is not bound to pay the price at any other particular place, he must pay it to the seller:

(a) at the seller's place of business; or

(b) if the payment is to be made against the handing over of the goods or of documents, at the place where the handing over takes place.

(2) The seller must bear any increase in the expenses incidental to payment which is caused by a change in his place of business subsequent to the conclusion of the contract.

Article 58

(1) If the buyer is not bound to pay the price at any other specific time, he must pay it when the seller places either the goods or documents controlling their disposition at the buyer's disposal in accordance with the contract and this Convention. The seller may make such payment a condition for handing over the goods or documents.

(2) If the contract involves carriage of the goods, the seller may dispatch the goods on terms whereby the goods, or documents controlling their disposition, will not be handed over to the buyer except against payment of the price.

(3) The buyer is not bound to pay the price until he has had an opportunity to examine the goods, unless the procedures for delivery or payment agreed upon by the parties are inconsistent with his having such an opportunity.

Article 59   The buyer must pay the price on the date fixed by or determinable from the contract and this Convention without the need for any request or compliance with any formality on the part of the seller.

Section II Taking Delivery

Article 60 The buyer's obligation to take delivery consists:
(a) in doing all the acts which could reasonably be expected of him in order to enable the seller to make delivery; and
(b) in taking over the goods.

Section III Remedies for Breach of Contract by the Buyer

Article 61
(1) If the buyer fails to perform any of his obligations under the contract or this Convention, the seller may:
(a) exercise the rights provided in articles 62 to 65;
(b) claim damages as provided in articles 74 to 77.
(2) The seller is not deprived of any right he may have to claim damages by exercising his right to other remedies.
(3) No period of grace may be granted to the buyer by a court or arbitral tribunal when the seller resorts to a remedy for breach of contract.

Article 62 The seller may require the buyer to pay the price, take delivery or perform his other obligations, unless the seller has resorted to a remedy which is inconsistent with this requirement.

Article 63
(1) The seller may fix an additional period of time of reasonable length for performance by the buyer of his obligations.
(2) Unless the seller has received notice from the buyer that he will not perform within the period so fixed, the seller may not, during that period, resort to any remedy for breach of contract. However, the seller is not deprived thereby of any right he may have to claim damages for delay in performance.

Article 64
(1) The seller may declare the contract avoided:
(a) if the failure by the buyer to perform any of his obligations under the contract or this Convention amounts to a fundamental breach of contract; or
(b) if the buyer does not, within the additional period of time fixed by the seller in accordance with paragraph (1) of article 63, perform his obligation to pay the price or take delivery of the goods, or if he declares that he will not do so within the period so fixed.
(2) However, in cases where the buyer has paid the price, the seller loses the right to declare the contract avoided unless he does so:

(a) in respect of late performance by the buyer, before the seller has become aware that performance has been rendered; or

(b) in respect of any breach other than late performance by the buyer, within a reasonable time:

(i) after the seller knew or ought to have known of the breach; or

(ii) after the expiration of any additional period of time fixed by the seller in accordance with paragraph (1) of article 63, or after the buyer has declared that he will not perform his obligations within such an additional period.

Article 65

(1) If under the contract the buyer is to specify the form, measurement or other features of the goods and he fails to make such specification either on the date agreed upon or within a reasonable time after receipt of a request from the seller, the seller may, without prejudice to any other rights he may have, make the specification himself in accordance with the requirements of the buyer that may be known to him.

(2) If the seller makes the specification himself, he must inform the buyer of the details thereof and must fix a reasonable time within which the buyer may make a different specification. If, after receipt of such a communication, the buyer fails to do so within the time so fixed, the specification made by the seller is binding.

CHAPTER IV PASSING OF RISK

Article 66 Loss of or damage to the goods after the risk has passed to the buyer does not discharge him from his obligation to pay the price, unless the loss or damage is due to an act or omission of the seller.

Article 67

(1) If the contract of sale involves carriage of the goods and the seller is not bound to hand them over at a particular place, the risk passes to the buyer when the goods are handed over to the first carrier for transmission to the buyer in accordance with the contract of sale. If the seller is bound to hand the goods over to a carrier at a particular place, the risk does not pass to the buyer until the goods are handed over to the carrier at that place. The fact that the seller is authorized to retain documents controlling the disposition of the goods does not affect the passage of the risk.

(2) Nevertheless, the risk does not pass to the buyer until the goods are clearly identified to the contract, whether by markings on the goods, by shipping documents, by notice given to the buyer or otherwise.

Article 68 The risk in respect of goods sold in transit passes to the buyer from the time of the conclusion of the contract. However, if the circumstances so indicate, the risk is assumed by the buyer from the time the goods were handed over to the carrier who issued the documents embodying the contract of carriage. Nevertheless, if at the time of the conclusion of the contract of sale the seller knew or ought to have known that the goods had been lost or damaged and did not disclose this to the buyer, the loss or damage is at the risk of the seller.

Article 69

(1) In cases not within articles 67 and 68, the risk passes to the buyer when he takes over the goods or, if he does not do so in due time, from the time when the goods are placed at his disposal and he commits a breach of contract by failing to take delivery.

(2) However, if the buyer is bound to take over the goods at a place other than a place of business of the seller, the risk passes when delivery is due and the buyer is aware of the fact that the goods are placed at his disposal at that place.

(3) If the contract relates to goods not then identified, the goods are considered not to be placed at the disposal of the buyer until they are clearly identified to the contract.

Article 70 If the seller has committed a fundamental breach of contract, articles 67, 68 and 69 do not impair the remedies available to the buyer on account of the breach.

CHAPTER V PROVISIONS COMMON TO THE OBLIGATIONS OF THE SELLER AND OF BUYER

Section I Anticipatory Breach and Installment Contracts

Article 71

(1) A party may suspend the performance of his obligations if, after the conclusion of the contract, it becomes apparent that the other party will not perform a substantial part of his obligations as a result of:

(a) a serious deficiency in his ability of perform or in his creditworthiness; or

(b) his conduct in preparing to perform or in performing the contract.

(2) If the seller has already dispatched the goods before the grounds described in the preceding paragraph become evident, he may prevent the handing over of the goods to the buyer even though the buyer holds a document which entitles him to obtain them. The present paragraph relates only to the rights in the goods as between the buyer and the seller.

(3) A party suspending performance, whether before or after dispatch of the goods, must immediately give notice of the suspension to the other party and must continue with performance if the other party provides adequate assurance of his performance.

Article 72

(1) If prior to the date for performance of the contract it is clear that one of the parties will commit a fundamental breach of contract, the other party may declare the contract avoided.

(2) If time allows, the party intending to declare the contract avoided must give reasonable notice to the other party in order to permit him to provide adequate assurance of his performance.

(3) The requirements of the preceding paragraph do not apply if the other party has declared that he will not perform his obligations.

Article 73

(1) In the case of a contract for delivery of goods by installments, if the failure of one party to perform any of his obligations in respect of any installment constitutes a fundamental breach of contract with respect to that installment, the other party may declare the contract avoided with respect to that installment.

(2) If one party's failure to perform any of his obligations in respect of any installment gives the other party good grounds to conclude that a fundamental breach of contract will occur with respect to future installments, he may declare the contract avoided for the future, provided that he does so within a reasonable time.

(3) A buyer who declares the contract avoided in respect of any delivery may, at the same time, declare it avoided in respect of deliveries already made or of future deliveries if, by reason of their interdependence, those deliveries could not be used for the purpose contemplated by the parties at the time of the conclusion of the contract.

Section II Damages

Article 74 Damages for breach of contract by one party consist of a sum equal to the loss, including loss of profit, suffered by the other party as a consequence of the breach. Such damages may not exceed the loss which the party in breach foresaw or ought to have foreseen at the time of the conclusion of the contract, in the light of the facts and matters of which he then knew or ought to have known, as a possible consequence of the breach of contract.

Article 75 If the contract is avoided and if, in a reasonable manner and within a reasonable time after avoidance, the buyer has bought goods in replacement or the seller has resold the goods, the party claiming damages may recover the difference between the contract price and the price in the substitute transaction as well as any further damages recoverable under article 74.

Article 76

(1) If the contract is avoided and there is a current price for the goods, the party claiming damages may, if he has not made a purchase or resale under article 75, recover the difference between the price fixed by the contract and the current price at the time of avoidance as well as any further damages recoverable under article 74. If, however, the party claiming damages has avoided the contract after taking over the goods, the current price at the time of such taking over shall be applied instead of the current price at the time of avoidance.

(2) For the purposes of the preceding paragraph, the current price is the price prevailing at the place where delivery of the goods should have been made or, if there is

no current price at that place, the price at such other place as serves as a reasonable substitute, making due allowance for differences in the cost of transporting the goods.

Article 77 A party who relies on a breach of contract must take such measures as are reasonable in the circumstances to mitigate the loss, including loss of profit, resulting from the breach. If he fails to take such measures, the party in breach may claim a reduction in the damages in the amount by which the loss should have been mitigated.

Section III Interest

Article 78 If a party fails to pay the price or any other sum that is in arrears, the other party is entitled to interest on it, without prejudice to any claim for damages recoverable under article 74.

Section IV Exemptions

Article 79

(1) A party is not liable for a failure to perform any of his obligations if he proves that the failure was due to an impediment beyond his control and that he could not reasonably be expected to have taken the impediment into account at the time of the conclusion of the contract or to have avoided or overcome it or its consequences.

(2) If the party's failure is due to the failure by a third person whom he has engaged to perform the whole or a part of the contract, that party is exempt from liability only if:

(a) he is exempt under the preceding paragraph; and

(b) the person whom he has so engaged would be so exempt if the provisions of that paragraph were applied to him.

(3) The exemption provided by this article has effect for the period during which the impediment exists.

(4) The party who fails to perform must give notice to the other party of the impediment and its effect on his ability to perform. If the notice is not received by the other party within a reasonable time after the party who fails to perform knew or ought to have known of the impediment, he is liable for damages resulting from such nonreceipt.

(5) Nothing in this article prevents either party from exercising any right other than to claim damages under this Convention.

Article 80 A party may not rely on a failure of the other party to perform, to the extent that such failure was caused by the first party's act or omission.

Appendix 3 UN Convention of Contracts for the International Sale of Goods

Section V Effects of Avoidance

Article 81

(1) Avoidance of the contract releases both parties from their obligations under it, subject to any damages which may be due. Avoidance does not affect any provision of the contract for the settlement of disputes or any other provision of the contract governing the rights and obligations of the parties consequent upon the avoidance of the contract.

(2) A party who has performed the contract either wholly or in part may claim restitution from the other party of whatever the first party has supplied or paid under the contract. If both parties are bound to make restitution, they must do so concurrently.

Article 82

(1) The buyer loses the right to declare the contract avoided or to require the seller to deliver substitute goods if it is impossible for him to make restitution of the goods substantially in the condition in which he received them.

(2) The preceding paragraph does not apply:

(a) if the impossibility of making restitution of the goods or of making restitution of the goods substantially in the condition in which the buyer received them is not due to his act or omission;

(b) if the goods or part of the goods have perished or deteriorated as a result of the examination provided for in article 38; or

(c) if the goods or part of the goods have been sold in the normal course of business or have been consumed or transformed by the buyer in the course of normal use before he discovered or ought to have discovered the lack of conformity.

Article 83 A buyer who has lost the right to declare the contract avoided or to require the seller to deliver substitute goods in accordance with article 82 retains all other remedies under the contract and this Convention.

Article 84

(1) If the seller is bound to refund the price, he must also pay interest on it, from the date on which the price was paid.

(2) The buyer must account to the seller for all benefits which he has derived from the goods or part of them:

(a) if he must make restitution of the goods or part of them; or

(b) if it is impossible for him to make restitution of all or part of the goods or to make restitution of all or part of the goods substantially in the condition in which he received them, but he has nevertheless declared the contract avoided or required the seller to deliver substitute goods.

Section VI Preservation of the Goods

Article 85 If the buyer is in delay in taking delivery of the goods or, where payment of the price and delivery of the goods are to be made concurrently, if he fails to pay the price, and the seller is either in possession of the goods or otherwise able to control their disposition, the seller must take such steps as are reasonable in the circumstances to preserve them. He is entitled to retain them until he has been reimbursed his reasonable expenses by the buyer.

Article 86

(1) If the buyer has received the goods and intends to exercise any right under the contract or this Convention to reject them, he must take such steps to preserve them as are reasonable in the circumstances. He is entitled to retain them until he has been reimbursed his reasonable expenses by the seller.

(2) If goods dispatched to the buyer have been placed at his disposal at their destination and he exercises the right to reject them, he must take possession of them on behalf of the seller, provided that this can be done without payment of the price and without unreasonable inconvenience or unreasonable expense. This provision does not apply if the seller or a person authorized to take charge of the goods on his behalf is present at the destination. If the buyer takes possession of the goods under this paragraph, his rights and obligations are governed by the preceding paragraph.

Article 87

A party who is bound to take steps to preserve the goods may deposit them in a warehouse of a third person at the expense of the other party provided that the expense incurred is not unreasonable.

Article 88

(1) A party who is bound to preserve the goods in accordance with articles 85 or 86 may sell them by any appropriate means if there has been an unreasonable delay by the other party in taking possession of the goods or in taking them back or in paying the price or the cost of preservation, provided that reasonable notice of the intention to sell has been given to the other party.

(2) If the goods are subject to rapid deterioration or their preservation would involve unreasonable expense, a party who is bound to preserve the goods in accordance with article 85 or 86 must take reasonable measures to sell them. To the extent possible he must give notice to the other party of his intention to sell.

(3) A party selling the goods has the right to retain out of the proceeds of sale an amount equal to the reasonable expenses of preserving the goods, and of selling them. He must account to the other party for the balance.

Part IV Final Provisions

Article 89   The Secretary-General of the United Nations is hereby designated as the depositary for this Convention.

Article 90

This Convention does not prevail over any international agreement which has already been or may be entered into and which contains provisions concerning the matters governed by this Convention, provided that the parties have their places of business in States parties to such agreement.

Article 91

(1) This Convention is open for signature at the concluding meeting of the United Nations Conference on Contracts for the International Sale of Goods and will remain open for signature by all States at the Headquarters of the United Nations, New York until September 30, 1981.

(2) This Convention is subject to ratification, acceptance or approval by the signatory States.

(3) This Convention is open for accession by all States which are not signatory States as from the date it is open for signature.

(4) Instruments of ratification, acceptance, approval and accession are to be deposited with the Secretary-General of the United Nations.

Article 92

(1) A Contracting State may declare at the time of signature, ratification, acceptance, approval or accession that it will not be bound by Part II of this Convention or that it will not be bound by Part III of this Convention.

(2) A Contracting State which makes a declaration in accordance with the preceding paragraph in respect of Part II or Part III of this Convention is not to be considered a Contracting State within paragraph (1) of article 1 of this Convention in respect of matters governed by the part to which the declaration applies.

Article 93

(1) If a Contracting State has two or more territorial units in which, according to its constitution, different systems of law are applicable in relation to the matters dealt with in this Convention, it may, at the time of signature, ratification, acceptance, approval or accession, declare that this Convention is to extend to all its territorial units or only to one or more of them, and may amend its declaration by submitting another declaration at any time.

(2) These declarations are to be notified to the depositary and are to state expressly the territorial units to which the Convention extends.

(3) If, by virtue of a declaration under this article, this Convention extends to one or

more but not all of the territorial units of a Contracting State, and if the place of business of a party is located in that State, this place of business, for the purposes of this Convention, is considered not to be in a Contracting State, unless it is in a territorial unit to which the Convention extends.

(4) If a Contracting State makes no declaration under paragraph (1) of this article, the Convention is to extend to all territorial units of that State.

Article 94

(1) Two or more Contracting States which have the same or closely related legal rules on matters governed by this Convention may at any time declare that the Convention is not to apply to contracts of sale or to their formation where the parties have their places of business in those States. Such declarations may be made jointly or by reciprocal unilateral declarations.

(2) A Contracting State which has the same or closely related legal rules on matters governed by this Convention as one or more Non-Contracting States may at any time declare that the Convention is not to apply to contracts of sale or to their formation where the parties have their places of business in those states.

(3) If a State which is the object of a declaration under the preceding paragraph subsequently becomes a Contracting State, the declaration made will, as from the date on which the Convention enters into force in respect of the new Contracting State, have the effect of a declaration made under paragraph (1), provided that the new Contracting State joins in such declaration or makes a reciprocal unilateral declaration.

Article 95 Any State may declare at the time of the deposit of its instrument of ratification, acceptance, approval or accession that it will not be bound by subparagraph (1) (b) of article 1 of this Convention.

Article 96 A Contracting State whose legislation requires contracts of sale to be concluded in or evidenced by writing may at any time make a declaration in accordance with article 12 that any provision of article 11, article 29, or Part II of this Convention, that allows a contract of sale or its modification or termination by agreement or any offer, acceptance, or other indication of intention to be made in any form other than in writing, does not apply where any party has his place of business in that State.

Article 97

(1) Declarations made under this Convention at the time of signature are subject to confirmation upon ratification, acceptance or approval.

(2) Declarations and confirmations of declarations are to be in writing and be formally notified to the depositary.

(3) A declaration takes effect simultaneously with the entry into force of this Convention in respect of the State concerned. However, a declaration of which the depositary receives formal notification after such entry into force takes effect on the first day of the month following the expiration of six months after the date of its receipt by the

depositary. Reciprocal unilateral declarations under article 94 take effect on the first day of the month following the expiration of six months after the receipt of the latest declaration by the depositary.

(4) Any State which makes a declaration under this Convention may withdraw it at any time by a formal notification in writing addressed to the depositary. Such withdrawal is to take effect on the first day of the month following the expiration of six months after the date of the receipt of the notification by the depositary.

(5) A withdrawal of a declaration made under article 94 renders inoperative, as from the date on which the withdrawal takes effect, any reciprocal declaration made by another State under that article.

Article 98 No reservations are permitted except those expressly authorized in this Convention.

Article 99

(1) This Convention enters into force, subject to the provisions of paragraph (6) of this article, on the first day of the month following the expiration of twelve months after the date of deposit of the tenth instrument of ratification, acceptance, approval or accession, including an instrument which contains a declaration made under article 92.

(2) When a State ratifies, accepts, approves or accedes to this Convention after the deposit of the tenth instrument of ratification, acceptance, approval or accession, this Convention, with the exception of the part excluded, enters into force in respect of that State, subject to the provisions of paragraph (6) of this article, on the first day of the month following the expiration of twelve months after the date of the deposit of its instrument of ratification, acceptance, approval or accession.

(3) A State which ratifies, accepts, approves or accedes to this Convention and is a party to either or both the Convention relating to a Uniform Law on the Formation of Contracts for the International Sale of Goods done at The Hague on 1 July 1964 (1964 Hague Formation Convention) and the Convention relating to a Uniform Law on the International Sale of Goods done at The Hague on 1 July 1964 (1964 Hague Sales Convention) shall at the same time denounce, as the case may be, either or both the 1964 Hague Sales Convention and the 1964 Hague Formation Convention by notifying the Government of the Netherlands to that effect.

(4) A State party to the 1964 Hague Sales Convention which ratifies, accepts, approves or accedes to the present Convention and declares or has declared under article 92 that it will not be bound by Part II of this Convention shall at the time of ratification, acceptance, approval or accession denounce the 1964 Hague Sales Convention by notifying the Government of the Netherlands to that effect.

(5) A State party to the 1964 Hague Formation Convention which ratifies, accepts, approves or accedes to the present Convention and declares or has declared under article 92 that it will not be bound by Part III of this Convention shall at the time of ratification,

acceptance, approval or accession denounce the 1964 Hague Formation Convention by notifying the Government of the Netherlands to that effect.

(6) For the purpose of this article, ratifications, acceptances, approvals and accessions in respect of this Convention by States parties to the 1964 Hague Formation Convention or to the 1964 Hague Sales Convention shall not be effective until such denunciations as may be required on the part of those States in respect of the latter two Conventions have themselves become effective. The depositary of this Convention shall consult with the Government of the Netherlands, as the depositary of the 1964 Conventions, so as to ensure necessary coordination in this respect.

Article 100

(1) This Convention applies to the formation of a contract only when the proposal for concluding the contract is made on or after the date when the Convention enters into force in respect of the Contracting States referred to in subparagraph (1)(a) or the Contracting State referred to in subparagraph (1)(b) of article 1.

(2) This Convention applies only to contracts concluded on or after the date when the Convention enters into force in respect of the Contracting States referred to in subparagraph (1)(a) or the Contracting State referred to in subparagraph (1)(b) of article 1.

Article 101

(1) A Contracting State may denounce this Convention, or Part II or Part III of the Convention, by a formal notification in writing addressed to the depositary.

(2) The denunciation takes effect on the first day of the month following the expiration of twelve months after the notification is received by the depositary. Where a longer period for the denunciation to take effect is specified in the notification, the denunciation takes effect upon the expiration of such longer period after the notification is received by the depositary.

Done at Vienna, this day of eleventh day of April, one thousand nine hundred and eighty, in a single original, of which the Arabic, Chinese, English, French, Russian and Spanish texts are equally authentic.

In witness whereof the undersigned plenipotentiaries, being duly authorized by their respective Governments, have signed this Convention.

Appendix 4　List of Common Imports and Exports

live animals	活动物
meat and edible meat offal	肉及食用杂碎
fish and crustaceans	鱼、甲壳动物
molluscs and other aquatic invertebrates	软体动物及其他水生无脊椎动物
dairy products	乳品
birds' eggs	蛋品
natural honey	天然蜂蜜
edible products of animal origin	食用动物产品
vegetable products	植物产品
live trees and other plants	活树及其他活植物
bulbs, roots and the like	鳞茎、根及类似品
cut flowers	插花
ornamental foliage	装饰用簇叶
edible vegetables and roots and tubers	食用蔬菜、根及块
edible fruit and nuts	食用水果及坚果
peel of citrus fruit or melons	柑橘属水果或甜瓜的果皮
coffee, tea, mate	咖啡、茶、马黛茶
spices	调味香料
cereals	谷物
products of the milling industry	制粉工业产品
malt	麦芽
starches	淀粉
inulin	菊粉
wheat gluten	面筋
oil seeds and oleaginous fruits	含油子仁及果实
industrial or medicinal plants	工业用或药用植物
straw and fodder	稻草、秸秆及饲料
lac	虫胶
gums, resins	树胶、树脂
vegetable saps and extracts	植物液、汁
vegetable plaiting materials	编结用植物材料

animal or vegetable fats and oils	动植物油、脂
cleavage products	分解产品
prepared edible fats	食用油脂
animal or vegetable waxes	动植物蜡
prepared foodstuffs	食品
beverages	饮料
spirits	酒
vinegar	醋
tobacco	烟草
manufactured tobacco substitutes	烟草代用品的制品
sugar and sugar confectionery	糖及糖果
cocoa and cocoa preparations	可可及可可制品
preparations of cereals, flour, starch or milk	谷物、粮食粉、淀粉或乳的制品
pastry cooks' products	糕饼点心
miscellaneous edible preparations	杂项食品
residues and waste from the food industries	食品工业的残渣及废料
prepared animal fodder	配制的动物饲料
mineral products	矿产品
salt	盐
sulphur	硫黄
earth and stone	泥土及石料
plastering materials	石膏料
lime and cement	石灰及水泥
ores, slag and ash	矿砂、矿渣及矿灰
mineral fuels	矿物燃料
mineral oils	矿物油
crude petroleum	原油
bituminous substances	沥青物质
mineral waxes	矿物蜡
products of the chemical industry	化学工业产品
products of allied industries	相关工业的产品
inorganic chemicals	无机化学品
organic and inorganic compounds	有机及无机化合物
precious metals	贵金属
rare-earth metals	稀土金属
radioactive elements or isotopes	放射性元素及其同位素
organic chemicals	有机化学品
pharmaceutical products	药品
fertilizers	肥料

tanning or dyeing extracts	鞣料浸膏及染料浸膏
tannins and their derivatives	鞣酸及其衍生物
dyes, pigments and other coloring matter	染料、颜料及其他着色料
paints and varnishes	油漆及清漆
putty and other mastics	油灰及其他类似胶粘剂
inks	墨水、油墨
essential oils and resinoids	精油及香膏
perfumery preparations	芳香料制品
cosmetic or toilet preparations	化妆盥洗品
soap	肥皂
organic surface-active agents	有机表面活性剂
washing preparations	洗涤剂
lubricating preparations	润滑剂
artificial waxes	人造蜡
prepared waxes	调制蜡
polishing or scouring preparations	光洁剂
candles and similar articles	蜡烛及类似品
modelling pastes	塑型用膏
dental waxes	牙科用蜡
dental preparations with a basis of plaster	牙科用熟石膏制剂
albuminoidal substances	蛋白类物质
modified starches	改性淀粉
glues	胶
enzymes	酶
explosives	炸药
pyrotechnic products	烟火制品
matches	火柴
pyrophoric alloys	引火合金
combustible preparations	易燃材料制品
photographic and cinematographic goods	照相及电影用品
plastics and articles thereof	塑料及其制品
rubber and articles thereof	橡胶及其制品
raw hides and skins	生皮
leather	皮革
furskins and articles thereof	毛皮及其制品
saddlery and harness	鞍具及挽具
travel goods	旅行用品
handbags and similar containers	手提包及类似容器
articles of animal gut (other than silkworm gut)	动物肠线(蚕胶丝除外)制品

artificial fur and manufactures thereof	人造毛皮及其制品
wood and articles of wood	木及木制品
wood charcoal	木炭
cork and articles of cork	软木及软木制品
manufactures of straw	稻草、秸秆制品
manufactures of esparto	针茅制品
manufactures of plaiting materials	编结材料制品
basketware and wicker-work	篮筐及柳条编织品
pulp of wood	木浆
fibrous cellulosic material	纤维状纤维素浆
recovered (waste and scrap) paper	回收(废碎)纸
paperboard	纸板
printed books, newspapers	书籍、报纸
pictures and other products of the printing industry	印刷图画及其他印刷品
manuscripts, typescripts and plans	手稿、打字稿及设计图纸
textiles and textile articles	纺织原料及纺织制品
silk	蚕丝
wool, fine or coarse animal hair,	羊毛、动物细毛或粗毛
horsehair yarn and woven fabric	马毛纱线及其机织物
cotton	棉花
vegetable textile fibers	植物纺织纤维
paper yarn and woven fabrics of paper	纸纱线及其机织物
man-made filaments	化学纤维长丝
strip and the like of man-made textile materials	化学纤维纺织材料制扁条及类似品
man-made staple fibers	化学纤维短纤
wadding, felt and nonwovens	絮胎、毡呢及无纺织物
special yarns	特种纱线
twine, cordage, ropes and cables and articles thereof	线、绳、索、缆及其制品
carpets and other textile floor coverings	地毯及纺织材料的其他铺地制品
special woven fabrics	特种机织物
tufted textile fabrics	簇绒织物
lace	花边
tapestries	装饰毯
trimmings	装饰带
embroidery	刺绣品
impregnated textile fabrics	浸渍纺织物
coated textile fabrics	涂布纺织物

covered textile fabrics	包覆纺织物
laminated textile fabrics	层压的纺织物
textile articles of a kind suitable for industrial use	工业用纺织制品
knitted or crocheted fabrics	针织物及钩编织
apparel and clothing accessories	服装及衣着附件
worn clothing and worn textile articles	旧衣着及旧纺织品
rags	碎织物
footwear	鞋靴
headgear	帽类
umbrellas, sun umbrellas	雨伞、阳伞
walking-sticks	手杖
whips	鞭子
riding-crops	骑手短鞭
prepared feathers	已加工的羽毛
gaiters and the like	护腿和类似品
artificial flowers	人造花
articles of human hair	人发制品
articles made of feathers or of down	羽绒制品
asbestos	石棉
mica	云母
ceramic products	陶瓷产品
glass and glassware	玻璃及其制品
natural or cultured pearls	天然或养殖珍珠
precious or semiprecious stones	宝石或半宝石
metals clad with precious metal	包贵金属
imitation jewelry	仿首饰
base metals	贱金属
iron and steel	钢铁
articles of iron or steel	钢铁制品
copper and articles thereof	铜及其制品
nickel and articles thereof	镍及其制品
aluminum and articles thereof	铝及其制品
lead and articles thereof	铅及其制品
zinc and articles thereof	锌及其制品
tin and articles thereof	锡及其制品
cermet	金属陶瓷
tools, implements, cutlery, spoons and forks	工具、器具、利口器、餐匙、餐叉
hair dryers	吹风机
hand-drying apparatus	干手器

electric smoothing irons	电熨斗
microwave ovens	微波炉
electromagnetic ovens	电磁炉
electric rice cookers	电饭锅
electric frying pans	电炒锅
roaster oven	电烤箱
coffee or tea makers	咖啡壶或茶壶
drip coffee makers	滴液式咖啡机
steam espresso makers	蒸馏渗滤式咖啡机
pump espresso makers	泵压式咖啡机
toasters	烤面包器
household automated bread makers	家用自动面包机
slice pop-up toasters	片式烤面包机（多士炉）
electro-thermic water dispensers	电热饮水机
machinery and mechanical appliances	机器、机械器具
electrical equipment	电气设备
mobile communication base stations	移动通信基站
integrated circuits	集成电路
printed circuits	印刷电路
broadcasting equipment	广播设备
office machine parts and accessories	办公设备零附件
recorders and reproducers	录音机及放声机
television image recorders	电视图像录制设备
television image and sound reproducers	电视图像、声音重放设备
nuclear reactors	核反应堆
boilers	锅炉
electrical machinery and equipment and parts	电机、电气设备及其零件
vehicles	车辆
aircraft	航空器
spacecraft	航天器
vessels	船舶
transport equipment	运输设备
railway or tramway locomotives, rolling-stock	铁道及电车道机车、车辆
fixtures and fittings and parts thereof	固定装置及其零件
traffic signaling equipment	交通信号设备
ships, boats and floating structures	船舶及浮动结构体
optical instruments and apparatus	光学仪器及设备
photographic instruments and apparatus	照相仪器及设备
cinematographic instruments and apparatus	电影仪器及设备

Appendix 4　List of Common Imports and Exports

measuring instruments and apparatus	计量仪器及设备
precision instruments and apparatus	精密仪器及设备
medical instruments and apparatus	医疗仪器及设备
surgical instruments and apparatus	外科用仪器及设备
clocks and watches	钟表
musical instruments	乐器
arms and ammunition	武器、弹药
furniture	家具
bedding	寝具
mattresses	褥垫
mattress supports	弹簧床垫
cushions	软座垫
stuffed furnishings	填充制品
lamps and lighting fittings	灯具及照明装置
illuminated signs	发光标志
illuminated name-plates and the like	发光铭牌及类似品
prefabricated buildings	活动房屋
toys, games and sports requisites	玩具、游戏品、运动用品
works of art	艺术品
collectors' pieces and antiques	收藏品及古物

References

Alred, G. J., et al. *The Business Writer's Companion* [M]. Boston: Bedford/St. Martin's, 2002.

Bailey, E. P. *Writing & Speaking at Work: A Practical Guide for Business Communication* [M]. Upper Saddle River: Prentice Hall, 2002.

Brusaw, T. C., Gerald, J. A. & Walter, E. Oliu. *The Business Writer's Handbook* [M]. New York: St. Martin's Press, 1993.

Cooke, W. *Business English* [M]. Leckhampton: Stanley Thornes (Publishers) Ltd, 1990.

Emerson, B. Frances. *Technical Writing* [M]. Boston: Houghton Mifflin Company, 1987.

Gerson, J. S. & Steven, M. G. *Technical Writing: Process and Product* [M]. Beijing: Higher Education Press, 2004.

Geffner, A. B. *How to Write Better Business Letters* [M]. 3rd ed. Hauppauge: Barron's, 2000.

Guffey, M. E. *Essentials of Business Communication* [M]. Ohio: South-West College Publishing, 1995.

Guffey, M. E. *Essentials of Business Communication* [M]. 6th ed. Mason: South-Western, 2004.

Hatch, R. *Business Writing* [M]. Chicago: Science Research Associates, Inc., 1983.

Hemphill, D. P. *Business Communication with Writing Improvement Exercises* [M]. Upper Saddle River: Prentice Hall, 2001.

Kennedy, G. E. & Montgomery, T. T. *Technical and Professional Writing: Solving Problems at Work* [M]. Upper Saddle River: Prentice Hall, 2002.

Krizan, A. C. *Business Communication* [M]. 5th ed. Cincinnati: South-Western Thomas Learning, 2002.

Kurdyla, J. F. *Longman Model Business Letters for the 21st Century* [M]. Hong Kong: Pearson Education North Asia Ltd., 2000.

Lakes, F. *Business Letters for Busy People: Time Saving, Ready-to-Use Letters for Any Occasion* [M]. 4th ed. Upper Saddle River: Career Press, 2002.

Littlejohn, A. *Company to Company: A New Approach to Business Correspondence in English* [M]. Cambridge: Cambridge University Press, 1990.

Mehr, R. I. *Fundamentals of Insurance* [M]. Homewood: Richard D. Irwin, Inc., 1986.

Shery, Lindsell-Roberts. *Business Letter Writing* [M]. New York: Macmillian, 1995.

Stewart, M. M., et al. *Business English and Communication* [M]. New York: McGraw, Inc., 1978.

甘鸿. 外经贸英语函电[M]. 上海：上海科学技术文献出版社，1996.

兰天. 外贸英语函电[M]. 大连：东北财经大学出版社，1991.

李时民. 出口贸易[M]. 北京：北京大学出版社，2005.

刘伟奇,等. 国际商务单证实务[M]. 上海：复旦大学出版社，2005.

束光辉. 新编进出口贸易实务[M]. 北京：清华大学出版社，2006.

杨晋. 现代国际商务函电[M]. 天津：天津大学出版社，2007.

余心之,等. 新编外贸单证实务[M]. 北京：对外经济贸易大学出版社，2005.

张干周. 国际贸易函电[M]. 杭州：浙江大学出版社，2007.

诸葛霖,周泰祚. 外贸英语函电[M]. 北京：中国对外贸易出版社，1981.

庄学艺. 外贸业务与函电[M]. 上海：上海外语教育出版社，1988.

编委会. 2019年中华人民共和国海关进出口税则[M].北京:经济日报出版社,2019.

于强,金晓玲.UCP600与信用证操作实务指南[M].北京:经济日报出版社,2012.